Smartph...
Nati...

Smartphone Nation

Why We're All Addicted
to Screens and What
You Can Do About It

Kaitlyn Regehr

BLUEBIRD

First published 2025 by Bluebird
an imprint of Pan Macmillan
The Smithson, 6 Briset Street, London EC1M 5NR
EU representative: Macmillan Publishers Ireland Ltd, 1st Floor,
The Liffey Trust Centre, 117–126 Sheriff Street Upper,
Dublin 1, D01 YC43
Associated companies throughout the world
www.panmacmillan.com

HB ISBN 978-1-0350-6904-0
TPB ISBN 978-1-0350-6902-6

Copyright © Kaitlyn Regehr 2025

The right of Kaitlyn Regehr to be identified as the
author of this work has been asserted by her in accordance
with the Copyright, Designs and Patents Act 1988.

Illustrations © Amy Lines 2025

All rights reserved. No part of this publication may be reproduced,
stored in a retrieval system, or transmitted, in any form, or by any means
(electronic, mechanical, photocopying, recording or otherwise)
without the prior written permission of the publisher.

Pan Macmillan does not have any control over, or any responsibility for,
any author or third-party websites referred to in or on this book.

9 8 7 6 5 4 3 2

A CIP catalogue record for this book is available from the British Library.

Typeset in ITC Charter Std by Palimpsest Book Production Ltd, Falkirk, Stirlingshire
Printed and bound in India by Manipal Technologies Limited

This book is sold subject to the condition that it shall not, by way of
trade or otherwise, be lent, hired out, or otherwise circulated without
the publisher's prior consent in any form of binding or cover other than
that in which it is published and without a similar condition including
this condition being imposed on the subsequent purchaser.

Visit **www.panmacmillan.com/bluebird** to read more about all our books
and to buy them. You will also find features, author interviews and
news of any author events, and you can sign up for e-newsletters
so that you're always first to hear about our new releases.

For sale in the Indian subcontinent only

For my daughters.

Contents

1   *Introduction*

13   **Chapter 1**
The Digital Supermarket

29   **Chapter 2**
Acknowledging Our Addictions

65   **Chapter 3**
How Algorithms Make You Sick – And How You Can Get Well Soon

95   **Chapter 4**
The Safety Paradox and Why Screen Time Doesn't Work

111   **Chapter 5**
Digital Nutrition: Your Guide to Healthy Consumption

131   **Chapter 6**
An Ethical Internet: Regulation and Defunding Hate, Harm and Disinformation

159   Conclusion
164   Useful Resources and Numbers
167   Acknowledgements
171   Glossary of Terms
179   Endnotes

Introduction

My daughter wants a cat named Unicorn for her birthday. I resisted, I tried to debate, but the requests for Unicorn persisted. That is, they did. They did until the day when my four-year-old bounded through the front door with her friend. They spoke loudly about their preferred type of ice lollies; a mutual dislike for hair brushing; and then, 'Do you know what?' my daughter questioned, 'I'm getting a phone for my birthday.'

Somehow, in my daughter's imagination, the smartphone is a marker of maturity. A different mythical creature to be given when she reached the milestone of 'big girl' – the age of five – and in that moment Unicorn the cat melted away.

After that, I began to reflect on my own phone usage, particularly around my children. I wondered if, through the apparent flexibility of the digital workspace, I had begun to respond 'just quickly' to a few too many emails in front of my kids. I wondered if I should only work on a laptop in their presence. I considered if my love of capturing their life moments or 'sharenting' – a concept I teach to my graduate students – was no longer healthy. Or if in those tired, end-of-the-day moments when I scroll to soothe, my kid had been watching. And, in turn, what had I been watching? An eternal procession of things I should want, should need and should be. What is the sum of all this screen consumption? And how does it impact what I understand, know or even think?

The truth is, though I can make different choices about how I use my phone around my children and this book will cover that very point, and though my daughter won't get a phone this year, or probably for the better part of another decade, she has already begun to be swept up in the march of ever-changing technologies and I, like so many parents, need to begin to prepare her. I need to sow the seeds of critical screen engagement: what is healthy consumption and what is not? And I will have to begin to make choices about the types of screens she uses. When – if at all – do I get my child a phone? Should it be a smart one or a dumb one? Should I allow any apps? Which apps are good? Which are potentially harmful? Will her offline communication be stunted? How will I speak to her about unrealistic body ideals? Pornography? Predators? And even before she has a smartphone, how will I deal with the impacts of the Internet on the offline world she inhabits? Because, of course, harm doesn't stay on screens but rather bleeds out into school yards and onto streets.

These are things that wake me in the night. The things I try to solve at 3 am, when I shoot up, messy-haired and groggy, to type out some ideas on my phone – the very device at the root of my concern. Concern not just for my own children. Not just for all children. But for all of us – humans – as we sit in our information silos being served our daily dose of personalized content; one-sided arguments; things that close us down; things that limit us; or simply things that find the chink and pry into our most vulnerable selves making us feel threatened or just a little lesser than. This is the digital diet to which many of us – I would argue most of us – are now addicted.

I've written this book not because there isn't enough resource available on digital literacy, but rather because there is too much.[1]

As one exasperated teacher expressed at an event I attended recently, people are very worried about this issue, and equally, they are completely overwhelmed. 'They don't know where to start.' Much of the guidance is that we should be talking about these issues, particularly to our kids; which is difficult to do if you don't have the knowledge or context to actually have the conversation. That is, it's hard to have open conversations about technology if you don't understand said technology, or the landscape in which it operates. And so this is an information-building book, so that you can make informed decisions about your own usage, and for those you love. Then this book will give you the tools to upskill yourself to make your own usage safer. You'll learn how to game your algorithm – or practise 'algorithmic resistance';[2] how to change your own sharenting practices to safeguard and protect your kids, your finances and your own physical safety; how to catch disinformation; and how to move from being a passive user to being an active participant.

To be clear, I am not a psychiatrist. I am not a behaviour scientist. Or a neurologist. I am the Programme Director of Digital Humanities at University College London – a university often ranked among the ten best universities in the world. My colleagues are information scientists and statisticians. I look at social media's algorithmic processes and their cultural impacts – particularly on young people.[3] I follow the tech. My research has fed into legislation and policy reform. I've consulted on the Online Safety Act here in the UK – although admittedly, I think it needs more work. I've worked with the Metropolitan Police about the online indoctrination of young people into extremism. I was on the research team[4] that informed the new digital flashing legislation, which means it's now illegal for an adult to send a picture of their genitals to a child – shockingly, it wasn't before.[5] Internationally, I've mapped the impact of digital abuse on public health professionals during the pandemic.[6] In Canada, I've examined the impacts of viewing video evidence on criminal justice professions;[7] in Scotland, I've created peer-to-peer mentorship resources around online hate and misogyny with the Scottish Government.[8] I've launched materials for schools in England on algorithmic harm with the Association of School and College Leaders;[9] I've researched social media usage with hundreds of teens;[10] and I'm also a mum who wants to fix a problem. A big generation-defining problem.

If you're reading this book because you're worried about your own device usage, the questions I asked above are also relevant. How do you carve out healthy digital engagement? How do you take control so that you control your algorithms instead of – the default setting – them controlling you? And how can it be more straightforward like eating healthily? Though we might not always choose to, we generally know how to do it. Green = good; beige = less good; old Halloween candy sitting at the back of your desk drawer because you didn't have time for lunch = decidedly bad. Generally, with food, we know the basics, or we know what we should be doing. And, when we don't, we know where to go for guidance. A quick Google search gives 'five a day', or food guides and pyramids outlining portions of dairy and protein.

But when I was concerned about my family's digital diet (that is, what we were consuming online), I struggled to know what guidance to use about how to feed my kids – and also me, an adult – by way of screens. Historically, most of the guidance available focused on controlling the dose of digital engagement, or 'screen time' (a concept now often seen to be outdated – I'll get to this later). Similarly, for adults, most of the guidance on digital diets has, like in old-fashioned food diets, been about restriction. And just like contemporary discussions around the quality of food we consume, it is helpful to think about our digital consumption along these same terms. That is, although some screen usage is good (take FaceTiming your grandmother), it is the way that content is served and suggested to us, by way of algorithms, that can render digital consumption unhealthy and potentially harmful. So I began pulling together my own work and compiling the research and insights of colleagues, professionals, scholars and scientists, and I created something to help myself and my family navigate the digital terrain. I thought of myself as a digital nutritionist.

Digital Nutrition

Not long after this, I was in the Houses of Parliament. I was sharing my work on the way TikTok algorithms prioritize harm for young people and normalize disinformation. And then I paused. I looked at the lawmakers around the table and I explained, 'You know, this is simply a symptom of a much bigger issue. If you really want to keep young people healthy, if you want to be proactive rather than reactive, you need to be concerned about their digital health. They need digital nutrition.' And at that, one lawmaker spoke very steadily, very seriously and responded, 'We want this. We need this. Everyone does.' And, with this statement, I realized maybe it was time to share my personal family recipe for digital nutrition.

Historically, when educators talked about the online sphere, they used the term digital literacy or before that, media literacy. 'Digital literacy education' refers to teaching both technical and critical-thinking skills by which people can evaluate their engagement with the digital space and the content they consume within it. But there is a gap in this education – a lot of us 'old people' didn't grow up with smartphones, tablets or Internet connected screens, or consequently with any digital literacy education at all. And in the family context, for almost everything else that we parent around, we grew up with it and we draw on this knowledge. The activities in this book are designed to help you deeply understand how these processes are working for you and on you, so that you can start to build an innate understanding; and if you are a parent, you can then draw on that information so that you can parent more effectively. Many of the case studies in this book are about young people, who as the evidence suggests are feeling the impact of this screen-based lifestyle acutely. Take, for example, the 2023 report from the Children's Commissioner, which found that one in four young people consume pornography before the age of eleven;[11] or that Ofsted has suggested that young people are using pornography as an educational tool, which can shape norms and create unhealthy attitudes around sexual aggression.[12] Consensus within research regarding the links between mental health and social media remains mixed, but as Lord Darzi's report into the NHS states, it is 'highly unlikely that the dramatic rise in mental health needs is wholly unconnected from social media'.[13]

However, though a lot of the examples I use in this book are about kids and teens, the concepts are universal and can, and should, be applied to us all at any age. For we adults need boundaries too. We need to face our own addictions. And in doing so, venture to learn the underlying technicalities of these devices that we touch, that we stroke, and through these actions possibly even develop feelings of love. To break those addictions, we must understand how these devices are built to lock us in and hook us even if that might mean feeding us things that make us feel bad or make us sick or teach us mistruths.

Take for example, January 6th, 2021, when a mob of an estimated ten thousand people stormed Capitol Hill in Washington.[14] They were not the under-sixteen-year-olds we talk about when restricting social media usage. The vast majority were adults. Consenting. Voting. Adults. The events in Washington were widely reported as having been instigated on and by social media – not just because of President Trump's use of (then) Twitter, but also because of the way in which platforms allowed for the targeted circulation of material that whipped people into a state of rage – enough to want to topple their national structures.[15]

And yet this remains an almost unregulated space. And though there are some new regulations coming into effect,[16] they are limp and weak compared to regulations for almost everything else we consume. Almost everything else we consume is regulated. The food we eat, the medication we take, the cars we drive all need to be proven safe before they are allowed on the market. For the tech industry, this is much less true. Or rather, it doesn't exist to nearly the same degree as in other industries. One of the reasons for a lack of consumer protection in this area is that we aren't actually the consumers of social media. We are the product.[17] Rather, our minds and our attention are the product, which is sold to advertisers. It is they who are the consumers. Keeping our attention, feeding us whatever is the most attention-grabbing – even if this means allowing harm, hate or disinformation to thrive.[18] This is the business model. I'll discuss this, the 'attention economy'[19] that underpins this whole system in detail, in Chapter 1.

For now, though admittedly this all sounds a little dystopic, I want to make one thing clear. I am neither an anti-tech nor a pro-tech person. I'm a pro-information person. So we as users – or we as the product – can equip ourselves with the information we need to keep ourselves healthy online.

I am heartened to see grassroots movements in my own community and in those around the world which are questioning the power of technology companies and which, through local initiatives, are spurring on a cultural shift. Groups like Smartphone Free Childhood, or Wait Until the 8th in the US, Unplugged in Canada, No Es Momento in Mexico, or the Heads Up Alliance in Australia. These groups have run information-building webinars and encouraged lecture evenings where communities crowd into school gymnasiums to 'tech up'. They have instigated phone-free Fridays for families and encouraged us to think critically about the corporate structures behind digital media.[20] Children, teens, adults, all of us should think more carefully about algorithmic processes and the need to be critical of our screen consumption. We all need to mitigate, moderate and indeed 'ban' some forms of harmful usage. Personal moderation is an important first step (all to come later). These movements have marked a watershed moment of public awareness-building.[21] And now, there is more work to do.

On a macro level, moderation of use alone can get tech companies and legislators off the hook, which as the writer Nicole Aschoff has argued, can pull our attention away from the root of the issue: the unethical practices of big tech.[22] Moderation of use alone can also become a shortcut that requires minimal commitment or investment from either corporations or government. Similar to debates on ultra-processed foods, it's easier for companies to frame the problem as ours – that is, our relationship to food rather than the content of the food. And then sell us further products that help us with 'our problem'. Tech companies are happy to sell us products to help supposedly 'moderate' our use of an addiction they created for us. For example schools buying Apple software to lock down Apple iPads, because children are now so addicted they simply can't disconnect.[23]

On a more micro level the moderation of phone use doesn't account for usage on other Internet connected devices, such as tablets and laptops. Research by Ofcom (the UK's Office of Communication) has shown that 67% of three- to four-year-olds use a tablet to go online.[24] A Pew Research Centre study found that 89% of parents of a child aged five to eleven say their child watches videos on YouTube[25] – a platform that parents might not often constitute as social media but can share much of the same content. And so, moderation of use needs to be paired with incremental education[26] to prepare you and your kids for differing stages of digital usage when they inevitably come. Even if a young person doesn't use social media up until the age of fifteen, they will turn sixteen.[27] And so we as a society have a responsibility to pair moderation with information-building to equip young – and older – people to navigate this terrain.

We might wish for a different world. We as Gen X-ers or geriatric millennials nostalgically reminiscing about our Nokias and their supposed innocence. As parents, we worry about our own children. We long to replicate the weekends and summertimes of childhoods past. Summertimes where kids went rogue on BMX bikes and weren't allowed home until the streetlamps came on. An article in London's *Sunday Times* from the summer of 2024 about smartphones references wanting to create a childhood summer like the one depicted in *Stand By Me*,[28] a film about summertime boyhood released forty years ago (1986), which in turn, depicts a childhood thirty years earlier (1959). We absolutely need more boundaries around tech. We do absolutely need more time off screens and more independent play for kids, as Jonathan Haidt has importantly advocated.[29] At the same time, we have a collective responsibility to inform ourselves about the digital world, so that we understand what not only our kids but also *we* as adults are currently living through. So before we get lost harkening back to an idyllic time, in a different country, as depicted by a Hollywood movie, we need to get to grips with the structures built to addict us and the rules of the attention economy under which we now live. We also need to acknowledge our responsibility as adults. That we ourselves are a part of the attention economy. And that, in turn, we often enter our children into this economy long before they have a device of their own. And if we are going to prepare ourselves and our kids to live healthier lives, we need to understand this.

Beyond Moderation

If previous conversations and advocacy have been about **step 1, moderation** or phone bans,[30] this book is focused on the next steps – steps 2 and 3. **Step 2 is information.** When the Internet first switched over to commercial providers in the mid-1990s and families began to purchase their first shared family PC, the concept of 'shoulder surfing' was introduced. The suggested approach was a way for parents to gently monitor their children's Internet usage; over their kids' shoulders. That is, while parents sat on the sofa and read the paper, they could glance at the large screen prominently atop a table in the living room. This guidance evolved with the technology – though only slightly. The concept of shoulder surfing was replaced by screen time to limit the time spent on TVs, computers, tablets, and phones to a set amount of daily usage.

But screen time guidance accounts only for the quantity of content consumed, not the quality. And it has done very little to account for adult usage.[31]

There are different types of screens and different types of screen times, and this needs to be acknowledged before you can make appropriate decisions about screen usage. Many now break down time on screens into two categories: *Active Screen Time*, which involves cognitively engaging in screen-based activities; and *Passive Screen Time*, which includes scrolling and passive gazing.[32] These categories should, like a food guide,[33] be given different weightings across overall usage. I call this the Digital Diet Pyramid. In Chapter 5, I'll talk about the Digital Diet Pyramid, which outlines different types of digital engagement, and how different proportions of each type might support healthy digital consumption.

And with this guide in mind, we can make conscious choices of what we want to consume and make a change. We can enjoy the brilliance of the Internet, the information and connection-building, the opportunity to create something of our own: a business or an education; and also the just plain old fun or the outright hilarious, while also rejecting that which is untrue, harmful or that which impacts our well-being. And if you are a parent, this book will build your understanding, so that you can begin to seed these ideas with your family from an early age.

Step 3 is regulation and the defunding of harm, hate and disinformation. This is about pulling the financial cord on online harm and regulating the corporate structure on which social media is built. It's a broader conversation about challenging the current structure where tech companies are rewarded for keeping us 'hooked', that is, holding our attention for as long as possible. Holding that attention – or the 'attention economy'[34] – and getting those views or 'impressions' (the industry term) is crucial to the whole business model of social media.[35] These algorithmic models can allow harmful content to flourish. Sadly, disinformation can be more interesting or 'impressionable' than the truth, and harm and hate can hook into our emotions and fears. And so these algorithmic models create the fertile conditions to allow this content to thrive, to get us to stay just a little bit longer or better yet, react.

To many this will seem obvious. A given. I articulate this not because I'm the first one to say it.[36] But because I think it's important that we redirect some of the energy which has focused on asking tech to make their platforms safer – something they still should do – to follow a much more simplistic thread – the money. Or rather, the financial underpinnings that fuel this system.

We can take a stand. We can demand bold policies that attack these financial structures. We can move away from seeing this as a siloed, individualistic problem, but rather, as a collective problem that we can solve together. We can also have a greater awareness of how these processes work and step away from the trees – or in this case, the phone – to see the forest – a big attention-grabbing, seductive, addictive forest personalized just for you in a palm-sized glowing rectangle.[37] The hope is that with this collective knowledge we – a big societal we – can use it much more critically and in turn, advocate for change.

Many of the concepts in this book are unlikely to be relevant to my four-year-old daughter right now, but I can make more informed decisions about the screens and platforms she inhabits; and I can begin to introduce concepts about good-quality, active screen usage to help her to develop safe habits for the future. Screen consumption, just like food consumption, can be good or bad. Sometimes my daughter eats ice cream, and that's OK, but it would be a problem if that was all that I fed her. She also likes doughnuts, but I know she should really eat some vegetables. Just like in her offline world, in her online world, I make choices about appropriate content, games and activities and then the right dosages of each.

I can also make choices about my own screen usage around her, and carve out time to disconnect, in order to connect in the offline space. These moments, of course, remain very important for both of us. In these moments, I might decide the ice cream is OK – but maybe not the doughnut. In these moments I might try, yet again, to brush her hair, unsuccessfully. In these moments, we might talk through something she saw on a screen. And in a moment just like one of these, I ended up agreeing. I caved. And I now have a cat named Unicorn.

Chapter 1
The Digital Supermarket

September. Master's students crowd into a wood-panelled lecture theatre. It has hard-backed benches designed likely over a century before anyone owned a computer, let alone brought one to class. And it is here, as students precariously balance their MacBooks atop the ripped knees of light washed jeans, that I tell them about the Internet's techno-enthusiast beginnings. To start, I often show them an American infomercial from the early 1990s called 'The Kids' Guide to the Internet', which encouraged families to install the Internet on their home computer. The ad opens with a jingle, 'Take a spin. Now you're in with the Techno Set. We're going surfing on the Internet!'[1] and then cuts to a family in their living room. They sit on a sofa with geometric patterned throw cushions. Beside them is a Microsoft desktop computer. 'The Internet gave us a new world of exciting possibilities,' exclaims Peter, a boy with a blond mushroom cut and an ill-fitting polo shirt. 'Now that I've gotten on the Internet, I'd rather be on my computer than doing just about anything.' His parents smile proudly, as his mother beams, 'I haven't been able to get the kids off it ever since.' The family goes on to speak about how the children have a new global understanding, because they can 'talk to people all over the world on chatlines'. The pre-teens are shown slowly clicking one key at a time to write out an email to President Clinton. And visiting the

Smithsonian 'without ever leaving home', as pixelated images of the museum's archive load jerkily across the desktop screen. But ultimately, the parents are thrilled that their children's grades and communication skills have apparently improved, offering them a shimmering hope of a college education.

This infomercial acts as a time capsule showcasing the early promise of the Internet. And, in many ways, these promises were fulfilled. We are now much more connected to politicians. We can access information and the materials of great institutions remotely. Kids can (for better or for worse) chat to almost anyone anywhere in the world. But the question of whether the Internet has enlightened us is up for debate. That is, whether we are all benefitting from the sum value of global knowledge, or whether we are, as the media theorist Neil Postman argues, amusing ourselves to death – is complex.[2]

Regardless of whether it is primarily a tool or a toy, it, the Internet, is largely unregulated relative to any of our other tools or toys. Most of what we consume as citizens is heavily safeguarded by our government and regulatory structures, and though there are new legislations emerging to protect some aspects of use (which I'll get to) much of the regulation around our digital consumption falls short of measures routinely taken for other services and products.[3] One of the arguments for this is that these technologies are still new and emerging. But the World Wide Web, born in 1989, has for more than half of the world's population[4] been a constant since birth. For more than half of us, not only is it not 'new', they've never known life without it. And yet consumer protection in this space is still not fit for purpose.

This is different from most other products (food, medication, terrestrial TV) that we use or ingest as consumers. But perhaps that makes sense, for we are not the consumers here – advertisers are. We are not the consumers. We are the product. Our attention – our minds – are the product, which is being sold to these advertisers. This chapter does two things: it maps the evolution of the Web from a space driven by information-sharing to a space driven by advertising, and it outlines the lack of consumer protection and regulation overseeing this space.

That doesn't mean that you can't use these technologies. But if you want to play in this space, if you want to navigate this terrain, if you want to climb this mountain, you're essentially doing so without a harness. This doesn't mean that you can't take the risk, but there is a greater duty of responsibility and care for yourself and for any dependants that you have when using these services. You are not looked after, so you're going to have to look after yourself and those you love. And this book gives you the tools to do just that.

Consumer Protection

'Consumer protection' refers to the act of protecting consumers from unfair commercial practices. As Priya Ramda from the UK Department of Trade explained to me, it 'prohibits misleading actions, misleading omissions and bans a number of practices' – for example, faulty products, products or services which aren't as advertised or aren't sufficiently transparent or exhorting children by way of certain products like tobacco or alcohol. Regulations govern much of what we use or put into our bodies. Globally, regulations around medication and healthcare products are overseen by regulators, with an alphabet spaghetti of acronyms; from the MHRA in the UK,[5] the PDD in Canada,[6] the TGA in Australia,[7] the CDSCO in India[8] and the FDA in the US.[9] They are responsible for securing a safe supply chain for medicines and medical devices. Most importantly, with all of these organizations it can take years for new medicines to go through the research, clinical trials and licensing process to ensure they are safe and up to standard.[10] And though it is by no means perfect, the MHRA pledges that medication will not be accessible to us as consumers until it is deemed safe.[11]

The acronyms don't just end with health regulators. Internationally there are agencies which ensure that vehicles and their safety equipment are indeed safe. From the RVS in Australia,[12] the MoRT&H in India,[13] the NRCS in South Africa,[14] to the DVSA in the UK[15] it's standard to regulate the things we use in everyday life. We could look to products for children, which come with age recommendations and guidelines on small oesophagus-sized parts.[16] Or pre-digital, or 'traditional' media (television, radio and film), which has a much more structured regulation by way of Ofcom, which ensures standards on primetime viewing slots and a duty of care across broadcast media. This will be discussed in more detail later in this book.

For food safety, globally there are regulators which protect public health in relation to food.[17] There are checks and balances in place at a national level to ensure the government has the power to act in the consumers' interests at any stage in the food production and supply chain.[18] This means that food can't be labelled, advertised or presented in a way that is false or misleading. And so, though we could get into a more nuanced discussion about preservatives or ultra-processed food, you are unlikely to find arsenic in your orange juice or a razorblade in your bread roll in your weekly shop.

For digital technology, instead of testing to prove something is safe prior to hitting the market, the tech industry has not been called into question until its products are deemed to be unsafe. And that is different from almost everything else that we buy or put into our bodies. The Internet, and social media which followed it, were not tested – or rather, they were not tested by government agencies. And they are (for the most part) unregulated – in fact, this was the virtue of the Internet from its inception – a free speech utopia – unlike the terrestrial media that came before it.

What is important for us to all collectively understand is that regulations[19] that have been thought through and considered – regulations about what is healthy for us to watch – have effectively been thrown out of the window. For many of us now no longer watch terrestrial TV. Children for the most part are more likely to be found on YouTube or YouTube Kids.[20] And because kids are now less likely to be on children's viewing hours but rather on unregulated platforms on tablets (or phones), as former Google employee Tristan Harris[21] has argued, most of the quite-well-thought-through regulation around children's viewing no longer protects kids.[22] And this is the same for all of us with our online usage. This is not a space that was regulated for our best interests, but rather, it was manipulated by tech companies in order to hold our time and attention as long as possible for their financial gain.

Consumer Rights and Online Safety

There is however legislation over the digital space. The Consumer Rights Act of 2015 introduced the concept of 'digital content' and set out consumers' rights (for example when paying to download an app or TV series).[23] And there are, currently, further changes afoot. I myself contributed to elements of the Online Harms Bill, which became the Online Safety Act in 2023.[24] The Act has put in place a series of new legislations across a variety of areas of Internet safety. For example, it says that social media platforms will be expected to 'remove illegal content quickly.'[25] However, the Act does not currently include comprehensive measures to remove material which is categorized as 'legal but harmful'.[26] This includes content that does not meet a criminal threshold but may encourage, promote or provide instructions for suicide, self-harm or eating disorders.[27] Both the ways in which something is classified as harm and the speed at which it is removed – if at all – are points of contention making actually implementing the Act difficult. It also does not directly address the role of platforms in amplifying hate, harm and disinformation (an issue discussed in the next chapter).[28]

Legal expert Professor Claire McGlynn has argued that the Online Safety Act doesn't have the legal backing to actually make it work functionally[29] and others suggest that in its current form, the Act places emphasis on the users themselves to be responsible for flagging harmful content. It says that companies must 'provide parents and children with clear and accessible ways to report problems online when they do arise.'[30] The issue here is that it's a reactive rather than proactive approach. It assumes that there *is* harm and people – including children – will encounter it. It also assumes that social media companies are actually reactive to such reporting. In 2024 Dr Caitlin Shaughnessy, Dr Katharine Smales and I conducted the 'Digital Nutrition' research project about the smartphone experiences of teens across the UK. Time and time again, they told us that even when reporting harm, responses from social media platforms were shockingly inattentive.[31]

Perhaps to understand this lack of regulation fully, we need to return to the ideological origins of the World Wide Web: open access and freedom of speech. Many have asked if we even *want* full regulation of the Internet. For the Internet is of course many things. It's a space of connectivity and collectivity and at the very same time one of isolation and fragmentation. We've been given unprecedented access to the sum of human knowledge – as Wikipedia puts it[32] – and have platforms to speak from like never before. And perhaps this open access and lack of regulation are the very things that made it so beautiful in the first place.

The Web

Tim was eccentric. He didn't always wear shoes. And he used large hand gestures when talking – which he did very, very quickly. In fact, when he spoke at work, his team would hold up bits of paper reading 'Slow down, Tim'. His colleague Jenny Tennyson said they actually had a unit of measurement to gauge how fast somebody talked called the TimBL. One TimBL is the same rapidity of thought and speech as Tim. And 'nobody else ever reaches one TimBL'.

Tim was a contemplative type. At one of his first jobs developing software in Dorset, he would sit on the riverbank with a pint and a ploughman's lunch letting his feet dangle into the cool water while he thought about code. To work out a problem, he could be found lying on the grass looking up at the sky. Literally, blue sky thinking, a trait that some colleagues found somewhat frustrating – particularly when they had a joint task to do.[33] But Tim was working on his own personal project. The aim of this project was to find a way to be connected so that he – everyone – could share content across a new network of different computer systems. Tim was trying to make it easier for people who were separated geographically to share research, to share the information. He envisaged an elaborate information management system. Tim's project would be called the World Wide Web. And it ended up being quite a success.

Initially meant as a space for academics or 'geeks', Tim, now Sir Tim Berners-Lee, would develop what we all now experience as a world of content – images, information, culture, and life – all connected together. For Jenny, now CEO of Sir Tim Berners-Lee's Open Data Institute, one of the things that made the Web work was the fact that he gave it away. He didn't keep it for himself: a precious gem to be gazed upon only by a tight knit club of coders. Rather, as Jenny explains, he 'brought in everybody else to be part of that story.' If he had structured it differently, it wouldn't have spread in the same way and 'we wouldn't have what we have . . . he wants the Web to make the world a better place'.[34]

In 1995 the network or the 'Net' – the Internet being the global network of computers on which the Web runs – was turned over to commercial providers. That year an online bookstore launched. The idea was to algorithmically offer book suggestions to consumers to bring them back to the days of a local bookseller, who got to know consumers and knew their interests. It was named Amazon.[35] 1995 also saw the launch of a website devoted to antiques and finding old collectables, including the first item to be sold on the site: a broken laser pointer. This site would be named eBay.[36] And with these developments, the cultural landscape of the Internet began to take shape.

But the early Web was messy. A messy, creative, scrap book for the world: the digital equivalent of a community centre cork-board with posters for the church bazaar peeking out from underneath flyers trimmed with tear-off phone numbers in an endless cycle of new information and constant sharing. And there was something glorious in this hodgepodge, where no one and nothing was prioritized. We just all had access to the same community board and the same push pins to tack up and promote our own page. But back then the Web was small. And as it grew, there were more and more posters for ever more weird and wonderful versions of church bazaars, making the one you wanted – or needed – harder and harder to find.

Targeted

It was 1996. Larry Paige, a goofy guy from Michigan who smiled a lot, and Sergey Brin, who loved a good debate – both the sons of academics – started a joint thesis project. Inspired by the processes of academic peer-reviewing of research papers – something they were aware of from their parents – they set out to improve the way Web pages were found on the Internet.[37] The idea was that if you were searching for something on the Web it would be helpful to know if other people, your 'peers', had found it useful. If you are looking for a recipe on how to make a Chicken Kiev, you don't just want mentions of 'Chicken Kiev' – you want the page that other people have agreed 'this is the best Chicken Kiev recipe'. Exploiting the existing structures of the Web, they developed the process of page ranking: the more people pointed to a page the more central or highly indexed it would be.

Larry and Sergey wanted to build upon Tim's idea of connection. Their mission was to 'organise the world's information and make it universally accessible'.[38] They said they wanted to make the world better. Their motto was 'Don't be evil'.[39] And they eventually called their project Google – which may or may not have been a misspelling of the mathematical term Googol, meaning ten to the power of a hundred.[40]

Spelling errors aside, Google quickly embedded itself within the makeup of the Web, so much so that it became hard to understand where one began and the other ended. What is the Web without Google? Google became a noun and a verb, and it was entered into the *Oxford English Dictionary* in 2006. In 2002, the American Dialect Society chose it as the 'most useful word of the year'.[41] Google is now integrated into our lives, behaviours and cultural lexicon. And scholars have argued that it has changed the way we think about, access and process information.[42]

This ubiquity of Google, the everydayness of it, can sometimes give a sense that this technology is a neutral truth-giver. That through its page-ranking system we are being given unbiased, even scientific, information. But technology *is* biased. Because people are biased. And people build technology. This is known as *Algorithmic Bias*. The UK's Children's Commissioner defines 'algorithmic bias' as a process where algorithms are created in such a way that their results reinforce human or societal biases.[43] For example, in 2015 Amazon noticed that one of its mechanisms for recruitment seemed to be disproportionately rejecting female applicants, regardless of their qualifications.[44] Upon closer examination, they found that the machine-learning tool they were using was trained by observing patterns in applications received by the company over a ten-year period. Most applications had historically come from men, reflecting the male dominance within the industry, and so Amazon's system assumed this was the company's preference and that ideal candidates must be male. This is an example of the way in which machine-learning algorithms can reinforce and actually entrench historic or outdated prejudices. In fact, the UK government has come out to say that 'Algorithms make use of data about past behaviour, which means biases embedded in the data can be reinforced and strengthened over time.'[45]

Professor of Gender Studies, African American Studies, and Information Studies at UCLA, Safiya Noble has looked at the ways in which Google's search recommendations can reinforce prejudices.[46] She gives the example of how a search for the word 'Professor' pulled up very specific images of tweed-jacket-wearing old men that don't look anything like Professor Noble – or me for that matter. Similarly, a recent study that found that facial recognition systems are 32% more likely to mistake recognizing a black woman over a white male[47] (simply because data sets that train the technology have been 'pale and male')[48] or take issues of class and credit rating, which have also had concerns raised regarding algorithmic bias.[49] And the reason this all matters is because we often assume that technology is neutral. And because of that assumed neutrality, the 'facts' that arise from our quick searches for information are often unreflectively accepted as 'truths' and, over time, such repeated 'truths' become our reality.

And so the power that Google now has in shaping our collective thinking and understanding of information makes it far more complex than that community centre cork-board. I'm not saying that every time you do a Google search you need to go beyond the first page or that you need to fact-check everything you read. That would be exhausting. But it is important to understand that the idea that technology neutrally provides us with facts is false. And often, we are over-reliant on Google as the truth-giver.

There is a parallel history to Google's rise as ultimate truth-giver, a much more hidden one. If webpages are the store-front windows of the Web, its financial structures sit in the furnace room deep in the basement. In October of 2000, Google launched its first self-serve online advertising platform: AdWords – and Internet marketing, as we now know it, slid onto our screens.[50] Buyers could set how much they were willing to pay per thousand impressions, or rather the times that the ad was shown. And the highest bidder would appear higher on the page. In 2002, Google added a scoring system based on a combination of the price the advertiser was willing to pay and the ad's relevance.[51] And through this process, adverts in prominent spots became trusted by Google users. Google was the only platform using this scoring system to grant coveted spots of prominence and trust. And so its real estate became preferred amongst advertisers and its price per square centimetre skyrocketed.

But for most users, this gradual increase in adverts and the increased efficiency at targeting us were almost imperceptible. Advertising became intrinsically linked to Web searches and increasingly personalized approaches were barely noticeable. And how it was done was relatively opaque. Professor Shoshana Zuboff, in her seminal work, argues that Google pioneered the mining of 'human experience' by way of collecting data for economic gain.[52] That is, the profiling of us, everything about us, so that it can predict what you want to buy before you want to buy it.[53] Because you don't pay for Google's services and yet you are a central part of its revenue generation. Keep in mind that without user-generated content – that is, the content that you post, upload and update online, generally for no pay – Google could not perform its searches. Media scholar Christian Fuchs sets out how Google relies on us to produce content and engage with others' content in two key ways:

- First, we create content. Google stores and sorts this user-generated content that is uploaded to the Web.
- Next, we search for and engage with content. Google uses our searches to generate and store data. This data is used to create a model that can be used to personally target advertising back to us.

So, through this engagement we use Google's services. We use Google Maps and then write a restaurant review and upload an image of our meal; we translate something on Google Translate; we watch YouTube,[54] all of which creates data about us.[55] So, through our online behaviours, all our online behaviours, Google generates and stores data about its users. It then uses this information to target adverts to users' interests. The result is targeted advertising. That means that for Google – and social media more generally – the advertisers are actually the clients, and we, the users, are the product. Our attention – or rather, our mind – is the product. But are we fully the product? Can we be both the product and at the same time the consumer? In many ways we are. We are products to be mined, so that we can, in turn, be persuaded to consume more and more and more. Which is perhaps why in the tech industry a different term is used altogether. A term which as computer scientist Edward Tufte has pointed out is only found in two industries, tech and the illegal drugs trade: 'user'.[56]

And as users, all platforms are competing for our minds and to keep our minds on their platforms as long as possible.[57] How much time can they get us to spend on their platform? How much time can they get us to give? Because in that time, they can collect a lot of data – historically unprecedented amounts of data, as Zuboff tells us – and this allows them to make better and better predictions about who we are. And this very tailored and accurate view of their 'users' is incredibly valuable to advertisers.[58]

But is this all a problem? Is it really a big deal that brands want to sell us a new pair of trainers? Maybe it's actually quite helpful. You might indeed feel this way. Context is important here: it's been estimated that Internet users are now bombarded with thousands of ads – some have put this as high as 10,000 every day.[59] They might be harmless. But they can also be financially or emotionally exploitative. My team and I heard from participants who are constantly bombarded by ads for weight-loss products, and even if they reported the content, they told us, the ads were still pushed at them through these targeting mechanisms.

Even if you are painfully aware of the corporate constructs of digital platforms, the bottom line is that most people wouldn't give up free services to mitigate targeted advertising. And if you do want to minimize your exposure to ads, as one student in my master's class once said to me, 'We can't opt out' and be able to still function in our society. But there are some ways that you can search and share more safely and with greater consumer protections.

How to Avoid Targeted Advertising

1. **Use Different Browsers.** Just like a healthy balanced diet, it's good to use a variety of browsers for different activities. For example, if you use one browser for shopping and another for socializing and social media, cookies – the way that websites track you – will be stored differently.
2. **Do Not Track.** This is a feature that lets websites know that you don't want your behaviours to be tracked. They don't have to abide by it. But many will. You can find it in most browsers' settings. You can also turn on incognito browsing, which stops cookie tracking. You can find instructions about how to do this in the Google Help Centre. iCloud have a feature called 'private relay' which you can turn on in iCloud settings on iPhone. It lets you hide your IP address and browsing activity in safari so nobody – including Apple – can see who or what sites you are visiting.
3. **Limit Your Google Use.** There are some Google alternatives. You might want to look at DuckDuckGo or Firefox Focus.[60] These search engines do not track you to serve targeted ads. You could also look at Startpage.com which allows you to use Google without tracking your digital footprint.[61]
4. **Digital Spring Cleaning.** The new spring cleaning is uninspiring cleaning. If it no longer inspires or educates you: unfollow it. This includes exes, TV personalities or brands. You don't need to keep

seeing bathing suits if you already bought one and you are back from holiday. Unfollow accounts regularly to clean up your feed and narrow in on what you do want to see.

Terms of Service: Didn't Read

Digital Forensics expert David Benford suggests looking at 'Terms of Service: Didn't Read': TOSDR.org. This site aims to address the issue that almost no one reads the terms of service that we agree to all the time with the click of a button. You can search the site for a company and it will give you the key points about the terms of service ranked red, orange and green. This means you can see clearly which sites have asked you to agree to clauses which might be problematic. For example, 'content you post may be edited by the service for any reason'; that 'the service can read your private messages' or that 'deleted content is not really deleted'. You can find details for all big platforms on this site and it will help you to understand what you are agreeing to.

The Digital Supermarket – Conclusion

The 90s infomercial finishes with the mother explaining, 'As a parent, I've never been happier that my children ask their friends over for an Internet computer party.'[62] But then she gives a stern mom stare down the camera lens. 'I'd like to add a word about safety, though,' understanding that this is a tool to be used with caution. To close, she warns, 'You have to remember the Internet is not a regulated environment, so the quality and accuracy of various information can differ quite a bit. It may even be a concern if your children should access some of them.'

I always find this line one of the most important of them all. Here, the ad gives prospective users a caution – a warning label if you will: this is not regulated. This is not tested or vetted, 'quality and accuracy' are variable, and essentially, it might not be safe for children. I'm not sure we do this enough now. It is as if that 'unregulated' warning label has faded and peeled off after decades of use and we've never thought to reapply it.

But perhaps such warnings were never meant for us in the first place. We of course aren't the consumers, advertisers are. We – our minds – are what is for sale through these corporate models pioneered by Google.

We are not sufficiently protected, and these processes of product testing are not as simple as milk pasteurization. Because, here, we are not the milk drinkers, but rather, we are the milk. Our time and attention are something that can be commodified, bottled up and sold at any old corner shop – or at least the virtual equivalent. We can advocate for a social media that is based on more ethical finance models. Ones that don't treat human beings and their attention as a commodity that can be harvested.

Though the altruistic origins of sharing global knowledge are still somewhat present on the Internet, the messy, unpolished, un-monetized cork-board of ideas no longer exists. But let's think about us, 'the product' or 'the user', and what we can do to take a much more active role. First, let's talk about how we can choose healthier modes of consumption. How can we be honest with ourselves about our current digital diet? This is not to mitigate the need to responsibilize tech companies and regulators (I will get to this later in the book). But we can inform ourselves in order to understand these algorithmic processes so that we can move away from being passive products and into being active participants. This is something worth striving for. And this is something much closer to the participatory ideal dreamt up while looking at a blue sky.

Chapter 2
Acknowledging Our Addictions

Getting my first BlackBerry felt like the ultimate luxury. That trackball mouse and those clicks as my thumbs danced across the raised keys felt like 'status'. When BlackBerry launched out of Waterloo, Canada in 1999, it mainstreamed portable Internet for the world.[1] And, in turn, it made the concept of remote work possible. And though, perhaps culturally, we were not ready to fully exploit the work/life balance possibilities of this pocket-sized hardware, it freed us from the desk. And with this freedom of movement, BlackBerry changed the way we worked.

And if BlackBerry changed the way we work, eight years later in 2007, the iPhone changed the way we live. Apple pioneered touchscreen capabilities and it encouraged a boom in application development (or apps).[2] And that touchscreen, which we stroke, and with this touching develop feelings of love and dependence.[3] That touching that slides us off one app and then – somehow without us even knowing it – seamlessly onto another in a deliciously effortless trance. And it's not just the phone that cultivates this soothing scroll, but also its applications: the homestead of social media.

These new applications and the social media which these apps allowed to flourish also gave way to something unprecedented. We saw advancements in connectivity, and collectively people, regular people – working people, women, minorities, people with disabilities or people needing communities that could not be found in the offline world – were given platforms to speak from. We saw developments in citizen journalism and digital activism. These were meaningful systemic shifts to our society. Try to remember wanting to speak publicly before the Internet. You could stand on a soap box in the middle of a town square, or you could write a letter to the editor of a newspaper and hope that they published it. Ultimately, the platforms available for expression were limited. And as people were given these new platforms, the implications for activism and participatory democracy completely changed our understanding of the way the world works.

And at the same time, by way of these platforms, people also became more accessible than ever before, which led to complex social implications. Take for example, the fact we now live in information silos or 'you-loops'; or 'sharenting' and the way we datafy our kids; or 'truth decay' and the rise of disinformation. This chapter will unpack you-loops, sharenting and truth decay – all products of our smartphone addiction. But, first, it will trace the evolution of portable Internet and the way that the social media it brought forward utilized the 'attention economy' to addict us further.

You-loops, sharenting, truth decay and the attention economy are all products of our digital age but the overarching change that links all of these issues together is that social media has changed the way we think.

That is, it changed the way we access information, and process information. It's changed our taste formation and the way we formulate our beliefs (political and otherwise). And that makes the impact of social media bigger than BlackBerry changing the way we worked, or even the iPhone changing the way we live. Because to change the way we think is to change us.

The Attention Economy

In February of 2009, the social networking application Facebook launched a new feature. Housed in a light blue rectangle was a small pixelated white fist. Its thumb pointed upwards and beside it, one solitary word: 'like'.[4] The like button gained popularity immediately. A single click, easier than a comment, encouraged users to engage, swiftly and with ease. This streamlined interactions on Facebook, and other platforms quickly followed suit. This would mark the beginning of ranked, personalized news feeds, which would forever shape social media.[5]

Likes (and now a host of other responses, including love hearts and angry faces) can now be used as currency traded for popularity or sense of self-worth.[6] And, through a web of marketization, can even be monetized for financial gain. But likes are just one indicator of a greater 'attention economy', a concept first used by the economist Herbert Simon in 1971, when he wrote about the scarcity of attention in an information-rich world.[7] The Internet in its current corporate form is very much dependent on attention economics. Accruing 'likes' and maintaining our attention for as long as possible have become big business.

Researchers have mapped our obsession with both the *like economy*[8] and the *attention economy*[9] and discussed the dopamine hit received in our brains when the content we post is indeed, 'liked'.[10] This hit keeps us coming back again and again.

In these earlier years, Facebook's algorithm was based around 'liking' and clicks, which in turn determined which posts to prioritize. As such, people and brands looked to craft snappy titles or 'clickbait' led by platforms like Buzzfeed.[11] By 2013, social media companies began to see 'clickbait' fatigue, where users disliked misleading headlines, and in 2014 and 2015 Facebook changed the algorithm to downgrade clickbait by focusing on new metrics, such as the amount of time a user spent doing certain activities like watching a video or reading a story.[12]

Now the top of a Facebook user's feed – the top real estate – is based on thousands of data points made up of their online interactions, reactions and comments. The boxes further down the feed are also dictated by the algorithm. In 2021 the *Washington Post* pointed to arguments for 'a news feed that orders posts from newest to oldest is better for society. This wouldn't prioritize divisive content but could give greater space to more frequent low-engagement posters – such as that one distant friend with a new baby' – and arguably be less addictive.[13] This indeed might be a more ethical approach, but is harder to monetize and thus – for the time being – unlikely.

WHAT YOU CAN DO ABOUT IT
Understanding Data Collection

Knowledge is power. Being able to see some of the data stored – the data that shapes how algorithms map us – can often give a sense of the scope of the issue. Once a year, I ask my students to download their Facebook data. Facebook is the dinosaur of social media, and most students roll their eyes when I mention it. But this exercise is relevant for anyone who has ever had Facebook because it tends to house the earliest versions of our social media selves. It holds on to and archives the less Internet savvy, the less polished you. And so here, its 'oldness' is an asset.

One year, when I set this task, I saw one young woman scrolling through her downloaded data with an expression of dread across her face. 'You don't have to share if you don't want to,' I said to her. But she did want to. What this student – I'll call her Ella[14] – then shared I'll never forget. 'Right now,' she said (I'm paraphrasing slightly), 'I am looking at a message chain from when I was about thirteen years old, but the thing is I deleted the message chain shortly after.' She explained it was a message between her and her boyfriend at the time. 'And,' she said, 'what I'm staring at, is a picture I haven't seen since I deleted it when I was thirteen. And it's a picture of me. And I'm naked.'

Looking at what is being stored about us and how far back this storage goes can be important in informing the way that we choose to behave and operate online. For oftentimes these aren't actually private messages. But rather, they might only be private to us. To the tech industry, they might not be private. And they might not belong to Ella or any of us, but to them.

You can find the instructions on how to download your Facebook data at the Facebook help center using 'Accessing and downloading your information'. You can also download your Apple data by visiting Manage your Apple account at account.apple.com.[15]

The addictive qualities of these applications – this virtual nicotine – don't end with a 'like' but rather are built into the construction of social media on many levels. These processes include things like the refresh screen that keeps your finger going back again and again, as a constant compulsion, a process that has been described by an ex-Googler, Tristan Harris, as a slot machine where you might get a new box at the top of your page.[16] Other times, you might not. It is this potential for new content, which is not always fulfilled but sometimes might be, which feeds the addiction further. And keeping us addicted, or rather, holding our attention for as long as possible, is what can be sold to advertisers. Eyeballs at a high cost. And they are not just any eyeballs. They are your eyeballs. You – with your specific characteristics. That is to say, specific target demographics, who are fixated on their products, are valuable to advertisers. In fact, a new company, Amplified Intelligence, say they are currently shifting the advertising industry by measuring eye tracking across content.[17] This is to help advertisers distinguishing between 'active' viewing, looking straight at the ad, and 'passive attention', looking more generally at the screen, in what they call the 'human attention measurement business'.[18]

Holding that attention, getting those views or 'impressions', is crucial to the whole business model. Meta, which owns Instagram (who I'll get to in the next chapter), and Facebook, which pioneered this model, built their algorithms to keep users engaged. Recent information suggests that TikTok may be even more efficient at this. Information inadvertently released during a US lawsuit shows that an internal TikTok report identifies that the app can be addictive after the first thirty-five minutes of use[19] which as one unnamed TikTok executive stated:

The reason kids watch TikTok is because the algorithm is really good. But I think we need to be cognizant of what it might mean for other opportunities. And when I say other opportunities, I literally mean sleep, and eating, and moving around the room, and looking at someone in the eyes.[20]

My team and I, while conducting the Digital Nutrition research project, found young people time and time again referencing the hyper-addictive quality of TikTok and the ways it could 'hook' them and pull them away from just about anything else. As one teenager said to me:

you'll start watching something . . . . you'll end up forgetting and just sort of being there for hours until it's like night-time and you need to get up in the next couple of hours and you're already passed the amount of time you'd need to get a proper night's sleep.

The reason for the addictive quality is that algorithms work out content that will hook us; the content that grabs us. This creates an environment in which hate, harm and disinformation can thrive because, quite simply, it is more efficient at grabbing us. And disinformation is often just more interesting than truth. American legal scholar Jack Balkin has suggested that the attention economy encourages companies to prioritize things that hold viewers' attention, and that this content is less likely to be informative or educational, and more likely to be 'false, demagogic, conspiratorial, and incendiary, and to appeal to emotions such as fear, envy, anger, hatred, and distrust'.[21]

As whistleblower Frances Haugen has testified, Facebook have realized that 'if they change the algorithm to be safer, people will spend less time on the site, they'll click on less ads, they'll make less money.'[22] So, though these algorithms *could* be changed according to Haugen, that is, they could be altered to deprioritize inflammatory content, more often than not, they aren't. This isn't necessarily to say that companies are wilfully spreading harm. But they're not investing in changes to stop prioritizing harm. They are not doing enough to correct these processes[23] and have little financial incentive to do so, because ultimately, they are in competition with each other to show they are the most attention-grabbing of them all. And this proof of engagement is what they are selling to advertisers.

My report with colleagues from 2024 showed that TikTok's algorithm prioritized harmful content on young people's For

You pages. The way harm is actively pushed can further increase the obsession with the subject matter being offered.[24] Because according to ex-TikTok employee Andrew Kaung, the algorithms' fuel is engagement, regardless of whether it is positive or negative.[25]

But, this engagement is not just based upon our interactions with the content we are being 'fed' or even, in turn, us deciding that we 'like' it. This economic structure is also based upon us 'sharing' pieces of ourselves or 'sharing' pieces of those we love. And, if we are parents, this could have impacts on our children. In working to understand the structures that build our addictions and the rules of the attention economy, it's important to also acknowledge the implications of our digital addiction on others. We ourselves are a part of the attention economy, and many times introduce our children into this economy long before they have ever had a device of their own, through a practice known as 'sharenting'.

Sharenting

A woman is rolled into an operating theatre for a c-section. Her partner, diligently dressed in scrubs and cap, stands anxiously by her head, and leans down to her cheek with a supportive word. Meanwhile, the obstetrician performs the surgery behind a sheet raised above the woman's ribcage. When the doctor finally looks up, she gives the nurse a nod. The nurse puts a hand on the father's shoulder and warmly suggests, 'You can get your camera ready.' The father pulls his phone out of the pocket of his scrubs and timidly watches, mediated through the digital screen.

The sheet is dropped, and the doctor raises a red, gooey infant into the air. It's a boy. The child opens his mouth and screams. His tiny chest heaving to exhibit his newly functional lungs. The father taps his screen to capture a few photos. The midwife wraps the baby and brings him to the mother's face. The mother nuzzles her child who attempts to suck her nose. The father snaps a few more images. These will be this human's first digital record.

Moments later, the father will post an image of the baby, nuzzling and nose-sucking mummy, on a WhatsApp group, shared with their close family members. This will be the baby's first piece of digital data. That evening, the couple take a picture of the baby, now clean, swaddled and accessorized with a pale blue knitted hat. They decided on a caption: 'Welcome baby Finn. Our hearts are exploding with love. heart emoji, baby emoji, heart emoji'. Then they upload the picture to both their Instagram accounts. These will be the first public record of the baby on social media.

Researching parents' sharing practices in London and LA, Veronica Barassi has analysed how children's personal information is collected, archived and sold as unique profiles that can follow them for the entirety of their lives, by way of 'sharenting'.[26] Sharenting is the process through which parents share their children on social media and create a digital record of them. Some advocates argue that the sharing of the newborn Finn is prioritizing the entertainment of adults over the child's agency, but most Gen X and millennial parents would agree that it's entirely appropriate to opt for an Instagram birth announcement over the one in the newspaper that accompanied their own birth. Social norms now dictate that sharing your kids online is valued and celebrated – so much so that a 2010 US study suggested that 92% of children have an online presence by the age of two.[27]

A more recent report from the Children's Commissioner found that on average, by the age of thirteen, parents have posted 1,300 photos and videos of their child to social media. This data greatly increases when children themselves go onto social media, with on average, children posting to social media twenty-six times per day – a total of nearly 70,000 posts by age eighteen.[28]

Whether sharenting is a problem and/or what is the appropriate amount to share of your child on social media is an ongoing debate. Some legal scholars and children's rights activists have argued for legislation on sharenting, though few countries have actioned this in any meaningful way. Recently, there have been campaigns encouraging parents to think of how sharenting might relate to physical safety concerns. For example, in September of 2022, a series of media outlets ran stories encouraging parents to make safer and more nuanced choices around back-to-school photos. This campaign suggested that putting photos of your kids in their school uniforms on public social media platforms gives potential predators an indication of your child's daily location. Back-to-school posts are also often captioned with names and year group, which gives additional identifying information that could put them at risk. As part of the campaign, cyber security company McAfee warned of paedophiles making use of such images and circulating them on online networks. In America the Better Business Bureau (BBB) warns against the trend of first day photos where children hold up 'first day of school' signs which display personal information, including their name and grade, because of the threat they pose in relation to identity theft, financial loss and even safety.[29] Nevertheless, an estimated 53% of parents still shared back-to-school photos on social media in September of 2022 across the UK.[30]

In fact, the Children's Commissioner report on sharenting states that:

> *We all need to pause and think. At the very least, schools need to start educating their pupils about the importance of guarding personal information. Children and parents need*

Acknowledging Our Addictions 39

to be much more aware of what they share and consider the consequences . . . And crucially, the Government needs to monitor the situation and refine data protection legislation if needed, so that children are genuinely protected – especially as technology develops . . . Children are being 'datafied'.[31]

Although this report from 2018 is now a long time ago in the life span of a child, still governments have not sufficiently addressed this concern. As a general rule, posting images to public social media accounts that make your children easy to locate – as with back-to-school photos – can be an unsafe practice and should be considered carefully. The end of this section goes into these points in more detail. But physical safety is just one of the concerns related to sharenting. Issues related to datafication, digital labour, child rights and the monetizing of children are also factors to be aware of when sharing your kids. Public awareness is rising about this issue. In March 2025, the UK data watchdog, the Information Commissioner's Office (ICO) launched an investigation into TikTok's use of children's personal information.[32]

Wren Eleanor is a three-year-old girl. She often wears her blonde hair in two bunches atop her head. She likes trying new foods; playing with water balloons; and wearing 'mommy–daughter' matching outfits. She also has 17 million followers on TikTok.[33] It is estimated that the TikTok account through which her mother, Jaquelyn, posts content of the toddler generates about $13,000 US per post. Public concern broke out in the summer of 2022 when TikTok users suggested that images of the child in crop tops and bathing suits were not only sexualizing but that they opened Wren up to child predators.[34] Commenters pointed out that a video of Wren wearing an orange crop top had over 45,000 saves, and that a short film of Wren eating a hot dog was saved nearly 375,000 times. Finally, it was one user's suggestion that 'Wren Eleanor tampon' and 'Wren Eleanor pickle' were some of the popular searches that come up in the TikTok search bar that eventually led to comments being disabled on the account.[35]

The family vlogging industry – where families share content of their day-to-day lives – boomed in the 2010s.[36] In the 2020s, we have now entered what journalist Sarah Manavis refers to as the era of more 'ethical' family vlogging.[37] Here influ-parents claim 'transparency' about how their kids 'work' at 'content creation'. And supposedly the ways in which their children have personal agency and 'boundaries' and promise audiences that they would never force their kids to perform. But, regardless of the new cultural shift, for both the child and family influencers concrete guidance around ethical practice remains limited.

Highlighting cases like Wren's, Singapore-based scholar and social media critic Crystal Abidin has pointed out that this labour performed by child influencers within a parent's social media account falls outside the legal framework of child labour laws.[38] From this perspective the phenomenon can be likened to the child stars of the Hollywood studio system, tales of whom revolved around child performers supporting their entire families and then left penniless in adulthood. France is one of the few countries to have passed laws to regulate working hours and ensure that the children are recipients of the money made.[39] In France, the government must authorize approval before children can engage in online labour, according to the Library of Congress.[40] The law also covers the 'right to be forgotten', meaning that platforms will be obliged to take down content upon the child's request.[41] And in July of 2024, the state of Illinois added an amendment to its child labour law, requiring that children who appear on the social media profiles of so-called 'Influencer moms' are paid. Specifically: children under the age of sixteen should receive 15% of an influencer's gross earnings if they appear in at least 30% of monetized content online. Guardians must place these earnings into a trust for the child.[42] In the UK, legal expert, Dr Francis Rees of the University of Essex, advocates that child influencers do not share the same protections as child models or child actors and is advocating for a new set of guidelines.[43] For now, few to no laws exist, raising the question of whether, within the digital sphere, ethics around child labour are stuck in the workshops of Victorian London.

The 'Save Wren Eleanor' movement was a watershed moment in how we all think about the ethics of sharing online. More specifically, movements like Wren's have encouraged parents to think more critically about 'sharing' their kids. Of course, sharing your kids on a public TikTok or YouTube account, regardless of the number of followers, has potential repercussions. These are often linked to the scale of your following but regardless of the size of your account the repercussions of digital sharing are different to the ones posed by showing two colleagues a dog-eared school picture out of a wallet like my parents used to do. Issues of connectivity, spreadability and anonymity make monitoring who sees what and for what purpose difficult. For these reasons more and more parents are now choosing to lock down accounts, limit what they choose to share, or omit children's faces from photos.

In the majority of cases sharenting isn't done on a mass level, or for financial gain or in any way in conflict with child labour laws. Quite the opposite. It is done with love and pride. A sense of success. For parents, particularly those of us who have spent our adult lives quantifying our successes through virtual validation from friends or the 'like economy', the sharing of our children is a very natural practice. A way for us to mark our greatest achievement: our kids.

It isn't necessarily a bad practice, but what is important to understand is that when you are posting content of your children – or yourself for that matter – you are engaging in an exchange. You are offered services that enable you to easily share precious moments with friends and family, and in exchange you pay by creating a digital footprint for yourself and for your child. This footprint isn't necessarily harmful. In fact, one day your children might be grateful that you have taken so much care to cultivate a digital scrapbook of their early years, something that they will be able to treasure in adulthood. But the practice also might infringe on your child's rights to privacy through what sociologist, Deborah Lupton calls the 'data self',[44] and it will generate a data footprint of your child likely before they have the ability to consent to this happening.

The Fraud Issue

This sharing – of birth announcements, parties or even pets – can spill into other areas of concern. According to Barclays Bank, there are three key pieces of information used in identity theft: a person's name, date of birth and home address. These can be deduced through sharenting by way of photos or updates on social media accounts – for example, a photograph of a child on their birthday with a location tagged might give away all this personal information. With this information, criminals can make a start on accessing bank accounts or making credit applications. The Children's Commissioner has reported that children's data is being stored until they turn eighteen, after which fraud can commence.[45] And even if we are not parents or that worried about our own privacy, sharing things about ourselves can put our families at risk. A birthday post might put your Facebook-using mother at risk if her banking password is indeed that: your birthdate. In fact, Barclays Bank has forecast that by 2030 'sharenting' will account for two-thirds of identity fraud facing young people in the next decade and will cost £667 million per year.[46] The FBI reports that the amount of money people have lost from online crimes that targeted children has more than tripled, from half a million in 2022 to over $2 million in 2023.[47] Let me say this again: one of the largest banks in Britain estimates that two-thirds of identity fraud that will impact children's future finances will be because of what their parents are currently sharing about them online – sharenting being done right now.

With over 90% of American parents choosing to share their children on social media, the majority of children have grown up datafied from birth. From baby Finn's post-caesarean appearance on that family WhatsApp group – possibly even at his twelve-week ultrasound scan, or a snap of a positive pregnancy test – he can be found in the back pages of his parent's Instagram posts. And as such, we shouldn't be surprised if – or when – our children want to take control of their digital footprints and begin their own social media accounts.[48]

These inadvertent privacy infringements can also extend beyond our children, jeopardizing our homes and own personal safety. Take the classic story of a break-in caused by a vacation photo posted on Instagram (letting the world know you are out of the country for a week) or personal location sharing by way of running apps (publicly sharing the route you run on your own every day). These are just some of the many ways we can create vulnerabilities without meaning to. What is important is that whether or not we are parents, we should all collectively be making proactive, rather than reactive, conscious choices about our online usage. And if we are parents, that we have already begun talking to kids about how the online world works by the time they themselves are active participants (I'll get to this later). As twenty-first-century humans, we and our children all need to understand how the digital space works, and more importantly, what it does. Awareness of these processes is how you build critical thinking skills and build smart, aware and confident digital citizens.

Sharenting: What You Can Do About It

- **Lock down your personal accounts.** Check who can access your information on your social media platforms and update your privacy settings accordingly. Then you may wish to consider culling your list to only close friends and family. Alternatively, set up another closed account specifically for this purpose.
- **Pause before you post.** Take a moment to think though the possible implications of the post with regard to safety. Are there risks of online exposure or is there something about the post that might embarrass your child in the future? Ask yourself, are there ways that you could limit the identifiable or personal information in the post?
- **Ask.** If your child is old enough, it is important to respect their rights and ask permission before posting. This can be a good way of introducing the concept of consent.

Exercise: Security and Privacy: the basics

- **Stay updated.** Updating your devices makes them much less likely to be hacked. So update your devices, but also apps, games and wearables like smart watches and smart devices such as Alexa or Google Home. You should also have anti-virus software installed.
- **Password protected.** Ideally you should have a different password for every account you use. Preferably it should be long and with a mix of upper and lower case, numbers and special characters. More specifically, try not to use your name, families' names, where you live or your birthday as these are easy to guess. Log out of websites and apps when you finish using them.
- **Draw your boundaries.** Make video calls password-protected so only people you know can join. When you are on a video call

or posting pictures think about whether your surroundings give away personal information about you, like where you are. Some apps automatically record video so check your settings and cover your camera when you aren't using it. Check your location settings on apps.[49]

The Echo Chamber

Baby Finn is now fifteen years old; he is fascinated by Transformers and can spend hours sketching detailed drawings of the characters. He is self-described as a 'stay at home and play video games' type of guy. He wears headphones with a mic atop a mop of black hair. He has excellent focus and attention to detail. Finn is not a real teenager, but rather he is a composite character drawn from my research. That is, his characteristics, passions and experiences are from real people interviewed by my team in 2023.[50] Family members tell him he is a talented artist, and he dreams of one day being an animator. There is a sixth form not far from his house, which has a fantastic art programme, and they hold an interview admission day yearly. Finn is nervous about his interview and works tirelessly to prepare. Finally, after months of waiting, Finn receives a letter. He hasn't been accepted. He is heartbroken.

To cheer himself up, he goes on the online platform Discord looking for people speaking about Transformers. He stumbles upon a Discord server that he thinks is about Transformers. It is in part, but it is also discussing the current plight of young men. People on the forum are joking about women and minorities having all the advantages and that white boys have no opportunities any more. Finn thinks about this in relation to the recent letter and it makes a lot of sense. He starts to get really frustrated about it and keeps reading the posts from others. An hour later, while scrolling through TikTok, he sees a post lamenting the fact that it's the worst time in history to be a boy. It's funny – or not funny – because it's true, Finn thinks to himself. He lingers on the video for a few seconds longer than on most and TikTok's algorithm has a seed to grow. He is quickly fed another video on the subject, and then another. And these videos are ones that feed Finn's insecurity, his disappointment, and offer potential answers. They get him, they know him, making it harder and harder for him to stop scrolling.

A *filter bubble* is a concept proposed by digital activist Eli Pariser.[51] Pariser argues that there is no such thing as a singular Internet any more but rather that there are as many Internets as there are users. As algorithms continue their ever-increasing attempt to personalize our online experience and feed each of us more 'relevant' content everyone's digital world becomes entirely self-curated. This means you could be seeing completely different news, ideas, culture, and arguably facts than someone sitting next to you on a bus or on your own living-room sofa. Even if you are getting your news from reputable mainstream sources, by way of news apps (e.g. Apple News or Google News), the articles you are fed will likely be on specific topics and hold specific viewpoints algorithmically tailored for you. And this, can shape how you understand the world.

Pariser uses the term *You Loop* here,[52] which I like to apply to any algorithmic feed that shapes and ultimately limits the culture and information that we receive. Most of us consume much less radio or terrestrial TV (which selects a variety of content, arguably, with a relatively balanced view). Instead, with the promise of immediacy, choice and personalization, we turn to Spotify, Netflix or news apps – or, for teenagers it's Instagram, TikTok and YouTube. But now – even with all of the world's music and programming at our fingertips – do we actually hear and see much less? Less difference of opinion? Less diverse content? For example, the work of two film scholars, Neta Alexander[53] and Mattias Frey,[54] who have studied Netflix algorithms and described how Netflix uses both scrolling activity and viewing habits in the recommending process and then uses this information to buy or produce its own new content. So, not only is the culture you are offered on Netflix shaped though your data, but the cultural content it creates is also informed by algorithmic data. Algorithmic-itized culture all offered in an easily consumable datafied smoothie.

Pariser warns us about this seemingly smooth and entertaining reality. He says:

> *Media also shape identity. And as a result, these services may end up creating a good fit between you and your media by changing . . . you. If a self-fulfilling prophecy is a false definition of the world that through one's actions becomes true, we're now on the verge of self-fulfilling identities, in which the Internet's distorted picture of us becomes who we really are.*[55]

And as the process begins to shape who we are; not just kids like Finn, but all of us so-called 'grown-ups' – you-loops and filter bubbles can give way to echo chambers, which function by feeding each person a high dosage of information that confirms a very narrow world view. Echo chambers can take on the form of an addiction in a short period of time. You, like Finn, might have one off day, and this has given the algorithm one little seed of an idea to nurture and grow.[56] But back to Finn scrolling through TikTok. TikTok functions differently from the comparative old-timer that is Facebook. It is fast-paced, short-form video content, consumed at high dosages, which can be much more potent than the relatively static social media of a decade ago.

Because of this, scientists and educators alike have expressed ever-greater concerns about echo chambers' influence on the minds of youth along with the rapid rise of mis/disinformation on the Internet. Through platforms like TikTok, content that was once relegated to relatively niche forums is now to be algorithmically offered, and arguably pushed, on popular teen platforms. In a report I led with Dr Caitlin Shaughnessy and Professor Nicola Shaughnessy in 2024, we looked at the gamification of harmful content on TikTok.[57] We found that as people scroll and microdose on harmful content, it can feel like entertainment to them.[58] Content is presented as inspirational or in the form of memes and parodies, which can mask the toxic ideas or violence at its roots. And this content is pervasive, presented as bitesize, digestible and entertaining chunks: as one young man put it in our research, these memes are 'just everywhere . . .'.[59]

On Finn's tablet, Andrew Tate slides onto the screen. Tate, who has been banned from TikTok, still has clips that circulate widely on the platform. Tate has tweeted that women should share responsibility for their assaults and advocated that an appropriate response to infidelity is to 'bang out the machete, boom her in the face and grip her by the neck'. Tate spent time in prison on charges of rape and human trafficking. Following his arrest in 2022, a wave of panic swept across mainstream media noting his worrying fan-following of teenage boys and linked his ideology to the online community of incels[60] (involuntary celibates).[61] Typically, those in the incel community are young men who feel left out of relationships and society more generally and take to the Internet to voice feelings of frustration and, at times, desire for revenge.[62] Incel logic often positions women's upward mobility in society as the root of their unhappiness[63] and in some rare instances, members of the community have committed acts of mass violence.

At one point I consulted for the Metropolitan Police in this area and know all too well how young people, often with existing vulnerabilities, find their way to the online spaces looking for community. And they find the wrong ones. Generally, these are young people looking for belonging and they are trying to articulate a feeling of a loss of control. Loss of control over their future, their career prospects, their happiness. And here in these echo chambers they are offered answers. Answers about how the upward mobility of women and minorities will limit their opportunities. But rarely do these communities offer positive role models, a growth mindset or beneficial ways forward. And so, instead of feeling better, they can become indoctrinated into ideologies that ultimately make them more unhappy and unwell. In rare cases, this results in terrible repercussions for all involved.

However, there is a small comfort in knowing that a very small proportion of people (young and less young) will actualize violence in this way. And so this analysis is a bit unfair to kids like Finn. What's often being missed are more nuanced discussions; the ways in which online misogyny and incel discourses might offer a means for young men to voice a fear of loss of control at a time that is very bleak for all young people. It is in these gaps in understanding and educational approaches that we have entered the age when misogynistic content has become saturated into popular youth ecosystems.[64]

What this popularization effect is doing is making young people angrier and more unhappy. Accounts from community professionals that I have worked with have suggested that boys seem 'more agitated' and 'depressed'.[65] They have tendencies to act out aggressively and seem to be developing more prejudices.

Through the echo chamber – in this case the high dosages of hateful content – violent views are becoming normalized for young people and are becoming interwoven into daily life.[66]

There is, however, admirable work being done in this area. The report *The State of UK Boys: Understanding and Transforming Gender in the Lives of UK Boys* (2022)[67] and Education Scotland's Mentors in Violence Prevention (MVP) programme,[68] which I've worked on, offers peer-to-peer learning where older boys mentor younger boys about gender violence. This form of positive male role-modelling is where boys are not just told what they can't be but what they can. But however important these initiatives are, they are small turns of the dial. We need more.

Finn's story is just one example. There are of course, many, many different echo chambers, peddling different beliefs but employing the same digital processes. Fifteen-year-old Finn could also be Michael, aged seventy-two, who has done away with mainstream news, is only receiving information from alt application Telegram, and after an explosive outburst last Thanksgiving is no longer invited to his sister's house; or Deb, sixty-seven, a conspiracy theorist, who is still convinced that the Queen had Diana killed; or Laura, thirty-eight, who after being diagnosed with breast cancer began to follow a course of natural treatments pushed to her on Instagram instead of chemotherapy – she was a mum of two.

There are ways to talk to people, to adults in your life about these issues. We can step away from the minutiae of the arguments and speak about the broader structures that are facilitating these information pathways. It doesn't matter if it is Finn, Michael, Deb, Laura or you (in whatever echo chamber you may have found yourself in), what is important is to recognize these structures. And if someone in your life is in an echo chamber, rather than trying to debate them around the actual topic, try to help them step away and see the broader processes at play.

There are actions we all can take to protect ourselves and those we love from echo chambers. As parents, we need to be proactive and intervene early on to try and help young people to navigate their pull. For it is not just that silky touchscreen that cultivates this soothing scroll, but also its applications, which are tailored just for us – to exploit our hopes, fears and frustrations in an endless stream of constant renewal. There is an escape route from the echo chamber. The escape can come from you. You can be honest with yourself or talk to your family. You can acknowledge your own you-loops, filter bubbles and echo chambers. You can think critically about what you are consuming and encourage those you love to do the same. And, in turn, you can through this give them the tools they need to be more active in their, in all of our, digital engagement, resisting the role of passive product.

Echo Chambers: What You Can Do About Them

How to recognize an echo chamber.

A: If everyone and everything that you are interacting with online has the same opinion as you and you only see content that confirms your point of view. And if certain news stories, people and themes come up over and over again.

B: If you think you might be in an echo chamber, look for alternative sources and other points of view. You don't necessarily have to agree with them, but it is important to understand that they are there.

How you can do information-building about echo chambers with your kids.

1. **The Emperor's New Clothes.** BBC Bitesize uses the story of the Emperor's new clothes to introduce the concept of echo chambers.[69] This story can be a great way to talk to children about someone believing something they want to be true; and how everyone agreeing can make something seem more true or instil a (potentially untrue) point of view.
2. **Up for Debate.** Introducing the idea that healthy debate is a good thing can be done from an early age. You can introduce the value of listening to both sides of the story as a way to develop critical thinking. You can introduce healthy debates as a family – pick a subject that isn't too personal but you know your kids care about and keep it light. For example, you could debate the idea 'Teachers should have to wear school uniform', with one side arguing for it and the other against. Have some ground rules like 'try to back your argument up with evidence', 'you can't repeat the same point in different ways again and again' and 'you can't only use emotional arguments.'
3. **Source Decode.** For older children, you might want to look at news stories that are reported in multiple places and talk about how they are reported differently. Look at what stories aren't reported from some news outlets but are in others and talk about why that might be.
4. **Praise.** When your children use critical thinking, respect someone else's opinion or look for evidence to back something up, let them know they are developing valuable life skills and that you are proud of them.

How to talk to someone in your life who might be in an echo chamber

1. **Be proactive, not reactive.** Start conversations organically, rather than in reaction to a comment or event. This will set an objective tone. Make conversations short and often rather than one big event.
2. **Think big picture.** Focus the conversation on the overarching structures at play. Where possible, inspire agency around these topics by offering information about online processes and then let them do the critical thinking.
3. **Focus on the positive.** Focus on positive examples, role models and narratives. This is often much more powerful than talking about the negative examples. Talk to older children and teens about what they can be rather than what they can't.

Gaming

Gaming can be great tool for relaxing, developing problem-solving and fine motor skills and finding or maintaining community. For example, some might choose to stay in touch with friends and family by way of gaming. You can chat to kids about the value of playing games together with others present. Having groups of people together gaming can make for a social and community-building approach to games.

At the same time, gaming can also be a gateway where people (particularly young people) can be introduced to harm. And so informing yourself about the gaming landscape is important. Young people might encounter harm through adults gaming on the same platforms as children. Also, games can be a space where young people are introduced to sexism, misogyny and racist content through listening to others on voice chat or by going online to find gaming tips and stumbling across this content. To take a safe approach to your child's gaming habits think about these key features.

- **If a child is gaming online this can open them up to playing with adults they don't know.** Actively choose who you want (or who you want your child) to play with. If your child has a headset it is possible that they will be able to hear other players in the game, who could be adults. Voice chat is a space where many children can be introduced to sexually inappropriate content, swearing, misogynist and racist language. To avoid this, you might want to agree rules around only using headsets to talk to family and friends and choose games with limited voice chat functionality. You could also try implementing rules such as asking them to tell you who they are talking to every time you walk by.
- **Some games can show your location.** This means people playing a game can detect your physical location. Disable settings which allow anyone to play, or which detect other players in the same area. Make sure settings are in place to prevent recording and changes to avatars and nicknames.
- **Check the PEGI rating.** This provides age classifications for games like film ratings. Not all games need to be allowed. There are a lot of games out there. Kids don't need *all* of them. You can set limits around what games you think are appropriate. Also, take a look at AskAboutGames.com, which has a games guide to help you choose suitable games.
- **Be proactive around time.** Decide how long you want to spend on the platform. You can find family agreements which you can use to talk about boundaries and rules at AskAboutGames and the NSPCC.
- **Don't add credit card details to a game which will ask you for micropayments.** Only download from the official game website. Be aware of buying anything for your game from another website as it could contain a virus. Check the NSPCC website for information about scams.

- **Try to keep a shared space.** For younger children, games should be played in a shared place where parents can be aware of what is going on. Whenever possible keep gaming (and Internet access, generally) in a public place within the home, for example keep the doors open when they're playing alone in a room.
- **Talk to kids about sharing personal information.** Have conversations about being cautious of people offering gifts, rewards or compliments, or asking to keep things secret. You might want to address the fact that they shouldn't share personal details and images (which might reveal their location) including sexual ones; or move to a different, more private app.

The mental health charity Young Minds[70] suggests the following things that young people would like their parents to consider when talking to them about games:

1. Start by finding out what their experience is, rather than assuming gaming is 'bad'.
2. Ask them what they enjoy about gaming and what they get out of it, and show interest in what they have to say.
3. Recognize that gaming is a social thing they do with their friends; think about ways to make gaming more sociable if you are worried because your child spends lots of time gaming alone.
4. Try to find out what else is going on that might be causing them to game so much, rather than assuming gaming itself is the problem.
5. Look for a compromise.

Truth Decay

Southport is a Victorian seaside town in the north of England. It is typical of other northern towns built around a beach front. Its somewhat faded glory harkens back to a time before EasyJet, and package holidays. But on the morning of Monday the 29th of July, the first hours of the summer holidays in 2024, Southport was buzzing. Among the activities was a Taylor Swift Yoga and Dance Workshop for children aged two to six running at a local yoga studio, Hart Space. The poster for the class had pink and purple clouds and 'Taylor Swift' written in bright pink script. Hart Space itself feels like many yoga studios – a predominately female safe space. The neon sign on the wall reads, 'This Is Our Happy Place'. But this 'Happy Place' would sadly become the site of a horrific incident. The mass stabbing attack would leave two children and two adults injured and three children dead. The class, specifically a Taylor Swift dance class. The attack, arguably on empowered girlhood. The deaths of Elsie Dot (seven), Alice (nine) and Bebe (six) are a horrific tragedy.

Their killer was Axel Rudakubana. When police searched the teen's home they found 164,000 downloaded documents including extreme violent imagery and information[71] depicting content on Nazi Germany, and an al-Qaeda training manual[72] from which he used techniques when carrying out the acts of violence.[73] Before leaving home to carry out the attack he viewed the violent footage of an attempted murder of a bishop in Australia on X.[74] Australia's Internet regulator later reported it had requested that X take down the video, but X had only blocked it in Australia so that it was still possible to view it globally.[75]

After Rudakubana's attack, differing accounts began to circulate that the attacker was an undocumented immigrant (though Rudakubana was born in Cardiff) and Andrew Tate posted a call to arms:

Somebody Arrived in the UK on a boat. Nobody knew where he's from . . . I don't see any protests in the UK. Nobody is complaining . . . The soul of the Western man is so broken. When the invaders slaughter your daughters, you do absolutely fucking nothing.[76]

The next day, an angry mob surrounded a mosque in Southport. More than fifty police officers were injured in the violence. People ripped up paving stones and garden walls to throw at the police in anger, people who were apparently longing for a less violent time, for Britain of the past, like the beachfront not far from where they attacked.

What happened in Southport is devastating, but it doesn't exist in a silo. More than a decade and an ocean away from the events in Southport is the village of Sandy Hook.[77] This Connecticut town has leafy treelined pavements[78] and a picturesque main street where an American flag flies atop a 110-foot flagpole.[79] The village is also home to Sandy Hook Elementary School. A school where the principal, Dawn Hochsprung had once dressed up as a Sandy Hook Book Fairy – to inspire her first-graders to read.[80] Just a month later, on Friday 14 December 2012, Sandy Hook Elementary would become the site of a mass shooting, which would claim the lives of twenty children aged between six and seven years and six adult staff members including Dawn Hochsprung. The gunman, twenty-year-old Adam Lanza, was fascinated by previous mass shootings and spree killings, including the 1999 Columbine High School shooting.[81] Documents released by the FBI showed that he had also used a website where players could role-play the Columbine shooters, Eric Harris and Dylan Klebold.[82]

The youngest of the victims was six-year-old Noah Pozner. Noah loved superheroes[83] and bubble baths.[84] In December 2012, a half hour after his dad, Lenny, dropped him off at school, Noah was shot dead.[85]

Just days after the massacre, disinformation began to circulate online that the shooting had been staged by actors and was a ploy by the anti-gun movement.[86] One person who popularized these theories was Alex Jones, who ran the website Infowars along with associated YouTube content.[87] Jones repeatedly claimed:

> *Sandy Hook is a [sic] synthetic completely fake, with actors, in my view manufactured. I couldn't believe it at first, I knew they had actors there, but I thought they killed some real kids and it just shows how bold they are, that they clearly used actors.*[88]

When Lenny finally felt ready to post photos of Noah online, people left comments reading 'fake kid' and 'didn't die'.[89] People turned conspiracy theorists, who harassed the parents and siblings of a mass school shooting, people who doctored images of children's graves reading 'didn't die here'.[90]

Professor Lewis Griffin works with the UK's Home Office on disinformation. He explained to me that one of the most pervasive harms to our contemporary society is known as 'truth decay'. The term was coined by the Rand Foundation in 2018 to describe the undermining of evidence-making.[91] But to Lewis, truth had been in trouble long before the Rand report was written, 'fuelled by the Internet and social media and steered by polarization',[92] and he believes it is set to get worse.[93]

When we speak about truth decay and the slow insidious increase of systemic mis- or disinformation, we're not talking about one post one time, but rather the accumulative impact of constantly micro-dosing on untruths. Disinformation can be more attention-grabbing than truth and thus rewarded by the algorithm. This is truth decay. When loneliness, alienation, polarization and political unrest become the staple of our daily media diet. When, as we scroll, as we continuously consume small doses of disinformation – which cumulatively make up a very high dose – so our political discourses and our societal framework shift. The capability of this technology to capture attention is not weakening. It is only getting stronger. It will only get better and better at locking us in. And this is something we should all be collectively concerned about as we move deeper into individual echo chambers. The events in Southport and Sandy Hook are painful examples of the potential patterns of harm brought forth by echo chambers. Here we see people existing in echo chambers promoting and normalizing violence. Then they actualize this violence in horrific ways. These acts of violence are then spun into further echo chambers that can be used to shape new narratives of violence, which can further hurt the communities – and at times survivors – who have already suffered dearly.

The day after her daughter was killed and the night of the subsequent attack on the mosque, the mother of Elsie Dot took the time out of her grief to put a message on social media: 'This is the only thing that I will write, but please stop the violence in Southport tonight.'[94] She did not want her daughter's death to instigate more violence, to have her fate used to fuel anger and hate. Not for a Southport of the past. Not for a Southport now. And not in Elsie's name.

How to Spot Misinformation

+ **Seeing isn't believing.** Be critical of what you see online and think about where you are getting your information and news from. Use fact-checking where possible (see the exercise below for more information on this).
+ **Look around.** What's around the information? Do the fonts change often? That suggests the post has been pulled from multiple different sources, possibly by a bot. Are there lots of hyperlinks to other websites? Do the sender and/or website look genuine? How is the information presented? You can use Link Gopher to see what hyperlinks are embedded in the page, which

will give you an idea of where the creator of the page wants to send you.[95]

- **Spot the bot.** If a user's handle or account name has lots of incongruous letters or numbers it might be a bot. Be wary if the account is only resharing content (and lots of it . . .) or using the same phrase posted by multiple accounts. If you want to know more, you can do an image search for the profile photo and see if it is often used elsewhere, as this is often an indicator.

- **Image conscious.** Images can be taken out of their original context and be presented as news. Be aware by zooming in to check if the street signs, advertising, licence plates and shop signs appear to be in the language of or from the country where the poster or image claims it is. Some AI-created images will have writing on billboards or street signs which appears backwards. Also be aware of memes – but just because a photo of a well-known person is put together with a quote doesn't mean they've actually said it. It's also important to remember that AI makes it possible for images and videos to be deepfakes. Look closely at the image and see if it has unusual components like distorted details in the background, too many fingers on hands or people with plastic-looking faces.[96]

- **Just because you want it, doesn't make it so.** Sometimes when we want something to be true, we believe it is. Try to be aware of this type of confirmation bias. Also, just because you like and trust someone, it doesn't mean that what they send or show you is factual. You might forward something because it validates your opinions and beliefs – or because you think it is funny and ironic – and others may take this as fact.

- **Take a beat.** Before you comment or react to a post, ask who else is telling this story and whether you can find information from another perspective. Are there experts talking on the

Acknowledging Our Addictions

subject? You can also visit the Internet Matters site, which has a critical thinking guide and a Find the Fake news interactive quiz, as well as loads of other digital literacy content.

Here are some exercises to help you and your family understand fact-checking.

Finding a Fake

✚ Using www.sightengine.com you can put questionable images into their search, and they will give you a percentage relating to how likely the image is to be fake. This is a task that you can do by yourself or with others, including with quite young children in order to talk to them about misinformation.

✚ You can also do a reverse image search, where a photo is used to search instead of typing in text – you can use TinEye, Google or Bing.[97] This will help you to find information about the photo including if it has been used elsewhere.

Follow the Facts

✚ Look up a reputable fact-checking site like Full Fact (see https://fullfact.org).

✚ Select a fact-check topic that interests you and read the claim. Try first conducting your own search outside of the fact-checking site, to test your own research skills.

✚ Finally, read the fact-checking site's answer. Think about how they break down the claim and how you feel about their findings. Are you surprised?[98]

Acknowledging Our Addictions – Conclusion

Portable Internet, pioneered by BlackBerry, has allowed for a blurring of work and home. This was exacerbated during the pandemic, and many of us developed hybrid lives. Working from home means we are spending more time in the presence of friends and family, but at the same time involves integrating technologically facilitated moments of working into home life. And so we resort to multitasking: pushing a swing in a playground whilst answering an email. This isn't necessarily bad – we are likely spending more time at home with our kids or with people we love. But it does mean that we need technology ever present in order to facilitate this new reality.

Technologies powered by the attention economy and underpinned by a lack of regulation. Technologies that don't want you to just answer that one email but are specifically designed to move you from that email on to another application, that are built to encourage more and more digital usage. And that usage may prioritize ever more negative thinking patterns and behaviours. These patterns that could include you-loops, disinformation or truth decay. For some individuals, the existence of truth decay will have the gravest of consequences. We should continue to mourn, rage and lament what happened in that Taylor Swift dance class and the loss of Elsie Dot, Alice and Bebe, and Noah, Dawn and those who were killed at Sandy Hook, not only for those who loved them, but for all of us collectively. Because the loss of those lives is representative of a massive loss for the world. These events demonstrate tragic cycles where violence is digitally normalized, and then horrifically actualized, and further still spun out into new narratives of hate.

This isn't to suggest that everyone is going to commit acts of violence longing for a supposed Southport of the past. But these same attention-grabbing, addictive processes, are built to pull us all in – into potentially ever-deeper echo chambers.

But by informing ourselves of what's actually driving what we see every time we pick up our phones, we can become more critical and intentional about how we use them. That knowledge will strip you-loops and truth decay of some of their power. And we can, we must, make more informed decisions about how we are 'sharing' pieces of ourselves, or 'sharing' our children – datafying children – in order to help safeguard them now, and safeguard against the digital imprints that will forever follow their future selves. Check yourself. Make those boundaries. Break the habit.

Chapter 3

How Algorithms Make You Sick – and How You Can Get Well Soon

I've been kicked off morning radio – but I wouldn't change a thing about what I said. In 2021, I had been invited on to a national breakfast show to discuss findings from a new study on digital flashing, led by my colleague Professor Jessica Ringrose, Professor of the Sociology of Gender and Education at the Institute of Education, UCL. Jessica is an advocate and trailblazer and was the first person in the UK to conduct research on youth sexting, in 2011.[1] Our study found that the rates of digital flashing – that is, the unsolicited sending of sexualized images – to people, particularly young women and girls, was incredibly high (75% of the girls in our focus groups had experienced it by the age of 15).[2]

But then the morning radio show presenter cut me off and apologized to listeners.[3] It was explained to me that the subject – that is, young people receiving unsolicited nudes (often from adults) – was not appropriate listening at breakfast. I agree. In fact, I don't think it's appropriate at any meal – breakfast or otherwise.

If digital flashing isn't appropriate for adults to hear about on the radio, how much less appropriate is it for children to receive them on their personal screens? As we as adults sit and worry about feeling uncomfortable, it means young people are being left to navigate this reality alone. This phenomenon, where as a society we adults are uninformed or feel uncomfortable and so leave kids to deal with online harm unsupported, is not unique to the issue of digital flashing. In September of 2021, when Meta whistleblower Frances Haugen released Facebook's internal research,[4] she told the world that Facebook's research suggests that because parents did not grow up with these experiences, they don't feel equipped or educated enough to support their children and as a result kids are suffering alone. Haugen described an addict's narrative where children said they didn't feel good when they used Facebook's products (including Instagram) – linking their use to body dysmorphia and suicidal thoughts[5] – and yet they felt that they couldn't stop the habit.

Senator Josh Hawley drew attention to another former Facebook executive, at the US Senate Judiciary Committee hearing in January 2024. They had shared that Meta's internal research found that among girls between the ages of thirteen and fifteen, 37% reported they had been exposed to unwanted nudity on the platform in the last seven days; 24% had experienced unwanted sexual advances in the last seven days; and 17% had encountered self-harm content pushed at them in the last seven days.[6]

This chapter seeks to offer answers to this common cycle where children suffer through harm and the mental health implications of social media, across a wide range of platforms, in silence, because the adults in their lives don't have the information or tools to understand and talk about their digital experiences.

I also provide information for everyone about the potential impacts of these technologies from a health and well-being perspective. Discussing things like self-harm, pornography and body dysmorphia and the way they can create content silos impacting our mental health is a hard read. I know. But I'm going to ask you to stick with me. These conversations push up against the offline–online divide where we often view online harm – or rather, harm that exists on a screen – as somehow less 'real' or less abusive. I would, and will, argue that it's not.

Images and online content are very much 'real' and exist in the real world. They have the power to abuse, impact mental health and quite frankly, make us sick, and that goes for adults as well as children. But information is power. Being aware of how image-based abuse and online harm works gives you the ability to equip yourself and take back control. If we are collectively given tools and guidance to make proactive interventions into these topics, we can build a healthier society. That's why I ask you to stick with me on this one. Let's equip ourselves to make things better for young people, for us, for everyone.

Filtering

On 16 July 2010 Mike Krieger took a photo. The photo, taken from a large industrial Crittall window, is of a marina with a white boat bobbing alongside a jetty. The photo is on a slant, presumably to feel more 'artsy', and it is heavily filtered, amplified by dark saturated colours. At 1:26 pm Mike uploaded it, as the first ever post on a new application he had developed with his friend Kevin Systrom that they called Instagram.[7]

Instagram's beginnings operated in conversation with the early smartphone technology of the time. It responded to the fact that everyone now had a camera in their pocket (which was revolutionary), but that those cameras were far worse than the standard cameras which people owned (which was not so revolutionary). And so, to address the poor pixelated photo quality of early smartphones, Instagram pioneered a fast and easy way to alter images for aesthetic purposes: filters.

When Hannah Ray joined Instagram as the first international employee from London, she describes arriving for training in California to a pink sky. And that pink sky, quite different from the grey of London, felt to her like being in an Instagram filter. She then took a cab from the airport and drove past street signs labelled Valencia and Dog Patch – now the names of filters.[8] This California dream was the world of Instagram. The goal was a community of sharing through an application that would make things look and feel better – literally rosy. A truly lovely feedback loop that people enjoyed and allowed everyone to be an artist.

Instagram deliberately copied the look and feel of instant Polaroid cameras. It was meant to feel instant. In fact, in the app's early years, it was a massive faux pas if you took a photo and posted it later. And if you did so, you were expected to disclose the delay through hashtags such as #latergram. The culture of Instagram was about feeling in the moment. It wasn't meant to feel polished or worse, produced.

In 2012 Facebook bought Instagram and as the applications grew and evolved, Instagram moved away from the 'instant' ethos represented in its name. In fact, you could say that Instagram in its current form is the opposite of 'instant'. Now a staple of Instagram is that the posts are often polished. And that the filter function is no longer used to fix the poor camara quality but instead to fix things about ourselves.

The filters available have become more and more sophisticated. They can drastically alter people's appearances, offering virtual nose jobs and implants and weight and age reductions.[9] Here the traditional structures surrounding entertainment, glossy magazines, advertisements and truth are broken down, so it becomes hard to pull apart where one ends, and one begins. Media scholar Christian Fuchs describes it as a new stage of advertising making it hard to distinguish content, editorial and advertisement.[10]

And with these changes, the way we formulate our taste – our beliefs – our values can also change. Social commentators have argued that the reason why all 'independent' coffee shops look the same is because Instagram has shrunk the options available and dictated our taste.[11] Coffee shops, milk varieties and latte art might not seem like such a big deal, but what about politics, values and how we form our identity and sense of self – particularly in our early teen years?

A 2019 YouGov survey of over a thousand teenagers found that 40% per cent of them felt images on social media 'caused them to worry about their body image'.[12] This is particularly true for girls. What makes matters worse is that if the teenager is already vulnerable, they are at greater risk of being impacted by the social media-driven harms. A 2022 survey found that 91% of people with eating disorders encountered online content that was harmful to their condition.[13]

This paints a very different picture – pun intended – to the carefree pink sky or a photo of a marina with a saturated filter to cover up poor photo quality in July 2010. So much so that in 2022 some of the original employees from both Instagram and Facebook raised concern and regret at how the app had moved from a creative photo-sharing service to a stronghold of influencer culture.[14] They lamented the ways in which the filters which they created are now used to promote unrealistic body ideals and self-harm. The company's own internal research published by the *Wall Street Journal* suggests that Instagram makes body image issues worse for one in three teenage girls.[15] Other studies have shown how Instagram use is associated with lower levels of body appreciation in teen girls.[16]

Even more pointedly, former Facebook employee Frances Haugen suggested that older generations can't understand how intense and complex these processes are for young people and equally, how these phenomena are now intrinsically intertwined in the ways young people live. Because as she put it, 'teenagers are killing themselves because of Instagram'.[17]

WHAT YOU CAN DO ABOUT IT
Turning Your Phone to Greyscale

Turning your phone to greyscale is one of the quickest and easiest ways of understanding the impact of colour and images on our user experience. This will give you a sense of how colour and image quality play into the addictive nature of these devices. You can find instructions to do this by searching for 'greyscale' in the Google Help Centre for Android Phones and at Apple Support for iPhones.

From Online Harm to Self-Harm

Molly was the youngest of three sisters. She was an inquisitive type of girl, with eyes that sparkled. And through them she would take in the world and contemplate it quietly before arriving at an informed opinion. And though this world would only know Molly for fourteen years, one could tell that Molly was mesmerizing.[18]

In 2017, Molly's parents noticed that their daughter's transition from child to teen was accompanied by relatively normal teenage behaviour. They had, of course, had two daughters become teens shortly before her.[19] So when she spent more time in her room and became less engaged in her childhood interests – horses, to be specific – they chalked it up to puberty. Molly still participated in family activities and came down for meals, so there didn't appear to be anything particularly abnormal going on. Molly, for the most part, seemed to be doing OK. But Molly was not OK. Tragically, in November of that year, she took her own life.

It wasn't long after Molly's death that Ian, Molly's father, opened up his home computer and accessed some of Molly's social media accounts. At first, what he found was what you'd expect to find on a fourteen-year-old girl's Instagram feed: a bright and colourful stream of celebrities and popstars. But then Ian was hit with something deeply upsetting. Ian's screen became awash with red. He scrolled through graphic images depicting blood, cutting and fresh wounds, encouraging self-harm. The text on these posts encouraged anxiety, depression and even suicide.[20] This content isn't unique to Molly's feed. In fact, a 2020 survey took a sample of nearly fifteen thousand children in the UK aged eleven to sixteen and found that one in four had seen content about suicide.[21] The report which presented the survey concluded that pro-suicide content was not only widely available, but that it was the most frequently seen form of online harm by one in four children they surveyed.[22]

Accompanying the colour red on Molly's feed was black. Black sketches of sad girls feeling lost and helpless. One sketch Ian recounted when speaking to *The Guardian* was of a girl lying in bed cuddling a teddy bear with its eyes gouged out.[23] The post read 'the world is so cruel, and I don't want to see it anymore'.[24] These posts in isolation might not seem so bad. But social media consumption and its impact are about dosage: a high volume of small doses adds up. This can aggravate pre existing vulner abilities, locking more vulnerable children into echo chambers of harm. For example, a 2020 study found that the likelihood of seeing self-harm content is 40% greater for those with mental health difficulties; 31% greater for autistic children; 30% greater for children with eating disorders; and 29% greater for children with experiences of being in care.[25] Researchers found that age, social isolation and digital competence all contribute to the extent of the online risks young people face. Additionally they have found that vulnerable young people have a higher exposure to unknown people because they seek out new friends or 'people like me' and this makes them targets of cyberbullying, cyberaggression and manipulation or coercion. But algorithms can also introduce new concepts even without pre-existing risk factors. As one fifteen-year-old explained to me at a roundtable discussion in 2024, 'I wasn't emo before. Then I saw it was cool to be emo on social media. So I decided to develop issues.' Being 'emo', emotional, blue, or angstful, is not a new teenage emotion[26] – far from it – but the ability to microdose on potentially incrementally more intense states of angst within an algorithmically personalized, unregulated silo (often well into the wee hours of the night) is new to this generation.

Having discovered this disturbing content on Molly's social media, Ian and the Russell family's wider community began to dig deeper to understand the root of the issue. Some of their family friends decided to report some of the content from Molly's feed to the platforms, assuming it would be helpful to alert companies to harmful content so that it could be removed. But the response from platforms was that the content did not breach their community guidelines.[27] And so the content remained online. Years later, in an interview with *The Guardian*, Ian would lament, 'I couldn't believe that platforms even considered that leaving this content online, in a place that thirteen-year-olds and upwards could find, was in any way safe.'[28]

Ian wanted to learn more about what happened to Molly and to do that he needed to get inside Molly's phone. Just weeks after Molly's death, and after failed attempts to receive any guidance from Apple online support, Ian ventured to London's flagship location, the Apple Store on Regent Street. He walked off the central London street, through the glass doors and into the bright, white, cavernous modernist space. Inside he spoke to a staff member on the shop floor and asked if he could speak with someone about a sensitive matter. 'Just talk to me,' said the shop floor worker. 'I really want to talk to someone, possibly even in a private room somewhere,' replied Ian. 'No,' responded the shop worker, 'it's fine. Talk to me.' Ian, one can only assume, exhausted and exasperated, then stated, 'I want it unlocked because my daughter ended her life a few weeks ago. And I want to see what these phones will tell us about why.'[29] The rest of the conversation was not very productive and eventually Ian was on a call to Apple's support service based in Dublin, to process his customer complaint. In the end, Apple did not give Ian access to Molly's phone.

The politics around children's rights to digital privacy have been written about by scholars like Sonia Livingstone[30] – though I doubt these intricacies were part of Apple's decision. But Ian would eventually see inside Molly's phone, in fact, the world would. And Molly's impact on the world – her story and legacy – would not finish there. Five years after her death, the Molly Russell inquest would use the powers of the coroner's court to gain access to Molly's data. The court would be given a full picture of what Molly had consumed in the last six months of her life. This included 16,000 pieces of content, 2,100 of which were related to suicide, self-harm, anxiety and depression.[31] Thirty four Instagram accounts were pushed to Molly, without her actively seeking them out, that had depressive titles.[32] Some of the content was so upsetting that one member of the court had to leave the room when it was being shown. The inquest's consultant child psychiatrist, Dr Navin Venugopal, not only found that the content would have affected Molly but that he himself had lost weeks of sleep over its distressing nature.[33] As *The Guardian*'s Global Technology Editor Dan Milmo reported, those in the court were almost willing the fourteen-year-old Molly to 'put down your computer' and 'just look away . . . there's absolutely no way that a 14-year-old girl, let alone a 14-year-old girl suffering from depression, should be able to access this content.'[34] But of course, putting down – or never accessing – their computer is not an option for most fourteen-year-olds who go to school, and do homework, and God forbid, have a social life.

When the Head of Health and Well-Being policy at Meta, Elizabeth Lagone, testified over two days at the inquest, she defended her company's actions. She claimed that what Molly viewed was admissible content, that it was 'safe'[35] and that it was 'important to give people that voice' if they were expressing suicidal thoughts.[36] But this argument surrounding free speech and the rights of the person posting falls short. Because the argument at stake is not about the right to publication but rather dissemination. First of all, the fact that the content is deemed 'admissible' by Meta's own guidelines – the ones that they themselves wrote – is a hollow defence. Secondly, and even more importantly, the key argument at stake isn't about whether the person posting has the right to share their experience – this isn't in question – but rather whether Meta have the right to present and crucially to promote such content, particularly to young people.

The content that Molly saw, that was made available to her, and even suggested or 'fed' to her, is shaped by machine learning. Machine learning is a set of algorithms that draw patterns and learn from data to, in the case of social media, encourage the greatest user engagement. But what keeps you engaged might be different from what you actually want to see or what is good for you. When I met with Amir Malik, an industry leader formerly of Google and Microsoft who now advises the United Nations and the UK government on AI strategy, he explained this phenomenon as the following:

> *We're really predictable, which means that a search history on a person can go on to . . . forecast what you are going to do – a drug deal, crime, a holiday, suicide. The advertising algorithm works in such an effective way it can predict what you want to buy before you buy it . . . the colour of the coat, the trainers . . . So what about self-harm or suicide?*

And yet, the maturity of the regulator is simply not there. If regulators were to say, we know you know you have this information. 'We know you can probably predict if someone is likely to be suicidal and there is a duty of care to report that a teenager, a fourteen-year-old, is likely to be suicidal.' This could help safeguard young people. But ten years ago, and indeed still today, that channel hasn't been set up. That is to say, there is not that consistent line of communication between what tech companies know about us and their duty of care to report such information. Information that a teenager, a fourteen-year-old is likely to be suicidal.[37]

Lagone's testimony did not address her company's ethical responsibility to look at the way in which their technologies make harmful content accessible, and worse algorithmically offered to children. But what became clear is that their platform had suggested such content to a fourteen-year-old Molly which clearly caused her harm. As Ian read from Molly's notebook on the BBC in 2024:

Sometimes my mind is like a little boat in the middle of the sea in a big storm. I'm alone and all the waves are closing down on me, drowning me.[38]

At the end of the inquiry the coroner, Andrew Walker, said that one of the worst things about this content was that a lot of it sought to isolate people and discourage discussion to prevent those looking at it, those at risk, from seeking the help from their family or friends.[39] His final conclusion was that Molly died from an act of self-harm while suffering from depression and the negative effects of online content.[40]

It is these last words that make Molly's case groundbreaking. A global first, as the NSPCC children's charity would call it, and would further describe it as a 'big tobacco' moment.[41] Molly's case is the first to directly link social media's contribution to a young girl's death. In the press conference that followed, Ian Russell spoke of a hope for change. He talked about a wish to make the online world safer and to prevent future tragedies. Then, as he concluded, 'Finally,' his calm and steady voice broke, 'thank you, Molly, for being my daughter.'[42]

The Molly Rose Foundation, which was created in Molly's memory, has a wealth of resources and support routes with the aim of suicide prevention targeted at people under twenty-five.[43] Their resources include signposting towards specific help lines to help young people stay connected.[44] Ian Russell and the foundation advocate for greater digital literacy and greater emphasis on regulation.[45]

Following the inquest, one of the proposed mechanisms for the oversight of social media companies' conduct was the Online Safety Bill, which became the Online Safety Act.[46] The purpose of the bill was to introduce a duty of care over social media companies' content and ensure greater consumer protections to mitigate the impacts of processes like the algorithms that pushed harmful content towards Molly.[47] This bill is multifaceted, and some elements are essential but, regrettably, it falls pitifully short. Because there are things that social media companies could do to make harmful content less accessible. They can use techniques like dispersion, which makes content harder to find by children. They can decide that there is some content that should never be algorithmically offered to children; and they can – and should – revise community guidelines to encompass a broader spectrum of harmful content. And yet they are still not forced to do so.[48]

With this in mind, there are actions you can take with your family now to gain control over the potentially harmful content that might be algorithmically pushed to you or someone you love. This is linked to one of the closing remarks from the coroner in Molly's case. He said that one of the worst things about the content Molly consumed was that it discouraged discussion. And discussion is what we need. But how can we have conversations about such difficult issues?

I know this can feel hard. It might feel overwhelming to consider how we can protect our kids if the companies themselves, and the law, aren't doing so effectively. But by reading this, by informing yourself, you have taken the first steps. There is action you can take to help your kids now, or what might feel now like far-off future versions of themselves when they eventually need to navigate this terrain. Academic social media researchers now use a technique called the walk-through method.[49] That's when you have research participants open up their apps with you, the researcher, and they walk through or scroll through a typical period of usage. This way the researcher can understand what the individual is seeing. Generally, at the same time, the researcher asks the participant to engage in discussion about the content and how the content makes them feel. I think we should *all* be using the walk-through method in our lives – teens and adults alike.

WHAT YOU CAN DO ABOUT IT
The Walk-Through Method

With a partner or friend, open up one of your most regularly used social media applications, and walk through a normal period of usage.

This might sound scary or even embarrassing because algorithms often feel very intimate. That's because algorithms are built to know you – or at least your characteristics, likes, dislikes and desires. This idea of media consumption being so personalized is relatively new. Television viewing used to be a family experience. Before home television, the cinema represented an even broader communal experience, where members of the community would come together to collectively laugh and cry.

But the fact that our media usage is personal doesn't mean that you shouldn't talk about it. If there are parts of your social media feed that you are embarrassed to show your partner, you might want to think about why that is. For example, if your feed is awash with ads for cosmetic surgery, your partner might help you to question if this is the best thing for you.

When you are ready to do a walk-through method, here's what you need to do:

Choose one of your most heavily used applications (e.g. TikTok or Instagram), for one sitting, scrolling through a normal period of use. Note how you feel at the beginning of that session, then note how you feel at the end.

Ask each other:

1. Where are you spending your time?
2. What makes you feel good?
3. What posts made you feel bad?
4. What posts do you wish you saw less of?

The walk-through is also an exercise you can do with children, should they already be on social media platforms, or when they first start. A weekly walk-through will give you a good indication of what your child is consuming, and if there are things that your child is uncomfortable with or feeling concerned about, you can give them the opportunity to talk about it. You don't need to breach their privacy by looking at their private messages. This is about you being un-embarrassable, uncritical and unjudgemental and, rather, giving them the chance to think about their consumption and how they want to change what their algorithms are feeding them.

Teens may be more private about their own feeds, and this might be particularly so around issues of sexuality. It is worth considering this and being respectful. If a walk-through method isn't appropriate for your teenager, instead, you can try shared check-ins, where everyone shares the following:

1. 1 post that made you feel good,
2. 1 post that made you feel bad,
3. 1 post that you found interesting
4. and 1 post that you questioned.

Bullying

Molly had also been a target of online bullying.[50] Issues of body image and self-harm can be linked to experiences of bullying. It's worth being aware of these dynamics for young people, particularly girls. In our project 'Digital Nutrition', my team and I heard many stories of bullying at different levels of intensity. From kids going onto SnapMaps (the geo-locator function on Snapchat),[51] finding each other's houses and egging them; to young people being targeted through phone calls and threatened by peers; to girls being so afraid to say the wrong thing in friend groups that they were using Chat-GPT to formulate messages, our study saw accounts of bullying take different forms.[52]

In our research we concluded that the large group functionality of apps like WhatsApp, which gives the possibility of group chats amongst large communities (including entire school year groups), can increase bullying potential.[53] Large groups can create more anonymity, and this anonymity can be linked to higher levels of online bullying. If you or your child is struggling with this, it's worth encouraging close friends towards smaller groups, where closer more positive friendships can flourish. Often smaller groups allow for more meaningful and positive connections over larger more anonymous group chats. Better yet, you might get a small group to leave this technologically facilitated socializing altogether and work towards helping them find spaces of connection with peers off screens.

Here are some additional tips to address digital bullying.

For kids dealing with bullying:

- On WhatsApp you can change your group privacy settings.[54] Know that the default setting allows anyone to add you to any group. By actively changing your settings to 'my contacts' or 'my contacts except . . .' only the people you choose can add you to groups
- Make sure you know about support avenues like Childline and have a plan for how to report the behaviour to a supportive adult.

For parents dealing with bullying

+ Make sure your child knows how to report and block on the apps they are using.
+ Give your child space and time to talk about it with you. Talk to your child about positive online friendships.
+ Internet Matters has a set of resources about bullying for parents and carers to get support and to see other parents' stories.[55]
+ If your child is the victim of a crime including sexual harassment or blackmail you can report to the CEOP.[56] This is the branch of the National Crime Agency which deals with child exploitation and online protection.
+ Have digital check-ins – see the walk-through method in this chapter or encourage them to keep a digital journal to record how they feel.

Pornified

If body image, eating disorders and self-harm are the problems mostly associated with girls, pornography consumption is one of the major concerns associated with boys. Jai is eleven. He likes Marvel films and football. Jai doesn't have a phone. He has an iPad that his parents allow him to use. Together, as a family, they have decided that he is not ready for TikTok, but he uses YouTube and Instagram because he likes to follow sports personalities. Generally, this screen time happens in the family living room after dinner, and his parents, for the most part, can look over his shoulder and monitor the content he is seeing. Jai also spends time in the TV room where he takes the iPad, and he's begun spending more and more time in there. Jai, while scrolling through Instagram to watch sports highlights, receives a message from a porn bot. There is an image of a woman in a thong with a link for him to follow to see more.

Despite the conventional idea of boys seeking out porn through sites like Pornhub, they can first encounter pornographic material accidentally.[57] This can be through their Instagram and Snapchat accounts,[58] where they can be targeted by highly sexualized media. Professor Jessica Ringrose and I looked at the ways in which boys were targeted with pornographic content by porn bots also known as porn push, where young people are sent illicit content often by way of private messages.[59] Since this study, avenues for porn push have increased; for example, X now permits 'consensually produced' graphic content on its newsfeed.[60]

We are not the only ones who have found this. A 2020 study found that 62% of eleven- to thirteen-year-olds see pornography unintentionally.[61] The Children's Commissioner's report from 2023 found that rather than visiting adult porn sites, young people were most likely to be fed pornographic content on X followed by Instagram and Snapchat. The study found that the average age at which children first see pornography is thirteen, though 27% of respondents had seen it by eleven. And that pornography is now so normalized – that is, it is circulated so widely in the digital space – that children cannot 'opt out' of it but rather, all young people, at some point, will encounter pornography.[62]

So, let's assume that Jai has experienced porn push. Is this a problem? you might ask. Boys will be boys and is this really such a big deal?

This groundbreaking report by the Children's Commissioner in 2023 found that early exposure to pornography can have negative impacts upon young people's confidence and that children who have viewed pornography aged eleven or younger were significantly more likely to present lower self-esteem scores.[63] Porn consumption is also tied to poor body image in boys and girls.[64] And both boys and girls often watch porn as an education resource to understand how their bodies should look and how they are meant to behave in sex.[65] For example, a study from 2020 suggests that young people have reported learning about sex through porn including getting ideas for new things to try sexually, and learning what people expect from them sexually.[66] Girls in particular mentioned using pornography to learn how to meet boys' perceived expectations, although the boys who took part in this research did not mention having said expectations.[67]

But erotic entertainment is not new to the Internet. If we go back to the pre-Internet era: in the early 1990s, strip clubs were the sites of sophisticated work events, and the top shelf of the magazine rack was the ultimate forbidden fruit for a teenage boy. But the thing about sexual entertainment in the 1990s, whether that was a rolled-up dirty *Playboy* under the bed or a bootlegged VHS tape, is that variety was relatively limited. And that arguably, one developed more of a relationship with the performer on the tape or bunny in the centrefold. Lest we forget, most pornography of this age had some – albeit contrived – narrative, and *Playboy* actually had biographies and interviews with their models. The argument of whether or not these performers were empowered or objectified sits somewhat outside this discussion (though I'm happy to have it another time – preferably in the pub): rather, the point for now is that pre-highspeed Internet, X-rated entertainment was consumed in a different format, extremity and on a completely different scale than digital porn.[68] Contemporary pornography is fast-paced, often fragmented, and is quantifiably much more violent.[69]

A 2020 study that reviewed over four thousand porn scenes found that 45% of Pornhub scenes included physical aggression and 97% of the scenes showed abuse directed at women.[70] Indeed, the Children's Commissioner's report shows that young people are frequently exposed to violent pornography, depicting coercive, degrading or pain-inducing sex acts, usually towards women – 79% of them before the age of eighteen in fact.[71] Let's just let that sink in.

Significantly, and *this is where it gets really important*: young people felt that violent pornography impacted their ability to understand the difference between sexual pleasure and harm. The Children's Commissioner report stated that 47% of young people 'expect' sex to involve physical aggression such as airway restriction or slapping, and 42% assumed girls 'enjoy' acts of sexual violence.[72] And listen to this, researchers indicate that these assumptions are linked to the way young people are now having sex, with 47% – nearly half – having engaged in violent sex by the age of twenty-one.[73] This has led to a rise in domestic violence in youth relationships.[74] And both police and children involved in this study made direct links between abuse and the abuser's exposure to pornography. And so the UK Government Equalities Office concluded that pornography is a driver of sexual violence not only outside of but also inside of 'consensual' sexual relationships.[75]

Pornified youth cultures have also been linked to normalizing *Image Based Harassment*, the sending of unsolicited nudes, and *Image Based Abuse*, the non-consensual forwarding of someone else's nude images to others.[76] We know that there is now a culture of boys using nudes (specifically dick pics) to elicit nudes from girls. These can be pressurized exchanges, where girls can feel obligated to send an image back. Boys can also feel pressured from peers to show others that they have received these images as an indicator of what Professor Ringrose terms their 'masculinity status'. In some youth groups this pressure has become so intense that, as one teacher at a private boys' school explained to me in 2024, 'one student made a deepfake of a girl' in order to prove to his friends that he had been sent a nude. These dynamics have led to stories of teen girls' bodies being sent non-consensually around large social groups resulting in terrible reputational or mental-health implications for the victims.

And I realize I'm becoming a real downer here: Ofcom, the UK communications regulator, has released findings which show that it is now 'inevitable' for young children to be exposed to harmful and violent online content – violent sexualized content playing a big role in this.[77] There are of course discussions of how to mitigate the availability of pornography. For example, age verification on pornography sites. Though this has been slow to be implemented. A quick poll of my UCL master's students will tell you that all their Instagram accounts have their age recorded as much older than they are, simply because when they first opened their accounts in their pre-teen years, they lied.

There is an alternative model currently being trialled in Europe. It's called euConsent[78] and the way it works is to issue an electronic token based on your age and that way the verification technology isn't storing personal information. Utah in the US has passed a law requiring porn sites to take responsibility for what it terms 'reasonable steps' to verify the ages of users,[79] and the UK is in final stages of considering similar legislation,[80] which would put the onus on the porn industry.[81]

And so increasing age restrictions on pornography sites doesn't do a lot for Jai, who is experiencing porn push on social media platforms. And besides, Jai is about to be twelve and understandably the pull is becoming stronger and stronger. Jai is growing up and that's OK. He is allowed to be sexually curious. He is going to need support to ensure he engages with this content in a way that is critical, and safe for him and others around him. But this is not something just to consider for Jai or boys but for us all when we consider what such pornified landscapes might be doing to us all. How does it impact the dating scene? One only needs to look at the current debate on rough sex to be concerned about how connections can play out in adult circles.[82] Legal scholars have argued that this becomes problematic when defendants in murder trials use a 'rough sex gone wrong' defence, in which it is claimed that the woman's death was the result of consensual rough sex, playing into victim-blaming, similar to 'she was asking for it'.[83]

This is not to say that porn in and of itself is all bad and I by no means want to position seeing people's bodies or the expression of sexuality as inherently problematic. It's not. There should, of course, be space for healthy, age-appropriate content. It should also be acknowledged that in an adult and more grassroots context there are producers of female, feminist and LGBTQ+ pornography. But this is a small proportion of the market and is not representative of what the majority of people are viewing. What is key here is being able to contextualize and think critically about this content. Which is why education – or porn literacy – is so important.

Does porn literacy sound scary to you? Sure, talking about these issues can feel uncomfortable. Talking about them with your children might feel unbearable. You might think it's easier to keep your child offline altogether, so that you don't have to engage with these issues. Take away all screens: ban phones; throw out the iPad and have them do their homework on a mechanical typewriter. Let's test this idea.

Let's change Jai's profile slightly. Let's say that Jai has never been given a screen. His parents put their phones and laptops in a drawer when they come home, and they don't have an iPad. Jai goes to school. He has a best friend, Cole, who also doesn't have screens, which Jai's mum loves. But Cole does have an older brother, Leo. And one time when Jai is over at Cole's house, they see violent explicit content on Leo's laptop. This is an example of the inevitability of viewing porn outlined in the Ofcom report. Though you can work to limit and mitigate risk in a variety of healthy ways, you can't completely shield your children from explicit content. And ultimately, it's much better for children to hear about these issues from trusted adults first, in order to help them critically navigate it. Because if this is an inevitability for all young people, it's important to contextualize and address the problematic nature of a lot of this pornography landscape. It's important that they know that things which might feel frightening or shameful are not the norm in healthy relationships. And that violence within sex is not standard or required.

A previous Children's Commissioner Report, from 2021, offers advice from young people to parents about how to approach conversations about sex. It advises that parents do talk to their children about these issues and at a young age, and before they are given a smartphone.[84] For young people who don't have those conversations are likely to look to online pornography as a way to dictate their first sexual experiences. As parents we want to intercept this trend. To emphasize that porn is a spectacle like a Marvel film, which Jai likes. It's not real.

Porn Literacy

In the early 1950s programming was fast developing to populate America's new favourite home appliance, the television. Among some of the new programmes was one which particularly caught the imagination of American boys. It featured a man in blue tights with red briefs over the top and a red cape. His name by day, Clark Kent, his name by night, Superman. What followed was a boom as boys began trying to behave like Superman shortly after the launch of the programme.[85] Some of which was good: running around with a cape helping people. Some of it was less good: like trying to fly. The results were what you'd imagine: broken limbs, because they tried to be well, super; jumping off car garages or rooftops. See, home TVs were a relatively new invention. Before that families went to the cinema, which would have been much less frequent. So, up until this point, families and their children hadn't consumed such exciting, stimulating content on such a frequent basis. The eventual cure: one could tell boys it was just pretend. They could be told that TV shows weren't real. And then, after a while, they might stop jumping off things.

Though it's not exactly the same, similar principles can be applied to porn literacy. It's not meant to be real life, or about caring, loving relationships where two people look after each other and want to make each other feel good. It's like a Marvel film. The explicit content young people might see online is a different thing altogether. That means acknowledging the fact that feelings of desire are normal, but also that a lot of explicit content online is not representative of consensual relationships and shouldn't be used as an education tool.

If you have an older child, you might choose to talk about key theoretical debates. Ask them: 'Do you think it's possible to have feminist porn? Can you have inclusive porn? Is there such a thing?' These are ways to open up the conversation and make it clear that you respect their opinions and that you are a safe place to come to discuss these ideas.

At any age, these should not be big one-off serious talks. It's much better to take the pressure off and have frequent smaller conversations. These conversations can happen while driving in the car or when something naturally prompts the discussion.

So, Jai and his hypothetical school friend Cole are not real – they are composites from my research. But Dawn is real. Dawn is a real girl in sixth form (although this is not her real name), who Professor Ringrose and I interviewed in 2019.[86] We wrote up this research into a report for the Association of School and College Leaders[87] and published it in a book, *Teens, Nudes and Image Based Abuse*.[88] Dawn explained to us that when she ended a relationship, she asked her former partner to delete images of her from his phone, and he did it. This way she could feel safe moving out of the relationship. Reading this you might ask, but why do they need to send nudes at all?! First, we should acknowledge that digital sex is now part of relationship cultures (particularly youth relationship cultures), and that is often going to take the form of image exchange. So instead of having physical sex in the back of a car or in the park (eek!), image exchange provides a digital alternative. And therein lies a pull – some people might say that digital sex is in many ways safer: they are not going to get pregnant, and they're not going to get a sexually transmitted disease. And in many ways, when compared to the hypothetical park, it is more private. But it also has the potential to be much more public. And if we are going to create nurturing environments to speak to teenagers about these realities, we need to talk about that pull. And that is through discussion with their partner around boundaries and expectations of such exchanges.

The exchange above is representative of empowered and critical digital citizenship.[89] An awareness that images can be used for abusive purposes and that sending on images without someone's knowledge or permission is a non-consensual practice. This is the kind of awareness and communication that we should be striving towards. That is, a healthy, respectful relationship between two young people built on digital consent and careful critical awareness of how to navigate the online world.

WHAT YOU CAN DO ABOUT IT
Tips on Porn Literacy

1. **Stay calm – but be the first.** Slowly and calmly begin to seed conversations about online explicit content at an early age. Reassure your children that it is fine and perfectly normal to be curious about their bodies. These do not have to be big or heavy conversations and of course need to be delivered in age-appropriate ways. For example, some children might still be at the stage of learning about the functionality of sex (i.e. making babies), while others might be ready to talk about physical touch as part of a loving relationship and more laterally, the concept of pleasure. InternetMatters.org has a set of resources split into age groups about how you can talk to children about porn in an age-appropriate way at different stages.
2. **There's no shame.** Release your own shame around sex. Your child may not have built up any uncomfortableness around sex. They might experience a variety of different feelings or sensations when seeing something and that's OK. You can acknowledge that they might see some things online and that some of it they might like, but a lot of this content is not reflective of normal relationships. Let them know that if they see – or have seen – content that they feel uncomfortable with or they're unsure about, you are here. You are open. And you are not embarrassed to talk about it.
3. **Think Superman.** Explain that a lot of explicit content is a

performance. It is like a superhero film or a Marvel movie, if that's helpful. It's pretend. It doesn't reflect real experiences and it's often not reflective of most relationships.

4. **Talk About Consent.** You can start conversations about general consent early. For example, you can ask your child if it is OK to take their photo. If your child is of an age when they are becoming interested in intimacy or romantic relationships, speak to them about consensual behaviour and also about digital images. If they are sending images there need to be ground rules, and they should not pressure people to send images. Also, it is a violation of trust and in some cases illegal to show someone's image without their consent to others. This can additionally be true when faking an image or putting someone's face on an explicit image.

5. **What's Missing from Porn.** For more help with these conversations take a look at the Brook website, https://www.brook.org.uk/your-life/porn/. They outline ways into these conversations. For example, instead of talking about what is in porn, talk about what is missing from porn, such as consent, breaks and realistic body types.

Why Algorithms Make You Sick – Conclusion

Two months after I was kicked off the radio, Jessica and my research informed new legislation on digital flashing.[90] Now, it's illegal for an adult to send a photo of their genitals to a child in the UK. Perpetrators of cyberflashing could face up to two years in prison.[91] This law is of course focused on the individual perpetrator, rather than the platforms that allow such harm to be circulated. And as Amir Malik rightly pointed out to me, criminalizing individuals is one thing but criminalizing the platforms 'that allow the users to send the image' is another. That is to say, there is still no threat to these businesses' bottom lines or threat of legal repercussions to the tech companies that facilitate such an image being sent to a minor. This platform focus will be discussed in Chapter 6.

Nevertheless, the new legislation makes a statement in acknowledging that digital images have the power to abuse representing – even if only a micro – cultural shift. Just months after morning radio claimed the findings were not 'appropriate' or too uncomfortable, laws were being changed in order take online abuse more seriously, and subsequently to begin to protect kids.[92]

In many ways this new legalization is thanks to Molly. Because with every piece of advocacy, with every legislation around social media consumption, we should think of Molly. Molly's Inquest was one of the first to prove someone could die from the negative effects of online content. It suggested that what we see online can seep into, and impact, our offline well-being and behaviour. It was the first time – a global first as the NSPCC put it – that social media companies were held accountable in such a tangible way.[93] Molly proved that social media has the power to make you sick and, in some cases, it can kill you. And now, slowly, incrementally, the world is beginning to listen.

The exercises in this chapter have been designed to help us have discussions around these difficult topics. The walk-through method and porn literacy can be big asks. I know. They are not quick-fix filters that make the sky pink or everything rosy right away. But they will help you take control and make decisions about the digital world you want to see and live in. These are techniques that take time but they can ultimately help you and your kids have healthier relationships with tech. They will help to navigate the mental health consequences of online consumption.

Talking about these issues publicly, not just on the radio, but at home, protects kids. Do it for them. Do it for the collective. Do it for Molly.

Chapter 4

The Safety Paradox and Why Screen Time Doesn't Work

'My city is Russia now,' is how Iryna started her story to me. My team[1] and I have interviewed teens about their relationships with smartphones across very different types of school environments.[2] This school was a state school in a suburb of London with a high proportion of refugee children and as such was concerned about the way in which the students with existing vulnerabilities were made more susceptible to some of the harms of social media. We sat around circular tables with thirteen- and fourteen-year-old girls. Some girls wore hijabs, others crosses. Iryna had blonde hair that reached all the way down to the small of her back. She was thirteen. And she told the story about when, two years earlier in the winter of 2022, her city in Ukraine had been hit by a missile attack. And while she was under stress, while she was feeling scared and down, TikTok seemed to know. And it presented the eleven-year-old Iryna with depressive and eating disorder content. It appeared that TikTok's algorithm assumed that because Iryna was feeling anxious, because she was feeling scared, that perhaps this was the content that she would like to see.

Iryna told her mother. And they did develop a way together to help Iryna put screen-time limits on TikTok and moderate her usage. But they did not get rid of her smartphone. Why? Because at that point Iryna needed the smartphone to keep her safe. She needed to be able to access information about the conflict and when to take cover from attacks. She needed to be able to call her mother. She needed to be connected.

Iryna, a refugee child from Ukraine, is a very specific case. But her relationship to her phone has a pull that is ever-present for us all – particularly for parents. And though perhaps the situations aren't as grave, for the same reasons as Iryna's mother did when we give our children phones, it is often to keep them connected in order to keep them safe. We give them phones because of their geo-locator devices; because of Google maps; because we want our children to be able to call us; because we want them to avoid social isolation. This chapter is about how we can address two issues: the distinction between quantity and quality of screen time and 'the safety paradox'.[3] Here we are stuck between the pull where smartphones can make you both safe and at the same time unsafe. That is, physical safety and the way in which phones can address that need and on the other side, digital harm and the way in which phones can amplify this reality. And this is not just true for Ukraine during a missile strike, but also true for us all, much closer to home. Not just for this suburban girls' school, not just for minors, but for all of us as we look to have a more balanced and healthy lifestyle

The Safety Paradox

Secondary school: it's eleven-year-old Ewan's first day. His slight shoulders rattle around inside his boxy school blazer. It's too big, but it's the smallest his mum could find at the second-hand uniform sale. He's carrying a huge rucksack filled with snacks, just in case it feels too much to get in the lunch queue with the upper years. Or adults as they appear to Ewan. And, as he walks

The Safety Paradox and Why Screen Time Doesn't Work

up to the stern utilitarian building, he grips the sides of his trousers for support. This is it, he thinks: this is 'big school'.

But Ewan isn't just worried about being one of the youngest kids in the school. He's tiny compared to post-pubescent teenagers, albeit with the biggest rucksack – but there are other things that are going to change for Ewan at secondary school. He's going to have to manage a lot of details all on his own: what classroom he needs to get to; when the after-school clubs are available; and when he can try for the football team.

Luckily, the school has an app. Ewan can see that science club is on Tuesdays after school and that football team trials are on Thursday (although he knows he'll never actually make the team). The app also shows points and praise from his teachers, which gives Ewan a real boost. It's almost like a game.

Ewan doesn't have his own phone on which to check the app. He uses his mum's tablet at home. And she starts to wonder if she needs to get him his own device. The other thing that is different now for Ewan is that he travels to school on his own. Sometimes he stays at his dad's house. Sometimes, at his mum's. He gets the bus, and when the clocks go back that might be after sundown. Ewan likes to meet his best friend, Mo, so they can travel together, but sometimes in the after-school rush it's hard to find him. And it's for this constellation of reasons – the school's app, the connecting with friends, the travelling independently – that a few weeks into the school year, Ewan's mum goes into a shop on her local high street and buys a pay-as-you-go plan for Ewan. Now Ewan will have a smartphone. A smartphone to help him stay engaged with his education; a smartphone to help him connect; a smartphone to keep him safe.

And so this is the paradox. The paradox that phones can help build community and at same time destroy it; that phones can help support education but also distract from it; and that phones can keep you safe and also at the very same time make you unsafe. This paradox tends to be the greatest point of tension within the whole phone moderation argument. In particular, the safety paradox, which pulls young people in opposing directions in relation to their digital consumption, can be confusing for all involved. On one hand, young people are at times encouraged towards smartphones as a key piece of equipment to stay safe, and in our research this was often reported to be encouraged or mandated by their parents.[4] For many parents in our study, brick phones or 'dumb phones' (such as flip phones with no geolocation capabilities) were not seen to be as safe. Tracking was an important feature for parents as well as access to maps. However, as discussed in previous chapters, safety is also a key theme in relation to harmful content or unwanted contact from people they don't know.

In some places, where young people travel to school by a school bus or get dropped by their parents, this safety paradox might be less acute. Parents might feel less pressure to track or locate their children. But in places like urban centres, particularly ones that are sprawling, where young people often travel on public transport, often on their own, often in non-daylight hours, having a phone, having a tracking device, having map capabilities – things that adults often enjoy – can feel like an answer to this conundrum.

And it is for these reasons that we need a multi-pronged approach to this problem. Whether you choose to get a brick phone or a 'dumb phone'; or an Apple watch; or a tablet; or a smartphone: none of these choices should be at the cost of digital education and a wider understanding of the way these technologies are structured. So the question is not just about whether to get a phone, but how we can moderate, and inform, in order to keep us all healthy at every stage of our technological usage.

WHAT YOU CAN DO ABOUT IT
Alternatives to Smartphones

If you are looking for alternatives to smartphones, there are options available including smart watches that are trackable and have messaging functions, and new devices or 'kidsafe smartphones' are hitting the market and will continue to emerge. Here are some questions to help parents assess whether a device is appropriate for their family.[5]

1. **Safety.** Does it increase safety or hinder it? Some phones have sections that can be monitored by parents. Talk with your child about how much oversight is actually healthy and age appropriate (e.g. parent-enabled apps).
2. **Functionality.** What do you actually need the device for and what do you need it to do? Does it fit these requirements, e.g. basic communication and location tracking?
3. **Usage.** Does it have capacities that support a healthy digital diet, e.g. screen-time restrictions and downtime? Protecting children's privacy?
4. **Moderation.** Ask: how can I help my child to use this appropriately and moderately? Even phones built for kids can be distracting. As a review for a kids' smart watch noted, it was possible to turn off the friends chat but not the family chat, and grandparents kept messaging their grandchild in class.[6] Setting out boundaries around these devices is still important.

Smartphone Free Childhood has an up-to-date list of alternatives to smartphones which you can find here: https://smartphonefreechildhood.co.uk/alternatives.

Smartphones as Medical Devices

Smartphones have been instrumental in changing the day-to-day lives of people with certain conditions. Smartphones now have applications which are compatible with hearing aids[7] or cochlear implants, with assistive technology for people with visual impairment[8] and offer lifesaving technologies to those with type 1 diabetes, prescribed on the NHS.[9]

For these people, including children and young people, smartphones are essential tools and in some cases are needed all day, every day. Managing the elements of smartphones that are unhealthy or toxic presents an additional challenge for these people. For example, type 1 diabetics need to have their phone in their room at night to respond to the alerts to reduce potentially fatal high and low blood-sugar spikes, and so advice about keeping smartphones out of bedrooms at night or not having a smartphone doesn't apply. In these cases, taking a proactive approach to moderation, managing digital consumption, employing critical thinking about what is being consumed and taking advantage of settings options to disable and limit certain functions and apps becomes key.

Staying Safe in Our Online World

We can – and should – talk about regulating phones, how to cut back and not have them in schools at all times, but that can't take away from the fact that we still need to be educating young people about how to work and live with them and operate in the future. Because even if, as I said in the introduction, young people are held off social media usage until their sixteenth birthday that birthday will, of course, come.

And there is something else that should be noted about Gen Z in particular, something less micro or specific to individuals but rather something much more macro connecting this whole generation of young people: they were born into a world not just post-Internet, but post-smartphones. And though there is some recent research to suggest that Gen Z are not as digitally aware as we like to think (lacking in both professional and emotive tech skills)[10] there is a societal and corporate expectation of their digital nativeness. That is, there is a general sense that the jobs our kids will be asked to do, the roles they will fill, and much of their leadership opportunities will be in careers that don't exist yet. And that's not to say that today's kids need to learn technical skills at a very young age, but rather they were born into a digital world which is, for better or for worse, their birthright. And whether or not we believe this to be overly sensational, or whether or not we are happy with this idea, their work and lives will be much more hybrid than ours and the boundary between offline and online will be much more porous. And we have a responsibility as their parents and their educators to equip them to navigate it. Just like the offline world, we need to teach them how to be safe and that there are some things they should be highly critical of. Like street smarts – we need to teach screen smarts.

So, what do those tools look like? Traditional guidance for parents around screen usage has traditionally focused on controlling the dose of digital engagement, or 'screen time'. Ten years ago, parents were told that they should limit kids' screen usage to one or two hours a day.[11] Screen time is thought by many contemporary experts to be outdated as a concept. Because screen time doesn't account for the multitude of reasons young people use their devices. It also doesn't account for the quality or type of content being consumed. Not all screen time is equal, not all screen-based activities are equal. Even within the same platform, watching a National Geographic documentary is different from influencer content on YouTube shorts. For context, let's go back to the origins of digital video platforms and the beginnings of self-produced online entertainment.

Screen Time

It was Valentine's Day, 2005. 'It's one of those things about being a computer scientist. Valentine's Day is just another day,' Jawed would joke later.[12] And so because it was just any other day, Jawed with his friends Chad and Steve began work on a video-sharing platform. The idea was to address the fact that new mobile phones had video capabilities. But there was really no way of sharing those videos.

So video content was just sitting on phones in people's pockets. Sitting in people's pockets all over the world. The friends set their mind to streamlining video sharing. Two months later, they'd cracked it. And though there were some other video sites around, what Jawed and friends did – they did really well. It was a very good video-sharing platform.

When it became time to monetize this concept, the three friends looked back to the day of the platform's beginnings. And even though they knew very little about the topic, they decided upon dating. A video dating service. Perfect. The site went live on 23 April 2005.[13] And because the idea was for people to upload videos of themselves, videos of you, they called it *YouTube*. To invoke feelings of romance, they made the logo red. Their original tagline? 'Tune In, Hook Up'.

The Safety Paradox and Why Screen Time Doesn't Work 103

And then, nothing happened. Nothing. This may have been because the friends didn't really understand dating. For example, the site didn't give users the option to actually select the profile videos, but rather selected them at random for users.[14] But also no one was uploading videos. No one. The friends had effectively got the best house – and all the booze – to have a banging house party, but no one wanted to come. At one point, out of desperation to have any videos uploaded, they turned to Craig's List. Through a classified ad, the trio offered women in the Las Vegas and Los Angeles areas twenty dollars to upload just one video. The number of replies? Zero.

Narratives around the impetus behind the eventual pivot of the platform vary. In a commencement address to the University of Illinois in 2007, Jawed suggests that they decided to open up the platform and give users more 'freedom . . . so that they could decide what YouTube was.' It's also been reported that the friends wanted to be able to see the 2004 Superbowl halftime show, when Justin Timberlake ripped Janet Jackson's costume to expose her breast.[15] And the friends thought it would be good to have a place to share similar hard-to-find footage, perhaps of other people's nipples – nip clips if you will. Perhaps both narratives are true. Regardless, by December of 2005, YouTube had eight million views a day. The clips were limited to 100 megabytes each, which was equivalent to about thirty seconds of film on a camcorder and ten minutes from a mobile phone camera.[16] And these limitations would shape the quick, fast paced, easily digestible cultural format of YouTube that we still have today.

But whether or not the impetus to open up the scope of YouTube's content was driven by wanting to see more of Janet Jackson, it's worth recognizing YouTube's beginnings as a jocular space to express young adulthood – bro coder culture of the early 00s. Its origins were not a space of thoughtful curation but rather a space to 'Tune In' to 'Hook Up'. I don't share this history with any judgement. Although I do still want justice for Janet. It's just an interesting history, paired with the fact that YouTube is where the vast majority of children now consume entertainment: 89% of children aged five to eleven according to a recent US study.[17]

But perhaps we should think more critically about what this so-called child space does, particularly in relation to screen-time arguments. The problem with screen-time guidance, and the reason why many experts believe it to be outdated,[18] is because screen time assumes everything we consume – everything we put into our minds by way of screens – is equal. And perhaps it's time we all collectively challenged that.

Reya and Luna are seven-year-old twins. They go to a church school a short walk from where they live, and they are allowed an hour of screen time every day. They like different things and so they use this screen time in different ways. Reya watches YouTube Kids on an iPad with headphones and Luna generally watches TV. Luna often watches CBeebies, a BBC kids' channel. Today, Luna is watching *My World Kitchen*, a show about kids cooking meals from their international heritage. She finds the show comforting and the episode about Guyanese fishcakes reminds her of her granny. Luna's dad perches on the sofa arm beside the girls and the show prompts stories about his mum and his own childhood. Luna's chat with her dad is an example of 'active' co-viewing. This type of viewing encourages interaction, and education, which is now recommended by the American Paediatrics Association.[19] Here an interactive form of viewing might spark discussion and socialization simultaneously during screen time.

Meanwhile, Reya wears a pair of light-up cat-ear headphones connected to the tablet she holds on her lap. Her small spine arches down, curving her body into the now familiar shape of digital pre-teendom. In this pose, Reya engages in hyper-personal viewing. She watches short, fast-paced clips on YouTube Kids, which make her wiggle her shoulders in time to the music.

After a clip from *Gabby's Dollhouse*, which features a character that is half cat and half cupcake singing about sweet treats, a new clip is quickly offered. A kid, also about seven, squashes a browned and gooey marshmallow and a slab of chocolate between two Oreos, before shouting, 'Next time you go camping, instead of Graham crackers, USE OREOS!'

Then YouTube star Mr Beast showing off his new chocolate bar is presented to Reya.[20] Reya is bored. She opens a new web browser and types in 'Kittens'. This time, she finds herself on the main YouTube channel. Here she is shown a video of kittens sitting with their heads poking out of jars and then another video of more kittens. Next: another video, still more kittens. And then someone putting a kitten on a road and running it over with a truck. This makes Reya upset, and she will have trouble falling asleep for the rest of the week. And so, Reya and Luna's screen time, though quantitatively the same, is qualitatively different.

But how did this guidance about 'screen time' that most parents now use come about? It was mostly drawn from physical health research. There is good, strong evidence linking high levels of screen time and poorer physical health outcomes,[21] with studies from about a decade ago indicating that children with high levels of television and computer use are more likely to have a higher body mass index (BMI) and have increased risk for being overweight or obese and for type 2 diabetes.[22] Most of us can agree that physical activity and time off screens is good. Very good, in fact. And so, previously, systematic reviews in this area generally landed on the one to two hours' screen-time recommendation, with over two hours being a risk factor for overweight/obesity in children and adolescents.[23] This was, and is, good guidance to promote physical health. However, because this 'screen time' advice was related to physical health concerns it didn't include robust discussion around the quality or nature of the content and how that might be impacting mental health.

But what does this do for seven-year-olds Reya and Luna? Not much. It's not very helpful just to say screen time doesn't work without giving them – or rather, their parents – advice on what does. More recently, there have been attempts to distinguish between types of screen time, such as 'passive' and 'active' engagement. Some have pushed policy to take into account 'Active Screen Time',[24] which involves cognitively or physically engaging in screen-based activities, such as playing games or completing homework on a computer, and 'Passive Screen Time', which includes non-interactive viewing with low levels of intellectual and social engagement.[25]

In these ways, Luna and Reya's after-school screen times may both be one hour. The same amount of screen time but their experiences are very different. One is consuming curated, regulated content for children on live TV providing a diverse range of programming. She is engaged with a parent and uses the viewing as a jumping-off point for discussion and connection. The other's viewing is fragmented. It is short-form content with little focus on meaningful storylines or characters, she is isolated and it's for the most part unregulated.

It should go without saying that this needs to be balanced with offscreen activity. Getting kids moving, independent and engaged offline is important, even essential.[26] Television is not the best form of childcare, but age-appropriate, quality, regulated programming is often qualitatively different than putting your kid on an unregulated private screen, such as an iPad – one where it is easy to slide off this platform onto another platform where even the most minimal child restrictions are not in place. To address this, a focus on habits and behaviours, rather than absolute limits, was adopted as policy guidance in the UK in 2019, when the Royal College of Paediatrics and Child Health (RCPCH) released new information, based upon both the positive and negative aspects of screen time.[27]

Neurodiversity and Smartphones

For neurodivergent people screens can offer many positives. Whilst recognizing that neurodivergent people are not a homogeneous group, evidence suggests that screens can provide predictability, a sense of belonging within like-minded online communities and can be instrumental in helping to manage anxiety.[28] Screens can provide avenues for deep learning as well as gamified learning for people where traditional educational methods may not be suitable. And calendars, timers and reminder functions are essential for those who struggle with executive function.[29]

For more advice in this area take a look at Childnet's STAR SEND toolkit, available at https://www.childnet.com/resources/star-send-toolkit/.

Regardless of what type of screen choice you make as a family, it is worth thinking exactly that: it's a choice. You can make active choices and think critically about what your kids – and you – are watching. And just like healthy eating, you can start seeding these habits about heathy consumption from an early age. Because though today's parents were likely themselves plunked in front of screens as pacifiers to watch a parade of singing puppet characters in front of TV dinners, the spectrum of screen options available for your parents was vastly different. They didn't have to make many choices about screens, because often there were a couple of channels with programmed children's TV at certain times or even one 'children's hour'.[30] And those choices – that curated children's programming – were made for them. These were different screens. Different screens, showcasing different content and presenting different levels of accessibility and risk. And if we are as parents going to use screens to soothe, to quiet, or to effectively switch off our young, it's worth being more conscious about what we are doing and the way we are doing it.

It's also worth considering ways in which you can 'co-view' or make screen time more social, educational and creative.[31] That is, the times in which you can opt for 'active' viewing, when you move away from a personalized screen time to a more social one. Like Reya's dad who was watching with her and talking to his child about what she was watching. Alternately, you could be engaging Luna and using learning apps together, 'activizing' these screens and making decisions about what to click on and helping her to become active in her online engagement rather than a passive observer or 'user'.

The next chapter will give you tools to engage educational and age-appropriate active online exercises with your kids, as well as for yourself. For now, let me impress what I have already argued: digital content is often unregulated and so it is without the restrictions you find on children's viewing elsewhere, for example around promoting junk food. And I've discussed how it might be easy to slide off this platform onto another platform where those child restrictions are not in place. So with these concerns in mind here are some tips about adding more nuance to screen consumption.

WHAT YOU CAN DO ABOUT IT
Screen Consumption

Active v. Passive. Prioritize active and engaged viewing over passive viewing. This means content that encourages creativity and discussion. This supports active brain engagement, learning and communication skills. If you are using a tablet and your child is engaging with learning apps, review what apps you have on your child's device. If you have an older child, you can do this together, with the child's consent.

Communication. Find time to engage with your family about the content they are viewing, building social engagement.

Quality of the Content. Pay attention to what is being consumed. Question what the content offers. Ask: Is this educational? Is this content detrimental, pushing negative ideas or self-beliefs? Begin to think critically about what is being viewed and open up discussions about this with your child.

A throwback to terrestrial. Look for regulated children's programming. I encourage my own children to watch live TV on platforms like CBeebies and CBBC, as this provides a diversity of content curated by a children's programmer. Lots of time and advocacy has gone into producing children's educational TV by way of both the BBC and PBS in the US.

The Safety Paradox and Why Screen Time Doesn't Work – Conclusion

Back in the focus group at the suburban girls' school, Iryna had moved on to a new story. This one no longer about Ukraine but about deleting her older brother's account on X. As she put it: 'Excuse my language, but the thing is there was a sex reference and I was really not happy to see it.' She continued, 'He was angry and me, I was like, NO! . . . He was about seventeen and I was seven,' a statement that left the whole group of girls in hysterics. Developing early critical thinking about screen usage and building boundary formation through talking about these issues regularly as part of our habitual lives is something that we all should be doing. Of course we should not be over-reliant on screens. Time off them is generally better than on. When we are on them, we should be making active critical choices about the quality of what we are consuming, and in turn, what we are feeding to our children. Simultaneously, we are all caught in the complexity of the safety paradox, where we all try to balance the good of technology against the bad. To grapple with this, we need to pull apart the aspects of technology that keep us safe (the stuff we want) from the parts that harm us (the stuff we don't want). In choosing screens, devices, 'smart' or 'dumb' options, we should be asking: What do you actually need the device for and what do you need it to do? Does it increase safety or hinder it? What functions are you hoping to be able to use and why? Does it have capacities that support a healthy digital diet?

An information-building approach is needed for both young people and the general public, who themselves did not grow up with digital technology, so we develop at least a base knowledge of understanding of what is healthy and what is not. One that doesn't just rely only on the quantity of usage but the quality. And one that takes into account these inherent pulls – or paradoxes – that we all face around communication and isolation; education and distraction; safety and harm; and the way that screens facilitate both.

Chapter 5

Digital Nutrition: Your Guide to Healthy Consumption

It's Saturday night. I hold a paper cup of cider brandy and raise the heels of my dirt-stained Converse high tops in an attempt to peer over the crowd. It's in vain. So, I look up to watch a sea of mini-Chris Martins duplicated on glaring smartphone screens again and again and again to infinity. This is Glastonbury. We, a crowd a hundred thousand deep, wear light-up bracelets that are meant to pulse in coordination with the music. But the hundred thousand glowing mini-Chrises in their rectangular boxes shine brighter and somewhat dull the impact. After finishing Coldplay's 2014 dance hit, 'Sky Full of Stars', Chris – the real Chris – pauses. 'We are having the best time with you all and that's why we feel confident to ask you one small favour.' He kneels for impact. 'We'd like to play this song one more time . . . This time we'd like to ask if we could try it with no cellphones. No filming.' And, then:

> All you need for this is your phone in your pocket and your hands in the sky. Your phone in your pocket and your hands in the sky. Your phone in your pocket and your hands in the sky. That's the way we're gonna make the whole world fly.[1]

Chris Martin did not ask people to stop filming altogether, he just said, Let's play that song 'one more time' and try it differently.

Let's compare the experience both with and without a smartphone. And with this approach, which I understand has become a bit of a Coldplay schtick (used at most of their shows), I nevertheless watched people around me drop their screens and drop in. They didn't feel like something was being ripped away but rather they were offered an alternative approach. This is a form of information-building. This is digital literacy.

I say this fully aware that the notes about Chris Martin's statement on putting down one's phone were recorded in a field in rural Somerset – on my phone. There are amazing things about our hybrid lives that facilitate mobility, access and connection. But it does mean that we have technology ever present in order to facilitate this new reality, potentially alienating those around us. And if we are parents, potentially while modelling addictive habits. What follows in this chapter is a guide to personal healthy digital consumption, which in turn can help to inform choices we make for those around us. The contents of this chapter can help you build a deep awareness of your own consumption – an innate understanding – so that in turn you can pass this understanding on. We all need to think about healthy consumption – putting good-quality, positive and information-rich content into our minds – and this is how we can start.

Phone Fed

In 1994 the UK launched the national food model, which was revised and named 'the Eatwell Plate' in 2007.[2] This 'plate' resembled a pie chart populated with one large section of green vegetables and another with loaves of artisanal bread. This iconic plate would shape general understanding of healthy eating and become woven into our social lexicon. From Australia to Canada,

Portugal to Sweden, these circular sense checks opened up understanding of the quality and types of food we should be eating, expanding beyond the concept of 'dieting', limitation or restriction that once dominated nutrition discourse. More recent transitions have looked at the ways in which substances that appear 'like food' are in fact 'ultra-processed' to the extent that they lose their nutritional value and instead fuel addiction and obesity. The recent arguments around ultra-processed foods (UPFs) have pointed to the idea that although food can be presented as healthy in its form, packaging and marketing, the processes the food has gone through has distorted and changed its nutritional value, which makes it not only less nutritious but potentially harmful.[3]

Similarly to food, digital diet guidance needs to take a more nuanced approach.[4] Just like ultra-processed foods, although the core of digital usage can be good (i.e. educational, social, creative and interactive material) the process through which that material is served to us, by way of algorithms and content creators, can render it unhealthy and potentially harmful. When I spoke to my colleague Dr Photini Vrikki about this metaphor while waiting for our departmental kettle to boil, she likened it to the plastic wrapping of food. That is, the packaging of content, which like the microplastics seeping into your prepackaged muffin can seep into us.

Academics from different fields have put forward the concept of a 'digital diet' to help think through the role of digital environments in developing public-health policy.[5] In particular, Amy Orben from MRC Cognition and Brain Sciences Unit at the University of Cambridge has advocated for greater parallels between the study of food and the study of technologies. In her words we need to think about digital consumption in relation to '(a) what is being eaten, (b) the amount that is being eaten' and '(c) different food groups . . .'[6]

In the same way that not all foods are created equal, we should differentiate between types of content. In the last chapter, I talked about breaking down time on screens into two categories: *Active Screen Time*, which is often like healthy food and involves cognitively or physically engaging in screen-based activities; and *Passive Screen Time*, which is often like junk food and includes scrolling and passive gazing.

Active screen time can have additional categories: **Education**, which might involve language games, maths tutorials and quizzes; **Creativity**, which can involve artmaking or reading; **Communication**, involving keeping in touch with friends or family members; **Participation**, which refers to searching or gaming.[7]

Digital Diet Categories

+ **Education.** Digital technologies are now a central part of education and learning. Working to understand and identify trusted news and information sources is important. Many young people access much of their schoolwork via apps such as Google Classroom. Educational games can also be part of a healthy digital diet, such as those for numeracy, reading and new languages. Giving young people skills online to explore topics of interest to them, and how to do this safely and critically, can support their digital literacy.
+ **Creativity.** Digital tools can support creativity. Given the known links between creative activities and well-being, particularly for teenagers, it can be good to encourage positive opportunities to use technology to explore creative interests, such as photography, drawing or music.

- **Communication.** Communication is central to the use of technology, providing opportunities to seek and find communities among peers, as well as supporting people to feel safe by keeping in contact with family and friends.
- **Participation.** Gaming and participation online can be fun and a way to support fine motor skills, problem-solving and community. Such activities should still be monitored in relation to their age appropriateness and safety concerns (outlined in Chapter 2).
- **Passive.** The format of the never-ending scroll can encourage consumption of content in a passive way. This can sometimes help to relax or switch off but can be damaging when unhealthy or harmful content is delivered at high dosages. When seeking to use technology to switch off or relax, try to use long-form or curated content.

These categories should, like a food guide, be given different weightings across overall usage. First, it's important to understand the quality of the content that you are consuming. I suggest using the walk-through method outlined in Chapter 3 where you look at a period of usage.

Next, it's good to get a sense of the quantity of the digital content that you are consuming. You can do this in two ways: by observing your screen usage by way of a 'phone fed journal', and by checking your screen usage through the settings on your device (see instructions below). All together, these qualitative and quantitative exercises give an idea of what you are consuming and should give you a sense of how your consumption is impacting your mood and well-being.

WHAT YOU CAN DO ABOUT IT
Keep a 'Phone Fed Journal'

For a period of a couple of days make notes in a journal (or your notes on your phone) about your screen usage. Write down the following:

1. What you opened your phone to do.
2. Where you eventually ended up.
3. How long the session was.
4. You can also write down how your mood was at the end of the session. Did you feel bad, did you feel good?

After a couple of days, if you look back over your **phone fed journal** and find that you are uncomfortable with the amount of time spent (the quantity) or the overall content and the way it made you feel (the quality) of your consumption, let's think about changing that.

Using your screen time stats to understand your current digital diet

To help with your journal: both Android and Apple devices also have settings where you can see how much time you spend on your device and on individual apps. You can find instructions about how to change these settings by searching for Screen Time in the Google Help Centre for Android devices and at Apple Support for Apple devices.

Digital Diet Pyramid

The *Food Guide Pyramid* was first introduced to Americans in 1992.[8] Housed in a rather unappetizing black geometric shape, it organized food groups in a hierarchical order with six to eleven daily servings of breads, cereals, rice and pasta forming the base. At the peak of this pyramid perched butter and oils, with the guidance 'use sparingly'. Building off the work of Orban[9], my team and I use a pyramid shape[10] to take a hierarchical approach to the different types of digital engagement. It shows how different proportions of each type of screen consumption might support a healthy digital diet.

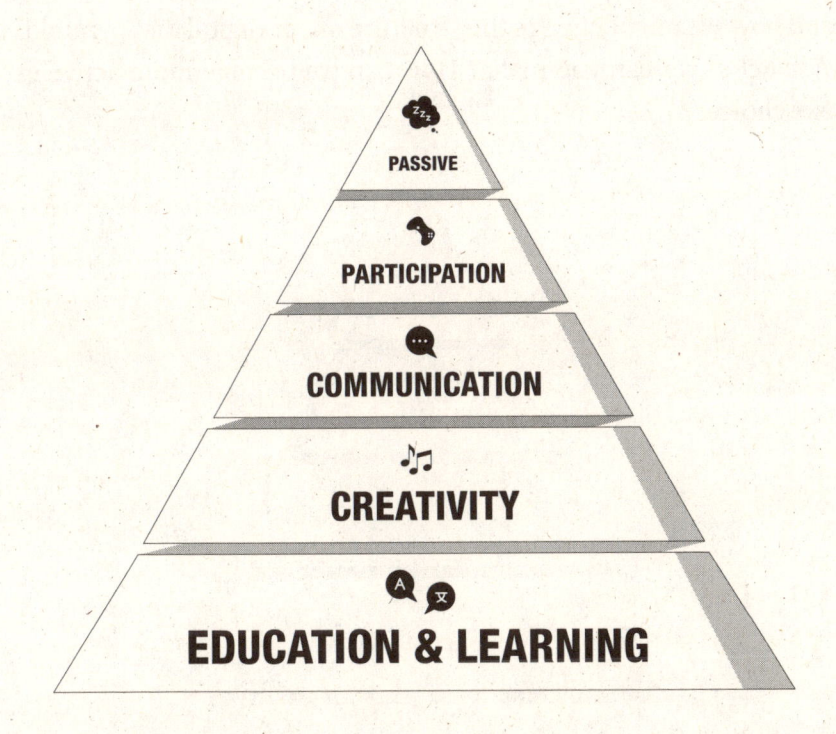

- PASSIVE
- PARTICIPATION
- COMMUNICATION
- CREATIVITY
- EDUCATION & LEARNING

Using this guide, you can start to think more critically for you and your family about what to prioritize with your screen consumption. Look over your 'phone fed journal' and ask yourself: What categories does my consumption fall into? If your consumption time is high and most of that consumption is sitting at the top of the pyramid, try to move your screen consumption lower down into a more active category.

There's a template below to create your own pyramid. You can use it to pencil in the different categories and where they fit hierarchically on your own current pyramid. Once you have filled it out, ask yourself: Am I happy with my current pyramid? Is there anything I'd like to change? Once you have done your own pyramid, you might also create a pyramid with others in your life. What this exercise does is ask us to think about what we consume digitally and how we might change the structure of our digital diet pyramid. What changes can you make? How can we become more active in our choices?

But it gets more complicated. And look, I realize this is all getting a bit dry and feeling equivalent to a flight attendant asking you to read the evacuation brochure before take-off (something you're never going to do). But bear with me here, I promise we'll take off soon. The pyramid also doesn't account for the easy slippages from healthy into unhealthy forms of usage. For this reason, it's worth thinking of the pyramid as a cone where positive and healthy forms of usage can slide into unhealthy forms of use. That is to say, for the most part, such crossovers between healthy and unhealthy usage do not have hard edges, but rather might imperceptibly seep into your feeds or habits over time. For example: education can slide around into misinformation. In this same way, creative expression might morph into filtering photos in the quest for unrealistic body ideals. Communication can become the site of trolling comments or cyberbullying. And participating in active gaming might cross over into unsafe spaces. Engaging with passive forms of entertainment can turn to doomscrolling or the 'brain rot'.

And particularly because this cone (see page 120) can allow for slippages into unhealthy or harmful forms of usage, we should make more active decisions about where we spend our time and attention. We can take more control over what is being fed to us in a much more active way. Ask: What do I want to see during my time on platforms? What do I want more of? And what do I want to reject? So that we are no longer just accepting what is algorithmically offered. But, rather, we have decided to teach the machine learning otherwise. This process is termed 'gaming the algorithm' or 'algorithmic resistance',[11] which Tiziano Bonini and Emilio Treré describe as the 'ability of the people to actively shape the outcome of algorithmic computation for their own benefit'[12] in order to push back against the attention economy. Bonini and Treré have researched a few key groups to look at how workers and specific industries are pushing back against the corporate tech constructs.[13] But algorithmic resistance – or 'gaming the algorithm' – is something we can all do in the personal or domestic space. It's something you can do, and do with others in your life, who are on social media, in order to take greater control.

Digital nutrition

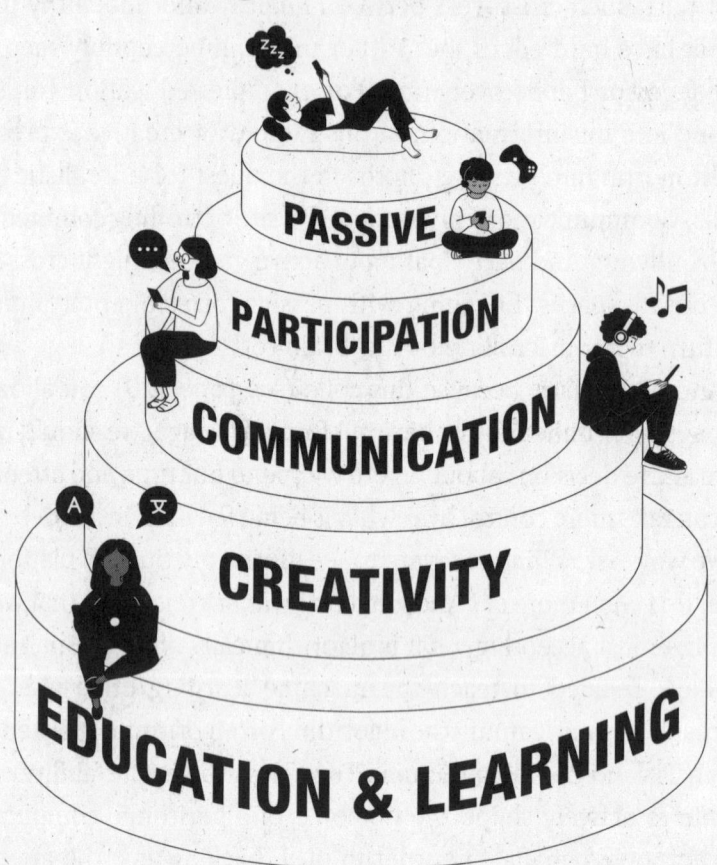

- PASSIVE
- PARTICIPATION
- COMMUNICATION
- CREATIVITY
- EDUCATION & LEARNING

PASSIVE
Non-interactive viewing with low levels of intellectual and social engagement are often used as a way to switch off. Such forms of relaxation are reasonable in moderation but the type of content being consumed should be considered and monitored.

! Avoid long sessions of consuming content with low levels of positive stimulation.

PARTICIPATION
Participation activities such as gaming can be a good way to have fun with friends, hone problem solving skills and as a way to relax.

! Be mindful of addictive qualities of some games and online gaming crossing into unsafe spaces.

EDUCATION & LEARNING
Digital tools are now crucial to education. Encourage use for research and homework and by using trusted news organisations.

! Misinformation or seeking out information about damaging practices.

COMMUNICATION
Healthy communities can support wellbeing, such as chatting with friends and family on invite only networks.

! Trolling, large unregulated group chats featuring bullying, sharing toxic content.

CREATIVITY
Art and music making practices and creativity can be supported by digital tools, such as graphics pads for drawing and music or film-making software.

! Filtering photos into unrealistic body ideals or creating disinformation.

Gaming your algorithm will look slightly different depending on the platform and what you are trying to achieve, but fundamentally, it's about moving away from the role of passive user to become an active participant. It is also worth noting that this is something you will need to do on a regular basis, in order to ensure algorithms don't slip away from your teachings, and you might need to evolve your practice as platforms adjust.

WHAT YOU CAN DO ABOUT IT
Algorithmic Resistance and How to Game Your Algorithm

1. **Make a choice.**
Make a clear choice about what you want to see on your feed. If you want cooking videos, great. If you are looking for old black and white films,

fab. If you want interior design and also some celeb gossip, cool. Just make a clear choice about what you want your perfect digital diet to be.

2. **Actively interact with things you want in your diet.**
Dedicate half an hour a week to training the machine learning by finding content that you want to see – content that you are passionate about or that makes you feel good. Actively search for things you like.

3. **Budget your attention.**
Next, not every piece of content that is fed to you deserves your time and attention. Your time and attention are money (literally, they're being sold), so become more discerning about what you want to give your attention to. Don't watch uninteresting, uninspiring content or content that makes you feel bad. Quickly move past it. And do not like, share or comment on things that don't fit into your new healthy digital diet. According to an ex-TikTok employee, even commenting that you don't like something can count as engagement.[14]

4. **Follow people who empower you.**
Don't follow accounts that make you feel bad or self-conscious. For example, this might mean unfollowing an underwear model who makes you feel bad about your own body and instead choosing to follow someone who represents you or who inspires you.

5. **Use privacy settings.**
Use privacy settings to control who can see your posts, comments and personal information. Where possible, keep your accounts private and restricted to friends or followers you trust. This might also mean turning off geo-locating on apps like Snapchat, so that tracking is disabled.

These steps taken together will begin to shift what is algorithmically fed to you on a daily basis and they will, in turn, change your digital diet.

Boundaries and Going Organic

'So many people just believe things that you see on TikTok. Like even my mum,' were the words of a matter-of-fact fifteen-year-old, who then went on to help her mum fact-check a news story on her TikTok feed.[15] To which another replied, 'I use a brick phone. It limits my screen time.'[16] Actively opting for 'brick phones', or what some have come to call 'going organic', has, in some teen circles, become quite hip. It tends to be a response to the addictive qualities of smartphones and represents an 'alt' movement distinguished from that of their tech-slaved Gen X parents.

This school, a London girls' school, was by far the most tech-heavy environment we as a research team had encountered.[17] All students have iPads, which they take to every class, and almost all their work is done on a screen. But at the same time, this school is heavily invested in digital literacy – that is education about digital processes and how to be critical of them. They have built a digital mentorship programme. Here girls run group sessions, where they speak to peers about challenges in the digital space. It's a programme that not only fosters community building, youth voice and leadership skills, but also enables teachers to stay up to date with pressing issues in this ever-developing terrain. This educational emphasis extends beyond students to students' parents, with their science teacher running sessions for parents throughout the term to 'tech them up', enabling digital education to spill out of the classroom and into the home, filling after-school time and weekends with healthy habits.

Along these lines, we have also met with teens who are neurodivergent, teens who are LGBTQ+ and teens who have chronic health conditions, all of whom found community through social media. Together, this school and these examples represent good stories of kids who have benefited from educational investment in these topics, creating healthy kids critically navigating tech. They represent an education approach paired with healthy self-regulation habits. They show how some members of Gen Z are working to enjoy the nutrients offered by the digital sphere while actively avoiding the junk food that might make them, and you, sick.

Peer-to-Peer Mentorship

Peer-to-peer learning programmes can be excellent for building community, youth voice and leadership skills. Around digital issues, they can also enable teachers and school leaders to stay up to date with pressing issues. Scotland's Mentors in Violence Prevention programme has been particularly successful across Scotland and specifically deals with gender violence. I have worked with Professor Nicola Shaughnessy and Angela McDonald on their digital misogyny training, where older kids lead sessions for younger kids around these issues. MVP supplies resources, and a wealth of peer-to-peer learning materials, which can be found on Education Scotland's website: https://education.gov.scot/news/new-mentors-in-violence-prevention-mvp-resource/.

In this book, I've talked about building a broader awareness of how algorithmic processes function. In this chapter, I've talked about equipping ourselves to make a change. Finally, I'd like to talk about – as the girls above demonstrate – how to set healthy boundaries around usage. That is, if you look at your **phone fed journal** and you are not so concerned about the content you are consuming but rather that you want less of it, let's talk about how to do that.

It's a good idea to make rules about times and places that are screen-free. That might mean when you come home from work, at meals, or in the bedroom. It's also worth considering a phone-free weekend in order to carve out time when phones are out of sight. This being said, some – if not a lot – of this consumption is simply unavoidable. It is intrinsically woven into contemporary society and there are hefty societal expectations around our engagement with these devices. Not just work but the admin of life – not just ours, but also for those we care for – are contained in these palm-sized rectangles. We need to text back, we need to answer, we need to buy ballet shoes for Tuesday's class and facilitate group Christmas drinks two and a half months in advance. I say this without irony – sort of. These are social norms, ones we might not want to shake.

What we can do is make active choices and communicate with those around us. That is to say, actively articulating what we are doing, why and for how long. If you have to respond to something on your phone that should take five minutes, stick to those five minutes. You might say to your friends or family members, 'I'm just doing this email for work and then I'm going to be back and focusing on you.' Setting a time boundary around these exercises can help prevent you from slipping into the inevitable checking of texts and then sliding onto Instagram, which means the five-minute activity has turned into a forty-minute session scrolling on your phone.

There are also a lot of tasks that we do on screens that are not for us but are for those around us, for example grocery shopping. These are activities that could be interactive activities, but we often don't allow them to be. We could engage our kids in these exercises. There was a time when we took our kids grocery shopping weekly, few people do this any more. Maybe this is an example of an online activity that could become an offline one. It's good to find opportunities to de-tech tasks where possible. Alternately, maybe you can engage your kids in the virtual grocery shop, so that they are active and making choices. Ask them, 'What should we have for supper on Tuesday?' And when you have finished the digital task, you actively choose to turn that device off.

These are social/behavioural changes we can make around our usage, but there are also technical tools you can use to enforce boundaries. Below are tips on how to moderate the amount of your usage along with limiting app usage and setting up controls.

WHAT YOU CAN DO ABOUT IT
Things you can do to mitigate your device usage

- **Decide your max.** Set a daily time limit for your most frequently used apps and stick to it. You can use your devices' limits (see below) to put these limits in place.
- **Stop pushing me.** Turn off push notifications which draw your attention to certain apps. At the same time, think about who you do want to hear from and adjust your settings so that you always get notifications from the people you want to hear from but not those you don't. You can even assign different ringtones to different people to aid with this.
- **Greyscale.** You can greyscale your phone (see Chapter 2) as a way to make you more mindful of the addictive qualities of smartphones.
- **Clean up your home screen.** Move social media apps off your main home screen. Or alternatively you can delete apps off your phone altogether and only access your social media channels by signing in via a web browser. Both of these techniques will dissuade you from sliding from a necessary task into doomscrolling.
- **Screen-free.** Make clear house rules about times and places that are screen-free. Whether that means when you come home from work, at meals, or in the bedroom, carve out times when phones are out of sight.

- **Limit your usage of individual apps.** Both Android and Apple devices have settings that allow you to limit how much time you spend on apps. You can find the instructions for this by searching for setting time limits or app limits at Google Help Centre for Android devices and at Apple Support for Apple devices.
- **Parental controls.** If you are a parent, when you finish setting limits for yourself, set up parental controls. There are layers of parental controls including limiting times on certain apps. The first layer is to set up controls at the Internet provider level. If you do this, it will block adult content for everyone in the household. The next layer is to set up controls at device level: the phone, iPad or games console. Lastly, you can set up controls at individual app level. You can find up-to-date sets of parental control guides for a wide range of devices and apps on the Internet Matters site: https://www.Internetmatters.org/parental-controls/. For gaming consoles there are a set of parental controls guides available at www.AskAboutGames.co.uk.

Remember, parental controls can only go so far. As children get older or more digitally savvy, they are likely to be able to get around parental controls quickly and easily. Parental controls also don't build critical digital citizens but rather function as a baby gate, and at some point, kids do need to learn to walk down the stairs. For these reasons, parental controls can be a strategy that is employed, but not the only one. You should still be aware of your child's online activity.

Digital Nutrition – Conclusion

After 'A Sky Full of Stars', a few around me dived into their pockets again, but most didn't. Many seemed to leave their glowing boxes tucked away in the bottoms of bags and backs of minds, setting personal boundaries around usage – if only for just that moment. The recording of a Coldplay concert is not social media consumption per se, but rather an intended consequence. The recording of Coldplay – all these mini-Chrises – is part of social media in that it reflects the cultural imperative to capture and upload experiences as a shared resource. It is part of it.

Some reading this book might argue they are not social-media users though they love the TikTok comedian a friend always sends through group chats. And they do use YouTube tutorials every time they need to bleed the radiators. Even if we believe ourselves to be above it all or undatafied, most likely, we are not. And so, as datafied digital citizens, we should commit time and energy to educating ourselves and in turn our kids about the online world. We should provide education so that they have the choice and agency to 'go organic', to know their limits, and to point out disinformation on parents' phones, eye rolling at our generational ignorance. This is a goal worth striving for.

This isn't meant to ruin all your fun. I know that sharing pictures of our kids or of our cats can feel amazing. It can bring techno-coloured joy to a rather grey workday. I'm simply suggesting that at the same time, we learn how to do a digital 'spring clean' (Chapter 1) and further, safeguard ourselves – and possibly those very kids and cats – against harm, unwanted or addictive content. To do this we can use tools. We can use screen-time functions on our devices. We can keep a phone-fed journal to track digital engagement. We can have digital check-ins. Regular digital check-ins, where both adults and teens share their screen-time experiences, like digital walk-through sessions, as described in Chapter 3.

And, finally, you can choose to take greater control. You can and should game your algorithms. You can decide what type of digital diet you want. The type of content you want to see. And then actively search for the topics you want more of. It's thirty years since the Eat Well Plate changed the UK's cultural awareness of food. Thirty years since it brought a concept of a balanced diet into the cultural zeitgeist. And it now feels high time we integrate new critical thinkings about what we consume by way of screens into public consciousness. Screens that – like food – have become essential to modern life. And screens over which we can have the power to change our relationships – so that we build active, nutritious online engagement. Digital nutrition. A balanced digital diet – for our 'feeds'.

Chapter 6

An Ethical Internet: Regulation and Defunding Hate, Harm and Disinformation

I'm in an industrial cafe in Hampstead. It has exposed structural steel, artfully fatigued wood floors and claims to provide 'professional coffee industry training'[1] for those leaving prison. At the counter, I order from a trendy looking person in a mustard-yellow woolly hat. We are inside and it's April, but I quickly push the thought out of my mind for fear my millennial might be showing, even if only to myself.[2]

I'm meeting with two of the founders of Smartphone Free Childhood, Daisy Greenwell and Joe Ryrie, along with one of their pioneering parent activists, Birdy. The couple, Daisy and Joe, had left London to build a more environmentally friendly family life around blackberries, beehives and rewilding.[3] Two months before our meeting, Daisy, fearing the pressure mounting to get her daughter a smartphone,[4] set up a WhatsApp group with friend Clare Fernyhough. The pair then took to Instagram and asked others to join the group. Longing for a 'people powered movement against the giant corporations', the group sought out 'parents united for a smartphone free childhood – it currently has 3 of us on it.' By the next day the WhatsApp group had maxed out at 1,000 members.[5] 'At the time of writing there are 175,000 members.'[6] The group asks parents to sign a pact to hold off giving children phones until the end of year nine[7] in order to shift social norms and remove pressures on children to need a smartphone in order to avoid social alienation.

Daisy is warm. A journalist and former commissioning editor at *The Times*[8] with a calming presence. But we weren't meeting about rewilding. Nor were we meeting about the ways in which they were looking to shift the dial of social media as an imperative in the socialization of early teens. We were meeting about a study I'd recently published, which suggested content consumed on TikTok was influencing boys' behaviour in school. And they wanted to talk 'causation'. Or rather, they wanted me, or someone like me, to prove causation.

Social media companies, and more latterly policy makers, have used the lack of causal evidence as a reason not to take action. In early 2024 when addressing the US Senate, including a group of bereaved families of teenagers, Mark Zuckerberg made the point that there is still no definitive finding that social media leads to harm. He stated, 'Scientific work has not shown a causal link between using social media and young people having worse mental health outcomes.'[9]

There is a push for further academic research to prove that social media is *the* 'cause' of recent negative socio-cultural shifts (polarized societies, poor mental health, anti-social behaviours... to name just a few). In a joint US–UK statement on the protection of children online in October of 2024, the UK government stated there was still 'limited research and evidence on the causal impact that social media has on children.'[10] For academic researchers, there is – rightly – a high bar for evidence to definitively prove that one thing directly causes another. And so there has been hesitancy among academics to engage with these simplistic 'headline' narratives. Harm is multifaceted, and is often compounded by lots of existing vulnerabilities and external factors. Dealing with complex research subjects (e.g. the developing adolescent brain, which exists in a nuanced and varied world) makes this very difficult. Because social media usage isn't like growing bacteria in a controlled, closed Petri dish.

'Causation is a tricky term,' I said. You see for much of the scientific world, the most effective way of determining 'causation' is the randomized controlled trial (RCT).[11] In RCTs, volunteer participants are randomly assigned, and then the two groups are compared on the outcome of interest. But for some situations, an RCT is just not possible. Take, for example, smoking. Though there have been RCTs around people who have stopped smoking to see the effects that this has on their health, an RCT seeking to prove that smoking definitively causes cancer is much harder and ethically problematic to conduct. No contemporary scientist is going to randomly assign a bunch of people and tell them they must smoke a pack of cigarettes every day, and others to a 'control' group, who are not allowed to smoke at all, and then watch them over an extended period to see if the two groups have different cancer rates. There is of course a huge 'naturalistic experiment' going on all the time because some people choose to smoke and others don't. However, even though those who choose to smoke do have higher cancer rates, because their groups are not randomly assigned by an experimenter, this naturalistic study is still likely be considered insufficient as incontrovertible proof of causation. For example (and completely hypothetically), it might be possible that people who are genetically prone to cancer are also genetically prone to nicotine addiction. If so, smoking would not be causing cancer. Rather, in this hypothetical scenario, something else (genetics) would be causing cancer and causing smoking in the same people.

Of course, there is lots of other converging evidence that can be brought to bear to make a strong logical case for why it is only sensible to conclude that smoking actually does cause cancer. But even then, we cannot say that cancer is an inevitable consequence of smoking. Some people smoke and don't get cancer. Others get cancer even if they have never smoked. So all we can do is make a logical argument that smoking meaningfully increases the probability of getting cancer. This means that many people and organizations[12] will state that smoking causes cancer (and we all know this to be true), but from a scientific perspective this is not definitive causation.

Similarly, it is going to be a more complex and subtle story in the link between social media use and mental health than is demanded by Zuckerberg's call for incontrovertible scientific evidence of a direct causal link. And, so long as governments continue to wait on causation as the apex of evidence, we are not going to be able to move anywhere around a socially complex problem – which is great for social media companies.

So Joe, Daisy and I talked about the things that we *can* do. What many amazing research projects have done is create evidence. And we can use that evidence to build an irrefutable case that social media increases the probability of these issues.[13] Amy Orben suggests it might pay to think about the state of adolescence and how issues that teens have always been more susceptible to (feeling down, risk taking, being prone to social pressure and anxiety) can bump up against or can be aggravated and amplified by social media usage.[14] This amplification doesn't have to be negative. Likes and finding community might feel amazing. But when it is bad, it can be really bad. And in these cases, and drawing on Orban's suggestion, we could surmise that it is not social media *causing* these issues, but that social media can make the natural state of adolescence *worse*. Let me pause on that. The question is not about whether social media causes these issues in teens but how much worse it can make being an adolescent. And, to a lesser degree, being any of us. How much worse does it make all our individual states of being? This is what we should be considering. This is what we should be talking to our kids about. This is what we should be calling out and shouting into the streets. Because it is in clearly defining it, pulling it apart and naming it, that we can start to distance ourselves.

So perhaps the argument isn't really what do we need to know more of. It's what to do with the information that we already have. Groups like Smartphone Free Childhood have done an incredible job to raise awareness about limiting phone usage for kids, educating parents on some of the harms of the online space and building communities of support. At the same time, as discussed previously, it's important to acknowledge that these issues are complex and the reasons why some kids might need a device: kids who access Childline via social media or online; kids with two homes; or SEND kids who use phones as medical devices.

But beyond these more personal accounts, so much of the focus of all these parent initiatives – like many grassroots movements – is to load the failings of corporate responsibility and government onto the community. That is, they are important movements, but ideally they shouldn't be necessary. Beyond personal responsibility, there is a much greater corporate and regulatory responsibility to solve these problems and it's high time we started looking in that direction. This chapter is focused in that direction, to break down the idea that this is a siloed, individualistic problem, but that rather, as a community, we can push advertisers and governments towards a more ethical approach. As algorithms become more sophisticated, so will the attention economy. It will get better and better at knowing us, so while using tools to mitigate the intensity of our addictions is crucial, there are much bigger changes that need to occur.

Chief Twit

He was carrying the kitchen sink. Dressed in his signature black jeans and a T-shirt, Elon Musk entered the glass doors of Twitter's head offices in October of 2022 with a sink. The reason for this was prop comedy. Musk then posted a clip with the text 'Entering Twitter HQ – Let that sink in!'[15] He later changed his Twitter profile to read 'Chief Twit',[16] and on the 28th of October, he posted that 'the bird is freed'.[17] Less than a year later, in July 2023, Musk would change Twitter's name, and that little blue bird would be free, or rather, crossed out and replaced by a minimalist, black 'X'.

Created in 2006, Twitter emerged as a new public sphere of political potential and impact. In 2011 scholars analysed 170,000 tweets from the Tunisian revolution and 230,000 from the Egyptian revolution and claimed, 'The revolutions were, indeed, tweeted'.[18] In 2014, #BlackLivesMatter (BLM) leapt to 93,000 tweets after the Ferguson verdict, when a white police officer was not charged with the fatal shooting of a black teenager. By 2016 the hashtag had been used more than twelve million times.[19] In 2015, JeSuisCharlie was (re)tweeted 6,500 times a minute the day after the terrorist attack on *Charlie Hebdo* magazine in Paris.[20] These movements are often cited as the beginnings of digital activism, which all happened on Twitter. And because of this boom in sharing, this truly unprecedented collectivizing[21] and communicating, media scholars have touted that these digital technologies have enabled a true freedom of the press:[22] more than we've ever seen before.

Of course, some have queried the effectiveness of digital activism. At times chalking it up to 'slacktivism'[23] for a lazy generation, where 'responding to an article in a blog can feel political'[24] but ultimately only 'feeds communication capitalism'.[25] Others suggest that the ability to do politics in private space has opened up access for different classes, rural communities, women and minorities to do politics. Indeed, when I query the ideas of digital activism within my own classrooms, often it is the students who are diverse – who are women, and are non-Western – who argue in favour of the power of digital politics, all started by a little blue bird. But Twitter's historic impact on politics is not just about digital activists, but also about politicians' use of the platform.

Trump's first presidency would be dubbed the 'Twitter presidency'. A space where the term 'rocket man' would be used in diplomacy with North Korea and where the late-night tweeting of the word 'Covfefe' (presumably a typo) would prompt his press secretary Sean Spicer to say that only a close circle knew 'what he meant'.[26] Some defined President Trump's use of Twitter as 'unpresidential'. To others, it was an innovation. As Rudolph Giuliani put it, the last presidential advancement in communication was the 'fireside chats of FDR or maybe the press conferences of John Kennedy'[27] and by way of Twitter, Trump – the '@real DonaldTrump' – communicated with his public.

But regardless, the relationship between Twitter and President Trump would become fractured. In 2020, in the midst of the second wave of BLM protests, Twitter hid one of President Trump's tweets stating that it 'glorifies violence'.[28] In 2021, following the storming of the capital in Washington, Twitter permanently suspended the former president's Twitter account, @realDonaldTrump, citing a 'further risk of incitement of violence.'[29]

Musk claims that one of the reasons behind his acquisition of Twitter – now X – was to enable a platform of free speech, and to re-establish a virtual 'town square'.[30] In doing so, Musk reinstated the accounts of banned users, including President Trump and a British far-right activist, Tommy Robinson. Musk also banned the word 'cisgender' as hate speech; and in response to an antisemitic post claiming 'Jewish communities' advocate 'hatred against whites' he commented: 'You have said the actual truth'.[31]

As X's content moderation continuously evolved, or arguably devolved, advertisers began to grow increasingly concerned about their brands appearing next to offensive content, harm, hate or disinformation. Musk later apologized for the 'actual truth' post of 15 November 2023, but in doing so, he also accused advertisers of 'blackmail'.[32] In an interview at the *New York Times* Dealbook Summit he said, 'if the company fails . . . it will fail because of an advertiser boycott' and further 'that will be what will bankrupt the company'.[33]

In the summer of 2024, Elon Musk's X filed a claim against GARM.[34] GARM (The Global Alliance for Responsible Media) was a voluntary initiative formed under the umbrella organization of the World Federation of Advertisers.[35] Launched in 2019, its purpose was to address digital safety following the attack on a mosque in Christchurch, New Zealand, which the killer live-streamed on Facebook. The idea behind GARM was to help advertisers avoid inadvertently supporting harmful or illegal content. According to GARM's website its formation also followed 'a slew of high-profile cases where brands' ads appeared next to illegal or harmful content such as promoting terrorism or child pornography',[36] creating both consumer and reputational issues for brands.

X claimed that through GARM, businesses were colluding to collectively withhold billions of advertising dollars from X.[37] GARM had over a hundred members. Four of them – Mars; the US pharmacy giant CVS; Danish company Orsted; and UK-based Unilever, whose products include Dove – were named as defendants in the suit filed by Musk in the summer of 2024.[38] This was an important trial in that it marked a stand in the way of corporate responsibility. The stakes of this trial felt big, and it felt as if it might give the legal system a chance to say something.

On 9 August 2024 GARM dissolved and posted the following:

> GARM is a small, not-for-profit initiative, and recent allegations that unfortunately misconstrue its purpose and activities have caused a distraction and significantly drained its resources and finances. WFA therefore is making the difficult decision to discontinue GARM activities.[39]

On 11 October 2024, X announced that it was 'pleased to have reached an agreement with Unilever and to continue our partnership with them on the platform'.[40]

GARM isn't the only organization to come up against X. X sued the non-profit Centre for Countering Digital Hate when it wrote about hate speech on the platform and suggested this dissuaded advertisers.[41] X has also begun litigation against Media Matters,[42] a watchdog group, who have pointed to pro-Nazi content appearing next to advertisements. But though most media attention has been focused on X and its relationship to advertisers, this is by no means a one-platform issue.

Google, as outlined in Chapter 1, drew the blueprint for the corporate ownership of tech companies, which other social media companies adopted and modified. The financing of Google through advertising, and the social media that followed it, seeped onto all platforms and became more and more advanced in an almost imperceptible way. It became a given. We accepted advertising as a mere annoyance. A slight buzz that was worth the rare sting, in order to have access to the that sweet, sweet honey. But through the sticky intoxication of the tech, we often forget what fuel funds this sugar rush. We can lament slow regulation, we can feel rage against unethical tech giants, but so rarely do we – as a society – question the source of funds that drive tech companies' need to dig deeper and deeper into our consciousness, holding our attention for just one more video. One more click. One more impression.

Ad agencies and commercial companies are paying for this, so that they can place adverts for their products next to content which people are engaging with, clicking on and reacting to it.[43] But though **advertisers** are the customers of **tech companies**, the **users** of tech platforms are, in turn, the customers of **advertisers**. And so therein lies the loop in which we exist. We are interdependent. As Professor Lewis Griffin has argued, this isn't new within the history of advertising, but 'What is different is the less stable relationship between the adverts and the luring media, and the platforms' disavowal of responsibility for that content.'[44]

But in this interdependence potentially lies power. Though we aren't the customers of tech, advertisers are reliant on us as the source of their revenue, and consequently, so is tech. And with this power, we can potentially vote with our feet, or clicks, a bit more. There have been some instances of successful initiatives in this space where the will of the people encouraged advertisers to take a stand. In 2019, a YouTuber, MattsWhatItIs, posted a video revealing what he described as a soft-core paedophilia ring and encouraged his fan base to report to companies putting their ads on the site with the hashtag YouTubeWakeUp. Major brands such as Disney, Epic Games, Nestlé and AT&T pulled their ads from the site within days of the controversy.[45] In response, YouTube took action and deleted more than four hundred channels.[46] This followed the 'adpocalypse' two years earlier, when Coca-Cola, Doctor Pepper, Johnson and Johnson and the UK government held or paused their advertisements on YouTube as a result of antisemitic, racist and hate speech on the platform.[47]

In 2020, after Twitter hid one of the President's tweets in relation to the BLM protests, Facebook took no similar action. Stop Hate For Profit emerged as a campaign challenging Facebook around its treatment of the incendiary post made by the President. Alongside more than a thousand companies such as Ben and Jerry's, Honda and Hershey, Stop Hate For Profit hit pause on ad spending on Facebook for July of 2020, in order to pressure Facebook to address racism across the platform.[48] This demonstrates ways that advertisers can employ more ethical approaches to technology. Stop Hate For Profit was primarily about one issue, one summer, but what if it had been longer?

GARM leaves a legacy: a set of categories around harmful and sensitive content, which are now well-established across social media platforms.[49] For example, in March of 2023, Meta, the parent company of Facebook and Instagram, launched 'brand suitability controls'.[50] Here it uses the guidelines laid out by GARM, where brands can exclude certain topics. Meta essentially gives three levels of brand controls:[51]

1) <u>Expanded Inventory</u> (the default setting), which shows ads next to all content that adheres to company policies.

2) <u>Moderate Inventory</u>, which 'excludes moderately sensitive content'. Meta specifies that this 'lowers your reach and may increase costs'.

3) <u>Limited Inventory</u>, which 'excludes additional sensitive content'. Meta specifies that this 'lowers your reach and may increase costs'.

What is crucial here is that brands are told that a more ethical approach will lower their reach and increase costs resulting in a poorer return on investment. And herein lies the fundamental flaw with this corporate structure laid out in plain sight. If you want to reduce harm, you will be less successful.

Perhaps it is worth looking to other models of incentivising advertisers.[52] For example, in the sustainability space, the 'B

Corp' certification is given to companies that can meet high standards of social and environmental performance, accountability and transparency.[53] We could decide that we need such models, to encourage ethical investments in social media on the part of brands and advertisers in the light of the continued lack of accountability on the part of platforms. We could look to models like B Corp or indeed look to build upon their pre-existing guidelines about social media investment because of course a by-product (quite literally) of the attention economy and the pressure to buy, buy, buy does indeed have huge environmental implications.[54]

WHAT YOU CAN DO ABOUT IT
The Environmental By-Products of Buying Products

Some former Amazon employees have begun speaking out against the streamlining of buying and the huge implications this has for the environment. The World Economic Forum tells us that, globally, we produce 92 million tonnes of textile waste each year. 400 million tonnes of plastic waste is produced annually according to the United Nations Environment Programme. And, in 2022, a global estimated total of 62 million tonnes of electrical and electronic equipment was produced, according to the World Health Organization.[55] If you want to address this in your own life, you might want to re-consider your online buying behaviours, where buying has become hyper-streamlined and easy, encouraging greater spending. You may choose to look to some pre-loved or vintage buying platforms. There are some rich communities to be found here.

An Ethical Internet 143

It's not just the ease of buying more and more goods that has an environmental impact. Digital usage can also have an impact. AI can use vast amounts of energy. For example, if all search queries were placed as generated AI queries, the impact on emissions would be huge: 60 times greater for CHAT GPT 3 and that is likely to become even higher as AI models become more sophisticated.[56] Creating 1,000 images with AI produces about the same amount of carbon dioxide as driving 4.1 miles in a typical petrol-powered car.[57] When starting a task or looking to buy a product, think about whether generative AI is the best tool to use. Dr Photini Vrikki suggests asking if your question or image prompt could be answered with a simple Google search? Even better, you could try Ecosia[58] a search engine that funds tree-planting projects in over thirty countries. Ecosia runs on renewable energy and helps local communities and biodiversity.

- There can be great community and camaradie to be found on pre-loved or vintage platforms. It's worth thinking about buying, selling or exchanging through these applications.
- Consider whether you need to use generative AI, which uses much more energy when completing an online task.
- Think of using Ecosia which funds tree planting projects and runs on renewable energy as a possible alternative to more mainstream search engines.

The early days of Twitter, its activism and the digital town square proposed by Elon Musk assume that we all have an equal space in the square. However, lawyer and Yale University lecturer Asha Rangappa suggests that Musk removing all content restrictions 'would harm democratic debate, rather than help it.'[59] Because social media platforms are not a town square but rather an algorithmically driven construct where the 'value' of an idea on social media isn't a reflection of how good it is, but rather how valuable it is to the attention economy. Users might have platforms to speak from like never before, but who hears them, who sees them and what content they keep company with, is determined by algorithms.

Movements like Stop Hate For Profit represent cracks in a much bigger silicon construct and very slight awakenings for us all as we start to question the current corporate structures. Because ultimately, advertisers are not the threat, nor is technology really, it's the attention economy's ability to hook into our most vulnerable selves. And this, slowly and incrementally, shifts our thinking. But people built these financial structures. And people can change them.

The corporate structure, the attention economy, has us all trapped in this machine because tech wants to make money from our attention, and we are willing to give it. And though social media companies might suggest they could make their algorithms safer, they suggest that this will result in lost access to audiences and at more expense. And through these means, brands are then disincentivized to use these tools.

But I don't say this to place blame on one platform or one industry, or even one government, but rather to encourage a collectivizing to make things better. To encourage a way forward, a holistic way forward, where different expertise can coalesce. Where we don't have to think of different interests as mutually exclusive, but actually that there is a way for companies to be profitable, while also keeping kids, us all, safe. This shouldn't be mutually exclusive. And if it is, if it really is mutually exclusive, then this is not a sustainable or safe industry and should be condemned by our governments and legal structures.

WHAT YOU CAN DO ABOUT IT
Making Ethical Choices Online

You can decide that you want to make more ethical choices around your online engagement.

1. Look for brands that are making active decisions for ethical online engagement. For example, they might say they are taking steps to fight disinformation, or they might be making conscious choices about where they place their adverts and what platforms they are choosing to avoid. These are good signs that they are thinking critically about ethics online.
2. Make clear choices about the platforms you give your time to. Don't stay on platforms that sit in opposition to your personal ethics. If you find a platform ethically objectionable, leave! Find alternatives and ask others to join you.

Pinterest and the Algorithmic Highroad[60]

During the height of the Covid pandemic Pinterest actively changed its algorithms in an attempt to tackle vaccine conspiracy in order to take a stand within the industry. When users searched for many health-related terms ('vaccines' or 'cancer cure') they were directed to bodies such as the World Health Organization (WHO), the US Centers for Disease Control and Prevention, and Vaccine Safety. It has taken a similar approach to climate disinformation, blocking this content to mitigate the spread of misleading or false claims. Pinterest's safety page states 'other platforms optimise engagement via content that triggers you to keep watching. We're taking a different approach.'[61] Of course, this might be easier for a platform that's mostly about home inspiration than for those designed to provoke debate, but if you are looking for a more ethical platform to get your social media fix, Pinterest is doing something a bit different.

A New (Or Maybe Old) Regulatory Model

Over a century ago, in Pittsburgh, Pennsylvania, two men had an idea.[62] The idea was a radio broadcast show, and with this, KDKA Pittsburgh was born. This would begin the first regular wireless broadcast in the United States.[63] The idea took off. Three years later, the US Congress began to issue hundreds of licences for radio broadcasts across the country. Two years after that, a Commission was sent from Britain to the United States to observe the radio industry. True to British form, seeing the American system as a waste of the medium's cultural potential, Britain built a different structure for organizing, funding and regulating this new communication tool. They called it the British Broadcasting Company, which became a corporation in 1927. The BBC's mandate would be to 'inform, educate, and entertain'[64] the public, in that order. In 1924, the six short pips to mark the start of the hour were heard for the first time.[65]

As commercial television became available, the basic business model and principles that were developed in radio were, for the most part, moved over to TV. The British model, where television could operate as a public service, was paid for by taxes. By contrast, the American commercial model was overseen by the Federal Communications Commission (the FCC) and was paid for by advertising. By the early 1970s, debates about how to balance the good elements of TV with the bad began to circulate in Washington. Questions were asked regarding the monopoly of the 'big three' channels, NBC, CBS and ABC. Further debates surrounding the impact of their content (particularly violent content) on people's off screen or 'real' lives emerged. In response, the FCC pressured networks to institute a family viewing hour in 1975.

An Ethical Internet 147

This period also led to the formation of the Public Broadcasting Service (PBS), whose content included expert informed children's programming such as *Sesame Street* and British imports like *Upstairs, Downstairs* and was in part paid for by the public through call-a-thons, where earnest impassioned presenters would ask audiences for 'pledges'. In one, from 1999, the presenter looks down the camera lens and encourages people to give, because that gift

> *makes it possible for us to stay clear of that commercial arrangement. Instead, we select our programmes for their value and content. That's why public television's children programmes have such a different feel from children's programmes on commercial stations.* Sesame Street, Barney and Friends, Mister Rogers' Neighborhood. *All of these programmes treat your children as people with a need for creative, educational television. With your help today we'll be able to bring your family a future full of the same kind of non-commercial, non-violent educational programmes.*[66]

I can remember watching these with my mother. I remember as she cradled the white Panasonic phone in the cruck of her neck, and moved the coiled cable to one side, to read out her credit card details – visibly moved by the idea of investing in educational viewing content for her daughter. For me. These were the things that Canadian parents did to replicate the children's viewing practices on the other side of the Atlantic. Content that was free from the 'commercial arrangement' or the attention economy. Content that treated kids, in this case me, 'as people'.

Using an old media model to govern the Internet, of course, requires us to acknowledge social media companies as just that – media companies. Where traditionally they have looked at themselves as digital indexers. That is, not the publishers of media, but rather automated librarians that categorize it. This clearly is no longer an adequate way to define these companies. They are not really tech companies, but rather like radio and TV before, they are companies that do algorithmically offer – and do publish or broadcast – content.

Moderation: Too Brutal for Broadcast

To a certain extent, tech companies argue that they do oversee content on their platforms by way of moderation and specifically, moderators. Moderators being the individuals who decide on whether content meets the platform's community guidelines. In November of 2024, BBC Radio 4 released a series that revealed the severe trauma being inflicted upon moderators, even those who train AI,[67] arguably working on the factory floor of the twenty-first century with insufficient health and safety. Many moderators have suffered from PTSD after viewing high dosages of harmful content including images of child sexual abuse, beheadings and violent content from war zones.

Former Facebook moderator and fellow at the Stanford Cyber Security Center David Willner recalled that 'the hardest part of content moderation is the images of things that really happened . . . really horrifying things.'[68] This is in line with some of my previous work on the ways in which video images of violent crime can lead to PTSD in criminal justice professionals who work with these materials – simply because viewing high-quality video of real abuse and real harm can lead to secondary trauma for the viewer.[69] But aside from the occupational hazards of this work, this type of moderation – where people watch and then take down content – isn't working sufficiently. My team's most recent project interviewed hundreds of young people in the summer of

2024 and almost all said they had seen what they classified as harmful content online.[70]

One of the issues with moderation is that it's basically a clean-up job after publication – it's mopping up the spill after someone has already slipped and hurt themselves. A system that according to UCLA's Sarah T. Roberts is an act of brand management to reassure tech companies' customers, advertisers, that they are taking action on the spaces in which advertisers' brands will appear but has little to do with the health and safety of users.[71]

When interviewed for this book, Tom Woolfenden, producer of the BBC Radio 4 series *The Moderators*, described the editorial guidelines[72] in making the programme and said that in the end, some of what the moderators reported seeing ended up on the cutting-room floor. It ended up on the cutting-room floor because as the programme's presenter Zoe Kleinman put it, it was just 'too brutal to broadcast'.[73] And herein lies the whole problem with the current structure.[74] Content that can be *viewed* by children was deemed too brutal to be *heard* by the primarily adult audience of BBC Radio 4. For BBC Radio 4 is a regulated space. Ian Russell made a similar point on *Good Morning Britain* when he brought in some of the harmful (but legal) content that Molly had seen on social media. He sat on the television breakfast programme, holding the images in a white envelope and explained that they couldn't be shown on TV because of broadcast regulations. They couldn't be shown on TV but they were freely available to view online including by children. And so, here again, we can see the chasm between what online is classified as 'free speech' (I'll get to this argument in a moment) and what in the terrestrial media is deemed 'too brutal for broadcast'. And it might be time for us as a society to start to question if we are comfortable with such a chasm, such a disconnect. Or, whether we want lawmakers to take action.

In the UK the Online Safety Act aims to put the burden on social media sites to increase moderation. However, the Internet Watch Foundation has criticized the way in which Ofcom is implementing the act.[75] And even with full, robust implementation the act remains insufficient – one of the reasons given time and time again for the lack of regulation is that it's very complicated.[76]

It is complicated, but we might look as a comparison to something like the ITU, the regulating body that governs satellite space. Literally, regulating 'space'. The ITU oversees the satellite systems that, among other things, provide broadband communications to large areas including entire regions or even continents. It oversees a satellite frequency registration process whereby an ITU member state sends a description of the radio frequencies planned to be used in a project of its satellite operators.[77] This regulation of the satellite system is complicated. And yet we do it. But, for now, though space might be regulated, your back pocket is less so because it's apparently too complicated.

In April of 2018, Mark Zuckerberg was questioned by the US Senate Commerce and Judiciary Committees on issues of privacy, data mining, Russian bots, the dissemination of fake news and Cambridge Analytica.[78]

But one of the most reported elements of the hearing was nothing to do with Mark Zuckerberg's answers, but rather the questions – questions from lawmakers who didn't know what to ask. Who didn't have the capacity to have the conversation. That is, that the questions asked by senators exposed a tremendous lack of knowledge and understanding. Senator Schatz asked, 'If I'm emailing within WhatsApp, does that ever inform your advertisers?'[79] Another led in with, 'My son, Charlie, who is thirteen is dedicated to Instagram so . . . he'd want to be sure I mentioned him while I was here with you.' Senator Hatch asked, 'How do you sustain a business model in which users don't pay for your services?' To which, Zuckerberg responded, 'Senator, we run ads'[80] – and then, allowed a smirk to creep across his face. That smirk, which almost became iconic and emblematic of the disconnect between big tech and policymakers and the way in which this disconnect allowed the tech companies to get away with, arguably, killing people. And it's that disconnect, that gulf, between tech and policy that we need to fill. It's a gulf that I, in my work – and others like me – try to fill, briefing lawmakers and feeding in on roundtables. But me and my colleagues, on our own, we are not enough.

There has been new awareness raising, new research and new hearings since 2018. In June of 2023, the *Wall Street Journal*, in collaboration with researchers at Stanford University and the University of Massachusetts Amherst, found that Instagram was connecting paedophiles with child sexual-abuse content. The *Wall Street Journal* exposed the ways in which the content was being algorithmically promoted,[81] such as promoting hashtags including #preteensex. In a senate judiciary committee in 2024, Senator Ted Cruz cited this report and further questioned:

> *Instagram also displayed the following warning screen to individuals who were searching for child abuse material: 'These results may contain images of child sexual abuse', and then you gave users two choices: 'Get resources. Or see results anyway.' Mr Zuckerberg, what the hell were you thinking?*[82]

It was at this hearing that Mark Zuckerberg did indeed turn to a group of families present who had lost children to social media-related harm and apologized. He turned to the crowd holding posters and sporting T-shirts depicting teens' faces – presumably faces that are no longer with us. Zuckerberg turned to them and said, 'I'm sorry.'[83]

Regulatory and media lawyer David Allen Green argues that determined governments can win battles with social media platforms because 'those who control the law can, if they want, control and tame any corporate in their jurisdiction.'[84] Singapore has implemented a 'Legally binding Code of Practice'; Brazil successfully banned and fined X so that it dealt with the dissemination of disinformation; and The Digital Safety Act in the EU can order access to platforms' algorithms,[85] which could be powerful as it spans all the member countries of the EU.

Mark Zuckerberg has voiced concern over international governments evolving policies, when he appealed to Trump in early 2025 to 'push back on governments around the world. They're going after American companies and pushing to censor more . . .'[86] Further, this fear of regulation is openly acknowledged in Meta's annual report:

> *regulatory or legislative actions or litigation concerning the manner in which we display content to our users, moderate content, provide our services to younger users, or are able to use data in various ways, including for advertising, or otherwise relating to content that is made available on our products, could adversely affect our financial results.*[87]

But whilst much of the rhetoric around this is about free speech, ultimately, the threat of regulation will hit Meta's financial bottom line. And as Green argues if governments push hard enough and legally require these companies to regulate their content, they will have to comply, no matter how costly it is to their bottom line – arguably the most effective way to force social media companies to react.

Free Speech

Free speech is one of the arguments often used in opposition to regulation on the Internet and something that has been positioned as one of the Internet's greatest assets from its inception. But the origins of free speech go back much further. Free speech is deeply rooted in American cultural identity. Early American newspapers were overseen by British colonial control and through most of the 1700s, American newspapers were published 'by authority' of the Royal Governor. Upon America's eventual independence, freedom of the press became formally established as the first amendment of the US constitution, signed in 1789.

As a result, the concept of free speech is something which is inherently tied to American identity in the way that you could say 'Liberty, Equality, Fraternity' is integral to French identity. Tech owners such as Elon Musk and Mark Zuckerberg use this emblem of America as a key argument against the idea of regulating their platforms. A patriotic ideal of the people (which also just happens to keep their financial and political interests intact).

But what does free speech look like in the digital space? Scholars Riemer and Peter have argued that discussions around free speech tend to focus on the point of censorship, where certain speech is prevented. So much of the focus on free speech in the social media landscape involves discussion of moderation and fact-checkers.[88] But, they argue, this isn't the only factor that we should be thinking about when it comes to free speech. They argue that free speech should be defined as speech that is free from both censorship *and* from algorithmic distortion. They point to the structures we've looked at in this book, prioritizing engaging content and segmenting audiences for targeted advertising, and argue that these models subject users' 'speech' to algorithmic amplification or suppression to certain audiences, all in the pursuit of profit. And this distortion is absent from discussions about free speech[89] which is convenient for those tech titans, who apparently hold it so dear.

It's also worth noting that here in the UK and many other democratic countries like Australia, India, South Africa and New Zealand,[90] it is a criminal offence to incite racial or religious hatred.[91] But not in the USA, where this is not the case, due to the first amendment.[92] But scholarly research has shown that hate speech does make its way onto social media platforms regularly. A case study of Elon Musk's takeover of Twitter using a data set of over ten million tweets saw an increase in hate speech following the relaxation of moderation.[93] And our own digital nutrition study found young people describing casual racism and sexist remarks being used in the comments of social media posts without repercussions.[94] But the idea that a regulated media system and free speech are mutually exclusive doesn't hold up. If that were the case, most newspapers, radio programming and television would not have enjoyed freedom of the press and we know that this is simply not so. We do have a free press. We do have journalistic and creative integrity on our TV screens. They can and do co-exist.

For policy makers to not look back at historical media models is at best a failure to sufficiently keep pace with technology and properly unpack these issues, or at worst, because politics itself is now so reliant on the attention economy for their own financial interests and political strategy, that they can't bear to part with it. Similarly, legal scholars[95] have suggested that social media platforms have a soft power, which is often exempt from legislative monitoring but rather define their own rules of what and how things should be monitored due to this regulatory gap. Given Elon Musk's government appointment and relationship to President Trump, it's arguable that this power is increasingly becoming less soft.

However wilful and calculated this lack of regulation has been in your own country or jurisdiction it has allowed for algorithms to take control. To create a status quo where we are worth more on screens than off them. And has made us into a disposable commodity. Tech companies have been allowed to frame this problem as something they can solve on their own, something they can solve within the industry, presumably without the help of policy makers and legislators. Legal structures and regulation could start to operate in the national interest – the interest of users. They could, but we are yet to see it happen effectively.

Parenting: A Public Health Warning

A Surgeon General's public health warning in America is not an everyday occurrence. They have been issued for cigarettes, AIDS and gun violence, and a call for a tobacco-style warning label on social media.[96] These were all to be expected. But the warning issued in October of 2024 was unusual. The US Surgeon General, Dr Vivek Murthy, put out an advisory on parenting.[97] Or rather, on the stress and mental-health implications of contemporary parenting. He suggested that parenting has become hyper-stressful and intensive, so much so that it's become an urgent public health crisis.[98]

The Surgeon General's report states that 70% of parents think that parenting is harder than it was twenty years ago and position technology as one of the reasons for this.[99] And, ironically, or maybe not so ironically, the Surgeon General suggests that a huge contributing factor to parents' stress is the cultural pressure around parenting. It cites a study that found 56% of parents felt they spent too much time on their phones – arguably being fed more cultural pressure about how to parent, as their social media feeds are flooded with parenting advice by experts on ways to turn every moment into a teachable one; endless Instafied toddlers in shades of beige – or ecru if you will; and carefully curated depictions of parenting success. And so we are in a social media-driven cycle where parents are stressed about kids' social media usage driven by their own social media usage.

Whether you're a parent or not, this information and the many things this book has covered are to give a sense of empowerment over these processes. Much time, attention and focus have been on implications of digital culture on young people, but we should not downplay or underestimate the impacts on adults.

These stressors of course should be contextualized within first-world privilege (they are not comparable to living through political unrest, famine or war).[100] But research also shows that continued micro-dosing on stress can have big impacts and puts us all at much more serious risks of mental illness, anxiety and depression.[101] We too doom-scroll. We too are vulnerable to forms of indoctrination, political or otherwise. We too can feel angry and enraged. We too can feel left out. Or feel like we don't have enough or that we are not enough.

And in addition to arming ourselves with the tools to take control over our digital lives, we also need to put pressure – a greater burden – on the others who should be engaging in corporate responsibility; those who should be building safer and more ethical technologies; and those who have pledged to act in the best interest of the public. Those who continue to load the responsibility on to parents and educators – because others aren't doing their job effectively. To leave it to us, who indeed might start to crack under this load.

An Ethical Internet – Conclusion

I said goodbye to Daisy, Joe and Birdy. I looked down at my flat white, sitting on a distressed wood table in that hip industrial cafe. A flat white in a hip cafe that looks like every flat white in every hip cafe, anywhere in the world because that is what we are algorithmically programmed to believe they should look like.[102]

My coffee – obviously – low stakes. Some of the themes outlined in this chapter, like threats to democracy, or the lack of regulation over child abuse material, are not. They are examples of the very sharp edge of this debate. The work of Daisy and Joe and the many parents and volunteers of Smartphone Free Childhood have raised awareness about phone usage for kids and early teens. This is important work. Limiting phone usage does not remove the need for digital literacy. This is still needed. As one tearful mum of a device-free fifteen-year-old recently said to me, 'The clock is ticking down to his birthday and I'm terrified.'

We parents, or any individual, can't do this alone. And according to the Surgeon General, we need to be mindful that we all might start to shake and buckle under the weight of the load.

Alone, we can't change the underlying corporate structures of the attention economy, which go beyond just the safeguarding of children to rather the safeguarding of all of us, as we give our collective consciousness to an Internet that is no longer the messy, free space of the early 00s or even the digital activist town square of Twitter's beginnings in the 2010s. Rather, who and what are prioritized and seen – for the most part – now serve a corporate purpose. But we can choose to support more ethical brands, investing more ethically in social media. We can also look to employ incentives for advertisers, like the B Corp model for sustainability.

As it stands, social media companies are still woefully unregulated, and we allow them to use the causation debate as a way to hold off regulation. And with this lack of regulation, they will continue to mine our minds and our experiences to see how much time, how much of our life we can give. For regulators, this assumes that nothing is 'too brutal for broadcast' and that tech should be allowed to regulate itself in a way we don't allow for most other industries: a reality that has often been chalked up to a lack of understanding on the part of regulators or fears of mitigating free speech – a free press. We can learn from historic regulatory structures. Perhaps even ones built over a century ago.

If we all decided we wanted such models in place, that we wanted more regulation and accountability, that we wanted greater control over how we spend our time and energy and more transparency about what shapes our opinions, so that *we* can determine what and how we think we could shift the status quo. We have such a power. These structures were built by humans and we humans – the users – can decide we need a change. We can. We should. We must.

Conclusion

Unicorn is an emotionally needy cat. Unicorn – full name Unicorn Pixie Sparkle (although not necessarily in that order) – grew into a rather large, fat cat, who spends most of her time draped across any surface on which I've tried to write this book. I suppose that's appropriate. Because in doing this, Unicorn – emblematic of the childhood innocence I was trying to preserve, when I gifted her as a birthday present in lieu of an electronic device – is a reminder of my own personal tensions around these issues. My own need to hold off screens, pretending I can forever fend off the pull of Apple products, which will inevitably cast a long shadow over my daughters' lives. I can't. This shadow will not necessarily be a negative one. But I – they – will need to be aware of its potential darkness in order to keep informed about ways to bring in the light.

Much of the regulatory discussion, advocacy and news coverage has focused on children's safety online – which indeed is important and is still worryingly inadequate. Less media attention has focused on its impact of these technologies on adults.[1] As if adults, en masse, did not attack a mosque in Southport after being fed disinformation online. As if adults were not the recipients of the deluge of social media-driven pressure around parenting – enough for the US Surgeon General to issue a public health warning. As if adults are not the ones sharing their children's personal lives on social media at such a rate that Barclays Bank has issued fraud warnings for the year 2030. As if adult health and well-being – adult minds – should fend for themselves. As adults (parents or otherwise) we can work to understand our own current usage. We didn't grow up with these digital technologies, so that innate parenting knowledge (that we draw on for almost everything else with parenting) often isn't there. But really working to understand our digital usage can help build knowledge about how these processes work, so that in turn we can make informed choices for us, and for our families.

1. First, we should look qualitatively at our usage using the **walkthrough method** (Chapter 3) with a partner or someone we trust to open up conversations about personal usage.
2. Next, we can look quantitatively at the amount of our usage through keeping a **phone fed journal** or looking at our weekly usage in our device settings (Chapter 5). This allows us to consider the quantity and types of our digital usage.
3. Then, taking the quality and quantity of our usage together, we can make active choices about what we want our digital diet to look like. If we simply want to be consuming less, we might think about **greyscaling** our phone (Chapter 3) or setting time limits so that our five-minute email doesn't become an Insta doom-scroll session. If we want better quality content, we can do a **spring clean** (Chapter 1) and we can **game our algorithm** practising **algorithmic resistance** (Chapter 5), so that we become an active participant with greater control over the content we want to see.

If you have older children on social media, you can include them in these practices. If your children are younger you can begin to seed these ideas in age-appropriate ways. My daughters are still small, but for now, I can be conscious of the ways in which I am datafying them. I can be mindful of how I engage in 'sharenting' (Chapter 2) and be aware of data shared that could be saved and used against them in the future. I can, and should, talk to them about the quality of the screen time (Chapter 4) that they consume, and cultivate shared time, where we communally view and chat about what we are consuming. Here I can begin to introduce the idea that we can have open conversations about what they see on screens, and if something is scary or feels bad, we can talk about it. They can come to me.

As they grow, I can start to introduce some themes like mistruths and disinformation. I might try to use **sightengine.com** (Chapter 2) to check an AI image, to talk about these topics. As they grow further, I can start to talk about echo chambers, and I can do **fact-checking** exercises (Chapter 2) when they are older still. Inevitably, the day will come when I will need to think about **porn literacy** (Chapter 3) and I will use fantasy or superhero films to help me to contextualize this as a performance rather than an educational resource. And I will need to balance the **safety paradox** (Chapter 4) and make conscious, informed choices for my kids with this in mind. All of this in the hopes that they become empowered digital citizens, ones who might choose to 'go organic' for one summer and roll their eyes at a previous generation who lived ridiculously unhealthy digital lives. Just as we did about our parents before us, driving unseatbelted and chain-smoking in hospital delivery rooms. I hope this is the case. I hope they will look back at our generation fumbling through our unhealthy relationships with screens, taking our daily dose of algorithmic hate and harm as exactly that: unseatbelted and farcically outdated.

As families or as households, we can think about our own collective boundaries and decide to take a weekend off. To put screens in a drawer for two days, sitting with our withdrawal symptoms, if only to show ourselves the extent of our addictions. I can – and do (I hate it) – inflict this tough love upon myself from time to time. But tough love and our own personal initiatives are not enough. We also need help from the structures that support and govern this domain. At a school level, we can support young people with awareness building and institute programmes like digital mentors (Chapter 4),[2] engaging young people in leadership and encouraging discussion about digital usage. At a community level we can encourage companies we support and those we work for to invest more responsibly in social media. We can encourage more brands and advertisers to take a stand and defund disinformation, hate and harm. And, at a social level, we can pressure government to increase regulation. We need to let policy makers know that we no longer accept this largely unregulated space (Chapter 6).

Because researchers have seen the other end of the machine, and how it can bombard young people – us all – with harmful content. As Amir Malik told me, 'The advertising algorithm works in such an effective way that it can predict what you want to buy before you buy it.'[3] We accept that they know what swimwear we will want next season; that we are pregnant before anyone else knows[4] – but do we also accept that they will know that our children are self-harming or suicidal? Do we accept this? Probably not – and yet there is no duty of care, no consistent line of communication between tech and governance to protect kids – us – before the fact. We accept the Online Safety Act as a clean-up job afterwards.

While I write this book as autumn of 2024 turns to the winter of 2025, some things have changed, and I've got some things wrong. I thought that the new Online Safety Act would have more legislatory might. It didn't. I thought that Unilever would win the fight against X and take a stand towards a more ethical brand investment on social media. They didn't. I didn't think Elon Musk would be given a prominent position in the US government or that Mark Zuckerburg would subsequently remove fact-checkers across Meta platforms.[5] All of this did indeed happen. For what further changes occur, post-publication, I ask for your understanding. The fast-moving nature of this subject means I will get some things wrong. But I wonder if there are some things that we can collectively get a bit more right?

In my master's class at UCL, my students were discussing misinformation. A German student raised her hand and reflected on a story told to her by her East German parents about an autumn some thirty-five years earlier. 'The TV news announced that the gates to the Berlin Wall were open,'[6] she said. And as a result, many East Germans began to make their way to those gates, assuming they were indeed, open. And the guard who was on duty at the time, seeing so many people believe that those gates were opening, that they should be open – in turn, opened them. And so in this story told by parents to a daughter who was now sitting in my class, a media-generated mistruth created reality.

This anecdote about something on the news in Eastern Europe in the late 1980s might feel far removed or a one-off event, but now we live in a world where such mistruths circulate infinite times a day on infinite screens, creating new truths and new realities. This family anecdote points out the power of media to create truth. But there is something else. This story also demonstrates the will of the people and the ways that legalization often follows that will.

When speaking about legalizing gay marriage on *The Ellen DeGeneres Show* in 2016, President Barack Obama said, 'the laws follow' but it 'started with folks like you',[7] suggesting that DeGeneres, a gay woman, and her TV show normalized same-sex relationships.[8] That is, the talk show moved the acceptance of same-sex couples into mainstream consciousness, and this changed public opinion; and policy follows public opinion. And we the people, for better or for worse, can pressure policy to create new models under which we want to live.

And so we find ourselves, the collective, as immensely powerful. Power that can be used for good. Because if the pressure of the people can push for policy shifts, then maybe we can see ourselves as much more powerful within these processes. We can decide that we no longer want the corporate structure of the attention economy. We can decide that we are worth more than our eyeballs and our children's eyeballs on screens. We can decide that we don't want to be locked in by technology that will become ever more advanced and efficient at manipulating us in order to hold us longer and longer and longer. We can decide that we want a change. We can decide.

Useful Resources and Numbers

On an individual and more granular problem level there is a wealth of information out there which allows you resources for yourself or discussion tools for ways to talk to your kids or others about different eventualities. They can be found here:

- Childnet www.childnet.com/sns
- Internet Matters www.Internetmatters.org
- NSPCC www.nspcc.org.uk/onlinesafety
- Parent Zone www.parentzone.org.uk
- Ask About Games www.askaboutgames.com
- Children's Commissioner www.childrenscommissioner.gov.uk
- Childline www.Childline.org.uk 0800 1111
- Young Minds www.youngminds.org.uk
- For SEND: https://www.childnet.com/resources/star-send-toolkit/star-films/

- For guidance on suicide prevention and to find a helpline: Molly Rose Foundation www.mollyrosefoundation.org
- If you think your child might be being sexually abused or encountering illegal activity online: CEOP www.ceopeducation.co.uk
- For anonymously reporting online child sexual abuse images and videos: Internet Watch Foundation www.iwf.org.uk
- If you are concerned about your child or your own mental health you should contact your GP or NHS services

Acknowledgements

First, to my brilliant research team – my teammates – Dr Katharine Smales and Dr Caitlin Shaughnessy your commitment to making the world safer, happier and healthier; and your ability to see the multifaceted possibilities of this work are remarkable. This project isn't possible without you.

In this book I draw from the work of activists, innovators and seminal researchers, including my past project collaborators, Professor Jessica Ringrose, Professor Nicola Shaughnessy, Professor Graham Glancy and Professor Cheryl Regehr. As well as Professor Oliver Duke Williams, Dr Photini Vrikki and all of the Digital Humanities Team in DIS at UCL, who support and inspire me in equal measure. I'm also grateful to colleagues, mentors, and friends – many of whom are all of the above – who contributed, influenced or encouraged: Professor Lewis Griffin, Professor Rosalind Murray, Professor Debbie Ging, Professor Elizabeth Shepherd, Dr Amy Orben, Dr Hetty Blades, Dr Sara De Benedictis, Professor Mattias Frey, Professor Peter Stanfield and Professor Glenn Regehr (with his merciless critical eye) – I thank you.

To my agents, the brilliant Rachel Mills – and the team at Rachel Mills Literary including Alexandra Cliff, Charlotte Denn, and Nick Ash – and of course, the wonderful Jonny Boy Fowler, all who had a vision for me and what this project could do, you are simply the best. To Jodie Lancet-Grant, my editor and metallic shoe enthusiast – thank you for seeing this not just as a book but also as part of a movement. To Joanna Prior and Lizzy Gray for championing this book, and further for investing in teacher materials and resources for schools. To Amy Lines, the fabulous designer who brought her imagination and creativity to digital diet diagramming. To Katy Denny and Nicholas Blake for your incredibly constructive, helpful and systematic guidance. To Alex Ellis and Will Upcott, for taking the time to read and offer your expert advice. And to Amy Winchester, Sian Gardiner, Dawn Burnett and the whole team at Bluebird, for your constant enthusiasm and for generally just getting it. For all of this, I am grateful.

To Samantha Zuckergood and Witney Frick at Dial Press, for seeing this as a 'matrix book' that could be part of a bigger change. To Martha Kanya-Forstner at Knopf Doubleday, for supporting this ESA girl and having a vision for the ways books can be tools of healing. And to all the team at Penguin Random House , thank you for taking this movement over the Atlantic and bringing me home.

To Gemma Stevenson and Priya Ramda at the Department for Business and Trade, who read and schooled me on food regulation, and consumer and competition policy, it is a great comfort to know brains like yours are in the civil service. To Angela McDonald, Education Scotland, MVP and the Prevent Programme, you are so good at what you do and thank you for including me as part of your team. To David Wilson and the National Education Union and to Margaret Mulholland and the Association of School and College Leaders, both of whom are fighting the good fight and are truly making tangible changes in children's lives across the country, it is such a pleasure to work with you. To Marissa Heintzman, who shared expertise and cakemaking, thank you. And to Dylan Glancy, thank you for schooling me on Canadian

Acknowledgements

policy and always being there – quite literally – I wouldn't have wanted to grow up next to anyone else.

To my students, past and present – some of your inspiration is reflected in this book – all of you keep me on my toes and up to date on all things Gen Z. To all the teachers and safeguarding leads at the schools who took part in the Digital Nutrition research project, you remain anonymous in compliance with research ethical guidelines, but you are not anonymous to me. I am in awe of all you do. And to the teenagers, who contributed to this research, thank you. Your experiences, insights and wisdom give me hope for the future.

To David Benford, your information on digital forensics both wows and terrifies me. I'm grateful for your contribution. To Amir Malik, your insights and clarity of thought amaze me. Thank you for sharing your knowledge. To John Paul, thank you for the epic ad insider perspectives and generally believing there is a way to make things better. To Tom Connaughton, thank you for your support, and sidewalk chats. To Tom Woolfenden, thank you for your kind input into all things 'Too Brutal to Broadcast'. To Matilda Temperley and the team at Somerset Cider Brandy, thank you for giving me my 'hands in the sky phone in my pocket' moment. And to Daisy and Joe and all the Smartphone Free Childhood community, for all your tireless advocacy, awareness raising and for giving insights of the power of people from the frontline. Thank you all!

To my community, who both look after my family and look after me – Alex, Alexia, Dani, Eloise, Emma, Essie, Francesca, Maggie, Maja, Laura, Lou, Paula, Rebecca, Tiffany, Steph, Shelley, Sina, Zoe – I appreciate you.

To my parents, who have always encouraged to think about how one's work can move beyond the academy in order to really help people. I love you. To my grandparents, who always wanted people to eat well, your teachings have underpinned the principles of this book. I miss you. To my daughters who drive me to try and solve this problem in the hopes their generation will be a healthier and more enlightened one. You are my sunshines. And to my husband, always, you are both my base and my belief.

Glossary of Terms

Algorithm
An algorithm is a step-by-step set of instructions designed to solve a problem or perform a task, similar to a roadmap or recipe. In the context of social media, it is a computational process that uses predefined rules and data to filter, rank, and recommend content (such as videos, users, or posts) to platform users. While not all social media algorithms are forms of artificial intelligence (AI), many incorporate machine learning techniques that analyse users' past interactions to predict and personalise the content they see, continuously refining recommendations based on ongoing user behaviour.

Attention economy
First used by Herbert Simon in 1971,[1] the attention economy in relation to digital technologies was described by James Williams in 2018 as typically being an ad-based business where the user is not directly the source of the revenue. Rather the user's attention is the product.[2] The information gathered about the user's attention – what they like or don't like as well as information about them including their age or location, for example – is used by technology companies to persuade companies to advertise on digital platforms or via their services. Academics have argued that

the attention economy business model incentivizes companies to render their platforms addictive.[3]

B Corp
A 'B Corp' certification is given to companies that can meet high standards of social and environmental performance, accountability, and transparency – not just for being environmental, but for being a business that has a positive impact on society that goes beyond just seeking profit.[4]

Baby Boomers
Baby Boomers define the generation of people born in the period between 1946 and 1964 when birth rates began a significant decline.[5] Sometimes called 'boomers', this bulge generation resulted in more teenagers than in previous generations, which drove the conception of teenagers as consumers and drivers of culture such as the massive popularity of television, The Beatles and Elvis Presley.[6] They were preceded by the Silent Generation where the range of birth years varies but begins with either 1925, 1928 or 1929 and ends with either 1942 or 1945.[7]

Body dysmorphia
The NHS defines body dysmorphia, also known as body dysmorphic disorder (BDD), as a mental health condition where a person spends a lot of time worrying about flaws in their appearance. These flaws are often unnoticeable to others.[8]

Bot
Merriam Webster defines a bot as a computer program that mimics human actions or performs automatic repetitive tasks.[9] Bots are sometimes used in customer service interactions, for example to respond to customer complaints. They can also be used for

malicious purposes and create security risks for organizations. On social media, bots are used to generate false activity through fake accounts or engagement. This can result in certain content's popularity rising or proliferating and misinformation spreading.[10]

Clickbait

Clickbait is a headline that is designed to encourage users to click a link to particular content. This headline is likely to pique users' curiosity or raise their emotions rather than presenting factual information. By following the link to this content, the website which the content is hosted on earns revenue from advertisers.

Cookie

The Information Commissioners' Office defines cookies as a small file of letters and numbers that is downloaded to your computer when you visit a website. Cookies are used by many websites and can do a number of things, e.g. remembering your preferences or recording what you have put in your shopping basket.[11]

Datafied

Scholars Deborah Lupton and Ben Williamson, in their 2017 paper 'The Datafied Child', defined the term datafied as how people, including children, are the objects of an increasing range of digitized surveillance practices that record details of their lives. Data might be collected via technologies, for example smartphones or tablets, but also wearable devices, smart speakers and social media platforms. In the case of children, they may engage in these practices themselves, but others may also do so on their behalf including parents, other caregivers, family members, friends, teachers and healthcare providers. Commercial organizations may also engage in this in order to capitalize on and profit from people's, including children's, personal information.

Deepfake

Deepfakes are created using artificial intelligence (AI) to manipulate either video or audio footage to create misleading content, making it appear as though someone is doing or saying something. Deepfakes can spread false information, ruin people's reputations or influence discussion about current affairs. They can also be used in scams, for example through cloning a person's voice to ask someone they know for money.

Digital native

The Cambridge Dictionary defines a digital native as someone who is very familiar with digital technology and computers because they have grown up with them.[12] There is some academic criticism surrounding this term;[13] nevertheless, 'digital native' is used regularly in public discourse.

Disinformation

The UK government defines disinformation as the deliberate creation and spreading of false and/or manipulated information that is intended to deceive and mislead people, either for the purposes of causing harm, or for political, personal or financial gain. Misinformation, by contrast, is the inadvertent spread of false information.[14]

Doomscrolling

Doomscrolling is a term used to describe spending a large amount of time consuming negative news stories. This is often, but not always, in the form of short-form videos or social media content.

Dumb phone
Also known as a brick phone, a dumb phone is a basic mobile phone that does not have the apps, cameras or other capabilities associated with smartphones.

Echo chamber
The limited exposure to a wide range of information encourages 'the formation of like-minded users framing and reinforcing a shared narrative, that is, echo chambers'.[15] These echo chambers create environments where people's opinions, political leanings and beliefs are reinforced by repeatedly interacting with others who share the same opinion.

Filter bubble
Eli Pariser coined the term 'filter bubble'. He described how the personalization techniques used by major tech platforms fundamentally alter the way we encounter ideas and information.[16] All major websites use some form of personalization to drive the content displayed to a user and so we are each surrounded by a unique collection of information online which is curated for us by algorithms.[17] Pariser argues that filter bubbles are invisible. When you decide to read a particular news source you generally know whether you are reading something with a liberal bias or a conservative one. But this becomes opaque when you are using a digital platform – you don't know how or why it has prioritized the information it is showing you. You also don't choose to enter this bubble as you do when you actively decide to watch a particular news channel – these personalized filters are presented *to you* rather than you choosing to engage with them. Pariser suggests that a filter bubble can be a very comfortable place but argues that

the things we compulsively click on aren't the same as the broad set of information we need to make educated decisions.

Gen X
Gen X is a shortening of Generation X and is the generation of people born between 1965 and 1980, between the Baby Boomers and Millennials. They were the first generation to grow up with personal computers and cable television, including MTV which broadcast music videos twenty-four hours a day. As a result, Gen X is sometimes referred to as the MTV Generation.[18]

Gen Z
Gen Z or Generation Z were born between 1997 and 2012. The iPhone launched in 2007 when the oldest Gen Z-ers were ten years old and as teenagers they had access to mobile devices, Wi-Fi, social media and on demand entertainment. The Pew Research Centre cites research which has shown dramatic shifts in youth behaviours, attitudes and lifestyles for this generation.[19]

Greyscale
Greyscale is when your screen is comprised of shades of black, white and grey as opposed to the colour screens which are ubiquitous.

Like economy
In the 'like economy' people's engagements with one another, through 'likes' or other engagement buttons, are transformed into data. This data about people's reactions to content can be used in turn to generate more traffic and engagement with content.[20]

Machine learning
Machine learning is a subfield of Artificial Intelligence.[21] It focuses on using data and algorithms to enable AI to imitate the way that

humans learn, gradually improving its accuracy.[22] An example of machine learning that you might come across every day is the last-minute recommendations made to you as you are about to check out of your supermarket shop. Using data about previous consumption behaviour, the retailer will recommend products that you might like during the checkout process.[23] Machine learning also uses data to change pricing models. For example, companies differentiate their pricing based on the demand, the amount of product available and other real time factors.

Millennial
The Pew Research Centre defines anyone born between 1981 and 1996 as a Millennial.[24] They became adults during economic recession and as the Internet became ubiquitous and social media and on demand entertainment developed as they grew up.

Misinformation
Misinformation is the inadvertent spread of false information, as opposed to disinformation, which is the deliberate creation of and dissemination of false or manipulated information.[25]

Social native
'Social native' is a term used by the economist Ben Marder to move away from the limits of the term 'digital native', which is mostly focused around the use of technology (those who grew up with touchpads and are fluent in emojis) to encompass the social realities of this generation, which have only known an instant-communication, relatively boundary-free social world. Marder suggests they are more individualistic, have more casual forms of communication and have higher expectations for their jobs and career prospects. At the same time, they are innovation focused.[26]

Truth decay

The term was coined by the Rand Foundation in 2018 to describe 'the undermining of evidence making'.[27]

You-loop

The filter bubble means that people are less aware of the diverse array of options and lifestyles; instead companies are using their algorithms to choose which options you are aware of. What you have clicked on in the past will determine what results you will see in future. This means that you can get stuck in a static, ever-narrowing version of yourself – an endless you-loop.[28] In this way you become stuck inside your own self-reinforcing point of view. This matters because without exposure or access to information or ideas our decision-making process is stunted as solutions to problems lie out of our sightline.[29]

Endnotes

Introduction

1 You can find digital literacy resources from a wide range of groups and organizations including government sources, industry supported initiatives, digital platforms, family centres and well-being guides and charities. For example, these would include UK Safer Internet Centre, Internet Matters, UK Council for Safer Internet, the Children's Commissioner, NSPCC, Childline, Childnet.com, ParentZone, BBC Bitesize, SWGfL, Internet Safety Brigade, Unicef, WHO, PEGI.com, AskAboutGames.com, family centres for Snapchat, Instagram, TikTok, Facebook, YouTube Kids parental guide, Meta, Google, Apple and Android.

2 Bonini, T. & Emiliano, T. (2024), *Algorithms of Resistance: The Everyday Fight Against Platform Power*, Cambridge, Massachusetts: The MIT Press, 1st ed.

3 This research was conducted as part of an Arts and Humanities Research Council (AHRC) funded, interdisciplinary project, hosted at University College, London (UCL) in partnership with the University of Kent, which explored the popularisation of online hate speech and misogyny, and its risks to young people. It was undertaken in collaboration with the Association of School and College Leaders (ASCL), who had identified concerns regarding young people's well-being and social media usage. Members of the team included Dr Caitlin Shaughnessy, Professor Nicola

Shaughnessy, Alfie Turner, Minzhu Zhao and Idil Cambazoglu. The full report is available here: https://www.ascl.org.uk/ASCL/media/ASCL/Help%20and%20advice/Inclusion/Safer-scrolling.pdf accessed 29th January 2025.

4   This study was led by my esteemed colleague Professor Jessica Ringrose at the Institute of Education, University of London. The findings were first launched in a report: J Ringrose, K Regehr and B Milne, 'Understanding and Combatting Youth Experiences of Image-Based Sexual Harassment and Abuse'. Available at https://www.ascl.org.uk/ASCL/media/ASCL/Our%20view/Campaigns/Understanding-and-combatting-youth-experiences-of-image-based-sexual-harassment-and-abuse-full-report.pdf. This work went on to inform the new cyber flashing legislation.

5   The first person to be jailed for cyberflashing was convicted on 19 March 2024 as reported by the Crown Prosecution Service: 'Prison sentence in first cyberflashing case', available at https://www.cps.gov.uk/east-england/news/prison-sentence-first-cyberflashing-case accessed 29 January 2025. It is worth noting that in the UK you have to prove the recipient didn't want to receive the image.

6   This project was led by Professor Cheryl Regehr at the University of Toronto. Regehr, K., Regehr, C., Goel, V., Sato, C., Lyons, K., Rudzicz, F. (2024), 'From the Screen to the Streets: Technology-Facilitated Violence Against Public Health Professionals', *Journal of Loss and Trauma* doi: 10.1080/15325024.2024.2406509.

7   Regehr, C., Regehr, K., Birze, A. & Duff, W. (2023), 'Troubling Records: Managing and Conserving Mediated Artifacts of Violent Crime', *Archivaria* 95 (Spring) 6–40. https://archivaria.ca/index.php/archivaria/article/view/13895; Regehr, C., Regehr, K. & Birze, A. (2022), 'Traumatic Residue, Mediated Remembering and Video Evidence of Sexual Violence: A Case Study', *International Journal of Law and Psychiatry* 81 (2) https://doi.org/10.1016/j.ijlp.2022.101778; Birze, A., Regehr, C. & Regehr, K. (2022), 'Organizational Support for the Potentially Traumatic Impact of Video Evidence of Violent Crime in the Criminal Justice System: "We're almost making more victims"',

International Review of Victimology, https://journals.sagepub.com/doi/10.1177/02697580221112436; Birze, A., Regehr, K. & Regehr, C. (2022), 'Workplace Trauma in a Digital Age: The Impact of Video Evidence of Violent Crime on Criminal Justice Professionals', *Journal of Interpersonal Violence* 38 (1–2) https://journals.sagepub.com/doi/10.1177/08862605221090571; Regehr, K., Regehr C., & Birze, A. (2021), Regehr, K., Regehr, C., Goel, V., Sato, C., Lyons, K., & Rudzicz, F. (2024). 'Technology-Facilitated Violence Against Public Health Professionals'. Journal of Loss and Trauma, 1–26. https://doi.org/10.1080/15325024.2024.2406509

8 The Mentors in Violence Prevention Team including Angela McDonald and Lorna Aitken do tremendous work to build peer-to-peer learning resources. I have had the pleasure of working with them on a number of projects. More information is available at https://education.gov.scot/news/new-mentors-in-violence-prevention-mvp-resource accessed 29 January 2025.

9 Regehr, K., Shaughnessy, C., Zhao, M. & Shaughnessy, N. (2024), 'Safer Scrolling: How algorithms popularise and gamify online hate and misogyny for young people', https://www.ascl.org.uk/ASCL/media/ASCL/Help%20and%20advice/Inclusion/Safer-scrolling.pdf accessed 29 January 2025.

10 The Digital Nutrition project was carried out over the Summer of 2024 with my colleagues Dr Caitlin Shaughnessy and Dr Katharine Smales and examined young people's relationship with their smartphone and gaps in digital literacy education. Regehr, Shaughnessy and Smales (2025), 'Digital Nutrition: rethinking digital literacy', in press.

11 In a January 2023 report the Children's Commissioner found that the average age at which children first see pornography is thirteen, though 27% of respondents had seen it by age eleven, and that pornography is now so normalized that children cannot 'opt out' of it (p. 5). Children's Commissioner, 'A lot of it is actually just abuse: Young people and pornography, available at https://www.childrenscommissioner.gov.uk/report/a-lot-of-it-is-actually-just-abuse-young-people-and-pornography/ accessed 9 July 2024.

12 Ofsted (June 2021), 'Review of sexual abuse in schools and colleges', available at https://www.gov.uk/government/publications/review-of-sexual-abuse-in-schools-and-colleges/review-of-sexual-abuse-in-schools-and-colleges#executive-summary-and-recommendations accessed 15 January 2025. The report says: 'Leaders we spoke to also highlighted the problems that easy access to pornography had created and how pornography had set unhealthy expectations of sexual relationships and shaped children and young people's perceptions of women and girls.' And 'A recent survey of over 1,000 undergraduates found that one third said they have 'learned more about sex from pornography than from formal education' (footnote 31). 'While research indicates that most children and young people recognise that pornography is unrealistic, a high percentage of them reported that they had used pornography as a source of information to learn about sex and sexual relationships in the past 12 months (60% of young men and 41% of young women). This is problematic when research indicates that much pornography depicts men as aggressive and controlling and women as submissive and sexually objectified.' And 'Although there is insufficient evidence to demonstrate that viewing pornography leads directly to harmful sexual behaviours, there is evidence to suggest that young people appear to become desensitised to its content over time and that it can shape unhealthy attitudes, such as acceptance of sexual aggression towards women.'

13 The Rt Hon. Professor the Lord Darzi of Denham OM KBE FRS FMedSci HonFREng (September 2024), 'Independent Investigation of the National Health Service in England', available at https://assets.publishing.service.gov.uk/media/66f42ae630536cb92748271f/Lord-Darzi-Independent-Investigation-of-the-National-Health-Service-in-England-Updated-25-September.pdf, p. 21, accessed 15 November 2024.

14 Zou, J. J. & Logan, E. B. (5 January 2022), 'Key facts to know about the Jan. 6 insurrection', *Los Angeles Times*, available at https://www.latimes.com/politics/story/2022-01-05/by-the-numbers-jan-6-anniversary accessed 17 October 2024; Duignan, B., 'January 6 U.S.

Capitol attack', *Britannica*, available at https://www.britannica.com/event/January-6-U-S-Capitol-attack accessed 17 October 2024; Remnick, D. (22 December 2022), 'The Devastating New History of the January 6th Insurrection', available at https://www.newyorker.com/news/american-chronicles/the-devastating-new-history-of-the-january-sixth-insurrection accessed 17 October 2024.

15 For a full account of this see Horwitz, J. (2023), *Broken Code: Inside Facebook and the Fight to Expose Its Toxic Secrets*, London: Torva; Cellan-Jones, R. (8 January 2021), 'Tech Tent: Did social media inspire Congress riot?', *BBC News*, available at https://www.bbc.co.uk/news/technology-55592752 accessed 18 October 2024; Suciu, P. (1 August 2022), 'Social Media Platforms And The Lessons Of January 6', Forbes.com, available at https://www.forbes.com/sites/petersuciu/2022/08/01/social-media-platforms-and-the-lessons-of-january-6/ accessed 18 October 2024; Donovan, J. and The Conversation US (6 January 2024), 'How Networked Incitement Fueled the January 6 Capitol Insurrection', Scientific American, available at https://www.scientificamerican.com/article/jan-6-was-an-example-of-networked-incitement/ accessed 18 October 2024.

16 In 2023 the UK passed the Online Safety Act, which aimed to make the UK the safest place in the world to be online. You can see more detail on the progress of the Act at Crawford, A. (27 October 2024), 'The Online Safety Act is one year old. Has it made children any safer?' *BBC News* available at https://www.bbc.co.uk/news/articles/c5y38z4pk9lo#:~:text=%E2%80%9CFrom%20December%2C%20tech%20firms%20will,creating%20a%20safer%20life%20online.%E2%80%9D accessed 27 November 2024.

17 This phrase is almost a cliché in industry circles these days. Likely taken from the Netflix documentary *The Social Dilemma* (2020), in which Tristan Harris says, 'If you are not paying for the product, then you are the product.'

18 Zuboff, S. (2019), *The Age of Surveillance Capitalism: The Fight for the Future at the New Frontier of Power*, London: Profile Books.

19 Simon, Herbert (1971), 'Designing Organizations for an Information Rich World', in M. Greenberger (ed.), *Computers, Communications and the Public Interest*, Baltimore, MD: The Johns Hopkins Press.

20 Some scholars have argued that these movements and more laterally school phone bans could start to raise more nuanced understandings of issues of the digital and begin to address issues of sustainability, pointing out that digital usage, particularly in education, is unsustainable and implicated in climate crisis. See Rahali, M., Kidron, B. & Livingstone, S. (September 2024), 'Smartphone policies in schools: What does the evidence say?', available at https://5rightsfoundation.com/resource/smartphone-policies-in-schools-what-does-the-evidence-say/ accessed 4 December 2024.

21 These movements have been spurred on by the work of Jonathan Haidt and his 2024 book *The Anxious Generation*, London: Allen Lane.

22 Aschoff, N. (2020), *The Smartphone Society: Technology, Power and Resistance in the New Gilded Age*, Boston, MA: Beacon Press.

23 Hari, J. (2022) *Stolen Focus: Why You Can't Pay Attention—And How to Think Deeply Again*, New York, Crown Publishing Group. Hari has been accused of poor citation practices and plagiarism in some of his work, but I think that this is a valid point.

24 As do 81% of those who have a child aged three to four and 57% of those who have a child aged two or younger. Ofcom (2020/1), 'Children and parents: media use and attitudes', report available at https://www.ofcom.org.uk/siteassets/resources/documents/research-and-data/media-literacy-research/children/childrens-media-literacy-2021/children-and-parents-media-use-and-attitudes-report-2020-21.pdf?v=326330 accessed 4 December 2024.

25 Pew Research Centre (2020), 'Parenting Children in the Age of Screens', available at https://www.pewresearch.org/internet/wp-content/uploads/sites/9/2020/07/PI_2020.07.28_kids-and-screens_FINAL.pdf accessed 18 October 2024.

26 Professor Andy Phippen argues that young people should learn to use smartphones with the support of adults around them in a nurturing environment. See Phippen, A. (September 2024),

'Conversation article: Should you give your child a "dumb" phone? They aren't the answer to fears over kids' social media use', available at https://blogs.bournemouth.ac.uk/research/2024/09/25/conversation-article-should-you-give-your-child-a-dumb-phone-they-arent-the-answer-to-fears-over-kids-social-media-use/ accessed 4 December 2024.

27 'How Australia's Social Media Ban will work', NPR, available at https://www.npr.org/2024/12/19/nx-s1-5231020/australia-top-regulator-kids-social-media-ban#:~:text=Australia%20passed%20one%20of%20the,responsible%20for%20verifying%20kids'%20ages accessed 15 January 2024.

28 Aitkenhead, D. (2024), 'What happened when I made my sons and their friends go without smartphones', *The Times*, available at https://www.thetimes.com/life-style/parenting/article/what-happened-when-i-made-my-sons-and-their-friends-go-without-smartphones-vpcnbj58d accessed 18 October 2024. It is also worth noting that *Stand By Me* is also a story of a childhood darkened by alcoholism; for one of the boys the trip is an escape from the neglect and darkness of his home.

29 Haidt, J. (2024), *The Anxious Generation*, London: Allen Lane.

30 Smartphone Free Childhood: available at https://smartphonefreechildhood.co.uk/ accessed 27 February 2025.

31 For more on this see Bond, E. & Phippen, A. (2022), *Safeguarding Adults Online: Perspectives on Rights to Participation*, Bristol: Bristol University Press.

32 Sweetser P. et al. (2012), 'Active Versus Passive Screen Time for Young Children', *Australasian Journal of Early Childhood*, vol. 34, issue 4, https://journals.sagepub.com/doi/10.1177/183693911203700413

33 Amy Orben first uses the 'digital diet' metaphor in, Orben, A. (2022) 'Digital Diet: A 21st century approach to understanding digital technologies and development', *Infant and Child Development*, 31(1), e2228

34 Simon, Herbert (1971), 'Designing Organizations for an Information-Rich World', in M. Greenberger (ed.), *Computers,*

Communications and the Public Interest, Baltimore, MD: The Johns Hopkins Press.

35 Zuboff, S. (2019), *The Age of Surveillance Capitalism: The Fight for the Future at the New Frontier of Power*, London: Profile Books.

36 Although I did do a study into the algorithmic harms of TikTok: Regehr, K., Shaughnessy, C., Zhao, M. & Shaughnessy, N. (2024), 'Safer Scrolling: How algorithms popularise and gamify online hate and misogyny for young people', https://www.ascl.org.uk/ASCL/media/ASCL/Help%20and%20advice/Inclusion/Safer-scrolling.pdf accessed 29 July 2024. See also Ribeiro, M. H., Blackburn, J., Bradlyn, B., De Cristofaro, E., Stringhini, G., Long, S., Greenberg, S., & Zannettou, S. (May 2021), 'The evolution of the manosphere across the web', in *Proceedings of the International AAAI Conference on Web and Social Media* (vol. 15, pp. 196–207); Reset Australia (2022), 'Algorithms as a weapon against women: How YouTube lures boys and young men into the "manosphere"', https://au.reset.tech/uploads/algorithms-as-a-weaponagainst-women-reset-australia.pdf; and Amnesty International (2023), 'Driven into Darkness', https://www.amnesty.org/en/documents/pol40/7350/2023/en/

37 In this book I draw from the work of activists, innovators, and seminal researchers, including project collaborators Professor Jessica Ringrose, and Professor Nicola Shaughnessy, Professor Lewis Griffin and digital forensics expert David Benford. The book is also informed by my ongoing work with policy makers, educational organisations such as the Association of School and College Leaders (ASCL) and the National Education Union (NEU) and ongoing research with Dr Caitlin Shaughnessy and Dr Katharine Smales in schools across the country as part of the digital nutrition project.

Chapter 1

1 The Kids' Guide to the Internet; early 1990s Internet commercial available at https://www.youtube.com/watch?v=A81IwlDeV6c accessed 20 December 2024.

2 Postman, N. ([1985] 2006), *Amusing Ourselves to Death: Public Discourse in the Age of Show Business*, London: Penguin.
3 At the time of writing, the 2023 Online Safety Act https://www.legislation.gov.uk/ukpga/2023/50 is being implemented in phases beginning in Spring 2025. You can see the progress of the Act here: Crawford, A. (27 October 2024), 'The Online Safety Act is one year old. Has it made children any safer?' BBC, available at https://www.bbc.co.uk/news/articles/c5y38z4pk9lo#:~:text=%E2%80%9CFrom%20December%2C%20tech%20firms%20will,creating%20a%20safer%20life%20online.%E2%80%9D accessed 27 November 2024. However, in the intervening time it has come under strong criticism, and there has been speculation that the Labour Party will change the act within two years of this parliament. See Swinford, S. (January 2023) 'Labour to Review the Online Safety Act Amid Riot Disinformation Fears', *The Times*, available at https://www.thetimes.com/article/labour-to-review-online-safety-act-amid-riot-disinformation-fears-bt82302kd accessed 28 January 2025; Helm, T., (January 2023) 'Labour pledges to toughen "weakened and gutted" online safety bill', *The Guardian* available at https://www.theguardian.com/technology/2023/jan/01/labour-pledges-toughen-online-safety-bill accessed 28 January 2025; Guest, P. (28th January 2023) 'The UK's Controversial Online Safety Act Is Now Law' available at https://www.wired.com/story/the-uks-controversial-online-safety-act-is-now-law/ accessed 28 January 2025.
4 Ang, C. (2021), 'Visualizing the World's Population by Age Group', available at https://www.visualcapitalist.com/the-worlds-population-2020-by-age/#google_vignette accessed 27 November 2024.
5 Medicines & Healthcare products Regulatory Agency, MHRA services & information for patients and healthcare professionals, available at https://www.gov.uk/government/collections/services-and-information accessed 4 December 2024.
6 Government of Canada, Health Canada, Drug products legislation and guidelines https://www.canada.ca/en/health-canada/services/drugs-health-products/drug-products/legislation-guidelines.html accessed 23 July 2024.

7 Australian government, Therapeutic Goods Administration, available at https://www.health.gov.au/contacts/therapeutic-goods-administration-tga#:~:text=The%20Therapeutic%20Goods%20Administration%20(TGA,medical%20devices%2C%20and%20diagnostic%20tests accessed 17 December 2024.

8 Central Drugs Standard Control Organisation, available at https://cdsco.gov.in/opencms/opencms/en/Home/#:~:text=The%20Central%20Drugs%20Standard%20Control,Authority%20(NRA)%20of%20India accessed 17 December 2024.

9 USA Food and Drug Administration (FDA), available at https://www.usa.gov/agencies/food-and-drug-administration#:~:text=The%20Food%20and%20Drug%20Administration,and%20products%20that%20emit%20radiation accessed 17 December 2024.

10 Medicines & Healthcare products Regulatory Agency, Clinical investigations guidance available at https://www.gov.uk/guidance/notify-mhra-about-a-clinical-investigation-for-a-medical-device accessed 4 December 2024

11 Medicines and Healthcare products Regulatory Agency, available at https://www.gov.uk/government/organisations/medicines-and-healthcare-products-regulatory-agency accessed 24 August 2024

12 Australian Government, Department of Infrastructure, Transport, Regional Development, Communications and the Arts, Vehicles, available at https://www.infrastructure.gov.au/infrastructure-transport-vehicles/vehicles/vehicle-design-regulation#:~:text=Vehicle%20design%20regulation%20%7C%20Department%20of,Development%2C%20Communications%20and%20the%20Arts accessed 17 December 2024.

13 Ministry of Road Transport and Highways, Automotive regulatory framework, available at https://igarr.com/vehicle-regulations-in-india/#:~:text=The%20Ministry%20of%20Road%20Transport,and%20vehicle%20regulations%20in%20India accessed 17 December 2024.

14 National Regulator for Compulsory Specifications, South Africa, available at https://www.nrcs.org.za/ accessed 17 December 2024.

15 Driver and Vehicle Standards Agency, available at https://www.gov.uk/government/publications/how-dvsa-makes-sure-businesses-make-or-sell-safe-vehicles-or-parts accessed 22 July 2024.
16 Toys (Safety) Regulations 2011: Great Britain, November 2023,
17 Whether it's the Food Standards Agency in the UK, the Canadian Food Inspection Agency or the Food Safety and Standards Authority of India. Food Standards Agency, UK, available at https://www.food.gov.uk/ accessed 17 December 2024; Government of Canada, Health Canada – Food and Drugs Act, available at https://www.canada.ca/en/health-canada/services/food-nutrition/legislation-guidelines.html accessed 23 July 2024; The Food Safety and Standards Authority of India (FSSAI), available at https://fssai.gov.in/cms/about-fssai.php#:~:text=FSSAI&text=The%20Food%20Safety%20and%20Standards,in%20various%20Ministries%20and%20Departments accessed 17 December 2024.
18 For food, the Food Safety Act was devised in 1990 in the UK. The 1990 Act is one of several pieces of legislation that underpin the work of the Food Standards Agency, the organisation through which the government has the power to act in the consumers' interests.
19 It may be worth distinguishing between the rules (regulations) that apply to those carrying out regulated activities or operating in a regulated sector (which usually includes some kind of licensing regime) and regulations that have more general application. For example, the General Product Safety Regulations 2005 apply to all consumer products unless there are specific rules in relation to that product elsewhere.
20 89% of parents of a child aged five to eleven say their child watches videos on YouTube, as do 81% of those who have a child aged three to four, and 57% of those who have a child aged two or younger, Pew Research Centre (2020), 'Parenting Children in the Age of Screens', p. 6, available at https://www.pewresearch.org/internet/wp-content/uploads/sites/9/2020/07/PI_2020.07.28_kids-and-screens_FINAL.pdf accessed 18 October 2024.
21 Center for Humane Technology: 'Who We Are', available at https://www.humanetech.com/who-we-are accessed 4 September 2024.

22. *The Social Dilemma* (2020), Netflix documentary available at https://www.netflix.com/gb/title/81254224.
23. Correspondence with Priya Ramda. Also see Citizens Advice, 'Examples of using the new consumer laws', available at https://www.citizensadvice.org.uk/Global/Migrated_Documents/corporate/cra2015-practicalexamples.pdf accessed 14 January 2024.
24. Online Safety Act 2023, available at https://www.legislation.gov.uk/ukpga/2023/50 accessed 4 December 2024.
25. House of Commons Library, November 2024, Online Safety Act 2023, available at https://commonslibrary.parliament.uk/research-briefings/cdp-2024-0138/#:~:text=The%20Online%20Safety%20Act%20received,sexual%20abuse%20material%20and%20grooming accessed 4 December 2024. See also 'Britain makes internet safer, as Online Safety Bill finished and ready to become law', published 19 September 2023, https://www.gov.uk/government/news/britain-makes-internet-safer-as-online-safety-bill-finished-and-ready-to-become-law accessed 4 September 2024.
26. Swinford, S. (January 2023) 'Labour to Review the Online Safety Act Amid Riot Disinformation Fears', *The Times*, available at https://www.thetimes.com/article/labour-to-review-online-safety-act-amid-riot-disinformation-fears-bt82302kd accessed 28 January 2025; Helm, T. (January 2023) Labour pledges to toughen 'weakened and gutted' online safety bill, *The Guardian*, available at https://www.theguardian.com/technology/2023/jan/01/labour-pledges-toughen-online-safety-bill accessed 28 January 2025; Guest, P. (28 January 2023) 'The UK's Controversial Online Safety Act Is Now Law', available at https://www.wired.com/story/the-uks-controversial-online-safety-act-is-now-law/ accessed 28 January 2025.
27. Online Safety Act Explainer, available at https://www.gov.uk/government/publications/online-safety-act-explainer/online-safety-act-explainer#:~:text=These%20categories%20of%20content%20are,self%2Dharm%20or%20eating%20disorders accessed 14 January 2024.

28 Woods, L. and Antoniou, A. (September 2024) 'Is the Online Safety Act "fit for purpose"?' available at https://blogs.lse.ac.uk/medialse/2024/09/03/is-the-online-safety-act-fit-for-purpose/#:~:text=In%20general%2C%20moreover%2C%20the%20Act,harmful%20content%20and%20connecting%20groups accessed 3 September 2024.

29 McGlynn, C. et al. (2024) 'Pornography, the Online Safety Act 2023 and the need for further reform', *Journal of Media Law*, https://doi.org/10.1080/17577632.2024.2357421 accessed 26 February 2025.

30 Online Safety Act: explainer, 8 May 2024, available at https://www.gov.uk/government/publications/online-safety-act-explainer accessed 4 December 2024.

31 Regehr, Shaughnessy and Smales (2025), 'Digital Nutrition: rethinking digital literacy', in press.

32 Wikipedia co-founder Jimmy Wales is quoted as saying, 'Imagine a world in which every single person on the planet is given free access to the sum of all human knowledge,' which is widely considered to be the Wikipedia mission statement. See Oxford Internet Institute, Oxford University (2016), 'Wikipedia's Ongoing Search for the Sum of All Human Knowledge', available at https://medium.com/oxford-university/wikipedia-s-ongoing-search-for-the-sum-of-all-human-knowledge-6216fb478bcf accessed 17 December 2024.

33 BBC Profile: Tim Berners-Lee, available at https://www.bbc.co.uk/sounds/play/m0003ch6?partner=uk.co.bbc&origin=share-mobile accessed 4 September 2024.

34 BBC Profile: Tim Berners-Lee, available at https://www.bbc.co.uk/sounds/play/m0003ch6?partner=uk.co.bbc&origin=share-mobile accessed 4 September 2024.

35 Hopkins, C. (1 May 2023), 'The History of Amazon and its Rise to Success', *Michigan Journal of Economics*, available at https://sites.lsa.umich.edu/mje/2023/05/01/the-history-of-amazon-and-its-rise-to-success/ tells us that On 5 July 1994, Amazon was officially founded under the name 'Cadabra' (as in abracadabra) by the young Princeton graduate Jeff Bezos in a garage space in his rental home in Bellevue, Washington. However, after just a few months,

Bezos switched the name to Amazon Inc. because of Cadabra's unappealing similarity to the word 'cadaver' (A&E Television Networks, 2015). Roughly a year later, the Amazon website was officially published as an online bookseller delivering to all fifty US states and to forty-five countries from that same garage space.

36 'Our History', eBay.com, available at https://www.ebayinc.com/company/our-history/ accessed 21 November 2024.

37 Batelle, J. (2005), 'The Birth of History', available at https://www.wired.com/2005/08/battelle/ accessed 18 October 2024; Witness History (30 September 2020), 'The founding of Google', available at https://podcasts.apple.com/gb/podcast/the-founding-of-google/id339986758?i=1000493065534, accessed 4 September 2024.

38 Witness History (30 September 2020), 'The founding of Google', available at https://podcasts.apple.com/gb/podcast/the-founding-of-google/id339986758?i=1000493065534 accessed 4 September 2024.

39 Cuthbertson, A. (May 2018), 'Google quietly removes "don't be evil" preface from code of conduct', *Independent*, available at https://www.independent.co.uk/tech/google-dont-be-evil-code-conduct-removed-alphabet-a8361276.html accessed 4 December 2024.

40 Witness History (30 September 2020), 'The founding of Google', available at https://podcasts.apple.com/gb/podcast/the-founding-of-google/id339986758?i=1000493065534 accessed 4 September 2024.

41 Heffernan, V. (15 November 2017), 'Just Google It: A Short History of a Newfound Verb', *Wired*, https://www.wired.com/story/just-google-it-a-short-history-of-a-newfound-verb/ accessed 24 August 2024.

42 Fuchs, C. (April 2021), *Social Media: A Critical Introduction*, Los Angeles: Sage Publications.

43 Children's Commissioner (November 2018), ' "Who Knows What about Me?" A Children's Commissioner report into the collection and sharing of children's data', p. 16, available at https://assets.childrenscommissioner.gov.uk/wpuploads/2018/11/cco-who-knows-what-about-me.pdf accessed 27 August 2024.

Endnotes

44. Dastin, J. (11 October 2018), 'Insight – Amazon scraps secret AI recruiting tool that showed bias against women', Reuters, available at https://www.reuters.com/article/us-amazon-com-jobs-automation-insight/amazon-scraps-secret-ai-recruiting-tool-that-showed-bias-against-women-idUSKCN1MK08G/ accessed 4 September 2024.
45. Centre for Data Ethics and Innovation Consultation, published November 2018, available at https://www.gov.uk/government/consultations/consultation-on-the-centre-for-data-ethics-and-innovation/centre-for-data-ethics-and-innovation-consultation accessed 24 August 2024.
46. Noble, S. (2018), *Algorithms of Oppression: How Search Engines Reinforce Racism*, New York: NYU Press.
47. Buolamwini, J. (2017, MIT Master's Thesis) 'Gender Shades: Intersectional Phenotypic and Demographic Evaluation of Face Datasets and Gender Classifiers'.
48. See page 101, Buolamwini, J. (2017, MIT Master's Thesis) 'Gender Shades: Intersectional Phenotypic and Demographic Evaluation of Face Datasets and Gender Classifiers'. Dr Buolamwini attributes this to 'pale male data sets' – data sets that primarily look a certain way and so the results work best for those types of faces. See also Joy Buolamwini, Timnit Gebru Proceedings of the 1st Conference on Fairness, Accountability and Transparency, PMLR 81:77-91, 2018.
49. O'Neil, C. (2017), *Weapons of Math Destruction: How Big Data Increases Inequality and Threatens Democracy*, London: Penguin.
50. Vizard, S. (28 October 2015), 'Google AdWords at 15: Moving beyond the last click', available at https://www.marketingweek.com/google-adwords-at-15-moving-beyond-the-last-click/ accessed 27 August 2024.
51. Bagshaw, T. (18 December 2023), 'The Evolution of Google AdWords – A $38 Billion Advertising Platform', available at https://www.wordstream.com/blog/ws/2012/06/05/evolution-of-adwords#:~:text=October%2023%2C%202000%2C%20will%20be,online%20advertising%20platform%20%E2%80%93%20Google%20AdWords accessed 4 September 2024.

52 Zuboff, S. (2019), *The Age of Surveillance Capitalism: The Fight for the Future at the New Frontier of Power*, London: Profile Books. If you are interested in surveillance capitalism, you might also be interested in data colonialism: see the work of Nick Couldry: 'Colonised by Data: The hollowing out of digital society', a talk at the Alexander von Humboldt Institute for internet and society. Available at https://www.youtube.com/watch?v=5tcK-XIMQqE accessed 21 November 2024.

53 Interview with Amir Malik.

54 YouTube is owned by Alphabet which is also the parent company of Google.

55 Fuchs, C. (April 2021), *Social Media: A Critical Introduction*, Los Angeles: Sage Publications.

56 Computer scientist Edward Tufte said, 'There are only two industries that call their customers "users": illegal drugs and software,' in *The Social Dilemma*, 2020, a Netflix documentary available at https://www.netflix.com/gb/title/81254224 accessed 17 January 2024.

57 Zuboff, S. (2019), *The Age of Surveillance Capitalism: The Fight for the Future at the New Frontier of Power*, London: Profile Books.

58 Zuboff, S. (2019), *The Age of Surveillance Capitalism: The Fight for the Future at the New Frontier of Power*, London: Profile Books.

59 Simms, A. & Murray, L. (2023), *Badvertising: Polluting Our Minds and Fuelling Climate Chaos*, London: Pluto Press.

60 With thanks to David Benford for this suggestion.

61 With thanks to David Benford for this suggestion.

62 Kids Guide to the Internet; early 1990s Internet commercial. available at https://www.youtube.com/watch?v=A81IwlDeV6c accessed 20 December 2024.

Chapter 2

1 The Canadian Press (2016), 'Timeline: 30 years of BlackBerry's ups and downs', available at https://www.ctvnews.ca/business/article/timeline-30-years-of-blackberrys-ups-and-downs/ accessed 3 September 2024.

2 Woggon, M. (20 July 2022), 'A Brief History of Touchscreen

Technology: From the iPhone to Multi-User Videowalls', https://www.forbes.com/councils/forbestechcouncil/2022/07/20/a-brief-history-of-touchscreen-technology-from-the-iphone-to-multi-user-videowalls/ accessed 27 August 2023.

3 Hertenstein, M. J., Verkamp, J. M., Kerestes, A. M. & Holmes, R. M. (2006), 'The communicative functions of touch in humans, nonhuman primates, and rats: A review and synthesis of the empirical research', *Genet., Social, General Psychol. Monographs*, vol. 132, no. 1, pp. 594, doi: 10.3200/mono.132.1.5-94. Academic study has long shown that touch constitutes one of the primary means of fostering intimacy between humans, including how stroking elicits positive emotions and modulates negative ones. More recent academic work has drawn links between the correlation between physically touching and emotionally feeling and how this can influence individuals' perceptions of companies, devices and online sites. e.g. White, M. (2022), *Touch Screen Theory*, Cambridge, MA: MIT Press.

4 Lapowsky, I. (4 February 2025), '15 Moments that Defined Facebook's First 15 Years', *Wired*, https://www.wired.com/story/facebook-15-defining-moments/ accessed 27 August 2024.

5 BBC, *In Depth* (October 2024), 'How have social media algorithms changed the way we interact?' available at https://www.bbc.co.uk/news/articles/cp8e4p4z97eo accessed 17 January 2024.

6 Gerlitz, C. & Helmond, A. (2013), 'The like economy: Social buttons and the data-intensive web', *New Media and Society*, vol. 15, issue 8, 1348–65, doi: 10.1177/1461444812472322.

7 Simon, H. (1971), 'Designing Organizations for an Information-Rich World', in M. Greenberger (ed.), *Computers, Communications and the Public Interest*, Baltimore MD: The Johns Hopkins Press.

8 Gerlitz, C. & Helmond, A. (November 2013), 'The Like Economy: Social Buttons and the Data-Intensive Web', *New Media & Society*, vol. 15, issue 8, 1348–65, doi: 10.1177/1461444812472322.

9 Simon, H. (1971), 'Designing Organizations for an Information-Rich World', in M. Greenberger (ed.), *Computers, Communications and the Public Interest*, Baltimore MD: The Johns Hopkins Press.

10 Lembke, A. (2021) *The Dopamine Nation*, London: Headline.

11 In conversation with Dr Photini Vriki.
12 *Washington Post* (2021), 'How Facebook Shapes Your Feed', available at https://www.washingtonpost.com/technology/interactive/2021/how-facebook-algorithm-works/ accessed 17 January 2024.
13 'How Facebook Shapes Your Feed', *Washington Post*, https://www.washingtonpost.com/technology/interactive/2021/how-facebook-algorithm-works
14 The student's name and some identifying details have been changed. The dialogue has also been altered to ensure anonymity.
15 Instructions correct at the time of going to press.
16 Center for Humane Technology available at https://www.humanetech.com accessed 4 September 2024.
17 Attention for Digital Advertising available at https://www.amplifiedintelligence.com.au/attention-for-website-and-digital-advertising/#:~:text=Using%20the%20in%2Dbuilt%20camera,tracks%20the%20collection%20participant's%20gaze accessed 17 January 2025.
18 'Amplified Intelligence, Global attention measurement leaders', available at https://www.youtube.com/watch?v=dIpLTpv9IZ0 accessed 17 January 2025.
19 Allyn, B. et al. (11 October 2024), 'TikTok executives know about app's effect on teens, lawsuit documents allege', NPR, available at https://www.npr.org/2024/10/11/g-s1-27676/tiktok-redacted-documents-in-teen-safety-lawsuit-revealed accessed 21 November 2024.
20 Allyn, B. et al. (11 October 2024), 'TikTok executives know about app's effect on teens, lawsuit documents allege', NPR, available at https://www.npr.org/2024/10/11/g-s1-27676/tiktok-redacted-documents-in-teen-safety-lawsuit-revealed accessed 21 November 2024.
21 Balkin, J. (2021), 'How to regulate (and not regulate) social media', *Journal of Free Speech Law*, 1 (1), 71–96, at p. 83, available at https://papers.ssrn.com/sol3/papers.cfm?abstract_id=3484114.
22 Pelly, S. (4 October 2021), 'Whistleblower: Facebook is misleading the public on progress against hate speech, violence,

Endnotes   197

misinformation', CBS News *60 Minutes*, available at https://www.cbsnews.com/news/facebook-whistleblower-frances-haugen-misinformation-public-60-minutes-2021-10-03/ accessed 30 August 2024. Horwitz (2023) *Broken Code* (p. 266) also gives an account of Facebook's leadership considering removing the 'like' button from Instagram as a result of fears that comparing 'likes' drove young girls to unhealthy comparisons with others. Internal research meant that this was rejected, but Horwitz writes: 'There were other drawbacks, too. Without a like count to signal which posts were popular, users were spending a little less time on the app and clicking on fewer ads. Revenue might fall as much as 1 percent.'

23 Horwitz, J. (2023), *Broken Code* contains numerous examples of Facebook not taking action to correct harmful processes on the platform – see in particular pp. 171; 186; 197–9; 226; 258. Also see Andrew Kaung's experiences at TikTok and Meta reported in: Spring, M., ' "It stains your brain": How social media algorithms show violence to boys', *BBC News*, 2 September 2024, https://www.bbc.co.uk/news/articles/c4gdqzxypdzo accessed 2 September 2024.

24 Regehr, K., Shaughnessy, C., Zhao, M. & Shaughnessy, N. (2024), 'Safer Scrolling: How algorithms popularise and gamify online hate and misogyny for young people', https://www.ascl.org.uk/ASCL/media/ASCL/Help%20and%20advice/Inclusion/Safer-scrolling.pdf accessed 29 July 2024.

25 Andrew Kaung in Spring, M., ' "It stains your brain": How social media algorithms show violence to boys', *BBC News*, 2 September 2024, https://www.bbc.co.uk/news/articles/c4gdqzxypdzo accessed 2 September 2024.

26 Barassi, V. (2020), *Child Data Citizen: How Tech Companies Are Profiling Us from before Birth* (1st ed.), Cambridge, MA: MIT Press. https://doi.org/10.7551/mitpress/12415.001.0001

27 AVG (2010), 'Welcome to the Online World', available at https://avg.typepad.com/files/digitalbirthsglobal.pdf accessed 4 September 2024.

28 Children's Commissioner (November 2028), 'Who Knows What about Me? A Children's Commissioner report into the collection

and sharing of children's data', p. 2, available at https://assets.childrenscommissioner.gov.uk/wpuploads/2018/11/cco-who-knows-what-about-me.pdf accessed 30 August 2024.

29. Better Business Bureau is a 112-year-old US organization which protects consumer rights. Reported *CBS News* (August 2024), 'BBB Warns Parents about Potential Dangers of Posting Back-to-School Photos', available at https://www.cbsnews.com/chicago/news/bbb-warns-parents-potential-dangers-back-to-school-photos/ accessed 11 January 2025.

30. Norris, R. (2022), 'The Politics of the Back to School Photo', *Grazia*, available at https://graziadaily.co.uk/life/real-life/politics-of-back-to-school-photo/ accessed 4 September 2024.

31. Children's Commissioner (November 2028), 'Who Knows What about Me? A Children's Commissioner report into the collection and sharing of children's data', p. 3, available at https://assets.childrenscommissioner.gov.uk/wpuploads/2018/11/cco-who-knows-what-about-me.pdf accessed 30 August 2024.

32. Gerken, T (3rd March 2025) TikTok investigated over use of children's data, BBC available at https://www.bbc.co.uk/news/articles/c62xxz141plo accessed 6th March 2025.

33. As of January 2025 her following is 16.6m.

34. Dickson, E. J. (20 July 2022), 'A Toddler on TikTok is Spawning a Massive Mom-Led Movement', available at https://www.rollingstone.com/culture/culture-news/tiktok-wren-eleanor-moms-controversy-1385182/ accessed 30 August 2024.

35. Kindelan, K. (2022), 'Parents remove videos of their kids from TikTok after "Wren Eleanor" warning', *ABC News*, available at https://abcnews.go.com/GMA/Family/wren-eleanor-tiktok-trend-sees-parents-removing-photos/story?id=87486106 accessed 17 January 2025.

36. Manavis, S. (30 November 2023), 'Family vlogging exploits children', available at https://www.newstatesman.com/culture/social-media/2023/11/family-vlogging-exploits-children accessed 30 August 2024.

37. Manavis, S. (30 November 2023), 'Family vlogging exploits

children', available at https://www.newstatesman.com/culture/social-media/2023/11/family-vlogging-exploits-children accessed 30 August 2024.

38 Abidin, C. (2017), 'Family goals: family influencers, calibrated amateurism, and justifying young digital labor', *Social Media + Society* 3(2): doi: 10.1177/2056305117707191

39 *BBC News* (7 October 2020), 'France passes new law to protect child influencers', available at https://www.bbc.co.uk/news/world-europe-54447491 accessed 30 August 2024.

40 Library of Congress, 'France: Parliament Adopts Law to Protect Child "Influencers" on Social Media', available at https://www.loc.gov/item/global-legal-monitor/2020-10-30/france-parliament-adopts-law-to-protect-child-influencers-on-social-media/ accessed 30 August 2024.

41 *BBC News* (7 October 2020), 'France passes new law to protect child influencers', available at https://www.bbc.co.uk/news/world-europe-54447491 accessed 30 August 2024.

42 Kato, B. (3 July 2024), 'Parenting influencers must pay their kids for using them in videos now: "You have to be ethical"', available at https://nypost.com/2024/07/03/lifestyle/parenting-influencers-must-pay-their-kids-for-using-them-in-videos-now-you-have-to-be-ethical/ accessed 30 August 2024.

43 University of Essex Research Project Dr Francis Rees Child Influencer Project – Ireland and the UK, available at https://www.essex.ac.uk/research-projects/child-influencer-project accessed 26 February 2025.

44 Lupton, D. (2016), *The Quantified Self*, Malden. MA: Polity.

45 Children's Commissioner, 'Who Knows What about Me? A Children's Commissioner report into the collection and sharing of children's data', November 2018, available at https://assets.childrenscommissioner.gov.uk/wpuploads/2018/11/cco-who-knows-what-about-me.pdf accessed 27 August 2024. p. 13 – 14

46 *BBC News* (21 May 2018), ' "Sharenting" puts young at risk of online fraud', available at https://www.bbc.co.uk/news/education-44153754 accessed 30 August 2024.

47 Federal Bureau of Investigation (FBI) Internet Crime Report 2023 available at https://www.ic3.gov/AnnualReport/Reports/2023_IC3Report.pdf reported in *Huffington Post* (August 2024) '4 Mistakes Parents Make When Posting Their Kids' First-Day-Of-School Photos' https://www.huffingtonpost.co.uk/entry/back-to-school-cybersecurity-risk_l_66d0de86e4b0b422df222e59 accessed 5th March 2025.

48 Most parents (73%) of all age groups reveal that they post or share photos, videos or information about their child online, and that almost 90% of those parents share them on their own social media accounts. Manotipya P. & Ghazinour K. (2020), 'Children's Online Privacy from Parents' Perspective', *Procedia Computer Science* vol. 177, pp. 178–85 https://doi.org/10.1016/j.procs.2020.10.026.

49 With thanks to David Benford.

50 This research was conducted as part of an AHRC project. The research team included Professor Nicola Shaughnessy, Dr Caitlin Shaughnessy, Minzhu Zhou, Idil Cambazoglu, and Alfie Turner who conducted digital ethnography and was a tremendous asset to this project.

51 Pariser, E. (2012), *The Filter Bubble: What the Internet Is Hiding from You*, London: Penguin.

52 Pariser, E. (2012), *The Filter Bubble: What the Internet Is Hiding from You*, London: Penguin.

53 Alexander, N. (2016), 'Catered to your Future Self: Netflix's "Predictive Personalization" and the Mathematization of Taste', in *The Netflix Effect: Technology and Entertainment in the 21st Century*, Daniel Smith-Rowsey and Kevin McDonald (eds.), London and New York: Bloomsbury Academic Publishing, pp. 81–100.

54 Frey, M. (2021), *Netflix Recommends: Algorithms, Flm Choice, and the History of Taste*, Oakland, California: University of California Press.

55 Pariser, E. (2012), *The Filter Bubble: What the Internet Is Hiding from You*, London: Penguin.

56 The whistleblower Frances Haugen uses this analogy in an interview with the BBC: BBC Three, The Instagram Effect (February 2022), available at https://www.bbc.co.uk/iplayer/episode/m00149j7/the-instagram-effect accessed 29 July 2024.

57 Regehr, K., Shaughnessy, C., Zhao, M. & Shaughnessy, N. (2024), 'Safer Scrolling: How algorithms popularise and gamify online hate and misogyny for young people', https://www.ascl.org.uk/ASCL/media/ASCL/Help%20and%20advice/Inclusion/Safer-scrolling.pdf accessed 29 July 2024.

58 According to Fitz-Walter, the term 'gamification' was coined in 2003 by Nick Pelling, but was not commonly used to describe gaming in training and education until 2010. Fitz-Walter, Z. (2013), 'A brief history of gamification', available at https://www.zacfitzwalter.com/articles/gamification-history accessed 22 October 2016. According to Christians (2018), game designer Pelling came up with the term after he had been tasked with developing a game-like interface for ATM and vending machines. Christians, G., 'The Origins and Future of Gamification', Senior Thesis, University of South Carolina, available at https://scholarcommons.sc.edu/cgi/viewcontent.cgi?article=1255&context=senior_theses

59 Regehr, K., Shaughnessy, C., Zhao, M. & Shaughnessy, N. (2024), 'Safer Scrolling: How algorithms popularise and gamify online hate and misogyny for young people', https://www.ascl.org.uk/ASCL/media/ASCL/Help%20and%20advice/Inclusion/Safer-scrolling.pdf accessed 29 July 2024.

60 Bratich, J., Banet-Weiser, S. (September 2019), 'From Pick-Up Artists to Incels: Con(fidence) Games, Networked Misogyny, and the Failure of Neoliberalism', *International Journal of Communication*, [S.l.], v. 13, p. 25, ISSN 1932-8036, available at https://ijoc.org/index.php/ijoc/article/view/13216 accessed 27 November 2024.

61 For more information about incel culture see Baker, C., Ging, D., Brandt Andreasen, M. (2024), 'Recommending Toxicity: The role of algorithmic recommender functions on YouTube Shorts and TikTok in promoting male supremacist influencers', available at https://antibullyingcentre.ie/recommending-toxicity-how-tiktok-and-youtube-shorts-are-bombarding-boys-and-men-with-misogynist-content/ accessed 29 November 2024.

62 Regehr, K. (2022), 'In(cel)doctrination: How technologically facilitated misogyny moves violence off screens and on to

streets', *New Media & Society*, 24(1), pp. 138–55 https://doi.org/10.1177/1461444820959019

63 Ging, D. (2019), 'Alphas, Betas, and Incels: Theorizing the Masculinities of the Manosphere', *Men and Masculinities*, 22(4), pp. 638–57. https://doi.org/10.1177/1097184X17706401

64 Regehr, K., Shaughnessy, C., Zhao, M. & Shaughnessy, N. (2024), 'Safer Scrolling: How algorithms popularise and gamify online hate and misogyny for young people', https://www.ascl.org.uk/ASCL/media/ASCL/Help%20and%20advice/Inclusion/Safer-scrolling.pdf accessed 29 July 2024.

65 Within my own consultancy work with school leaders.

66 Media studies scholars Debbie Ging and Euginia Siapera have argued that content like this is being normalized for young people. See Ging, D. & Siapera, E., eds (2019), *Gender Hate Online: Understanding the New Anti-Feminism*, London and Basingstoke: Palgrave Macmillan.

67 Equimundo (2022), *The State of UK Boys: Understanding and Transforming Gender in the Lives of UK Boys,* Washington, DC: Equimundo, available at https://www.equimundo.org/wp-content/uploads/2022/12/State-of-UK-Boys-Long-Report.pdf accessed 17 January 2025.

68 Mentors in Violence Prevention (MVP) programme, 1 January 2017, updated 25 April 2024, available at https://education.gov.scot/resources/mentors-in-violence-prevention-mvp/ accessed 30 August 2024.

69 BBC Bitesize, 'What are Echo Chambers?', available at https://www.bbc.co.uk/bitesize/articles/zbwkbqt#:~:text=The%20emperor%20always%20wanted%20the,that%20the%20hype%20was%20real accessed 17 January 2025.

70 Suggestions from young people as gathered by the Young Minds organization, available at https://www.youngminds.org.uk/parent/parents-a-z-mental-health-guide/gaming/ accessed 17 January 2025. For more information and resources for helping young people deal with their mental health and issues see https://www.youngminds.org.uk/

71. *Financial Times*, 'Southport and the "lone wolf" policy conundrum', https://www.ft.com/content/cf2f01b0-c8e7-4b40-9c03-3cee23e2c502.
72. *BBC News* (28 January 2025), 'Families "shocked" at missed chances to stop killer', https://www.bbc.co.uk/news/articles/c3w85yz0053o.
73. Cooney, C. (26 January 2025), 'Remove videos seen by Southport killer, Cooper says', *BBC News*, https://www.bbc.co.uk/news/articles/cz0lyy37jk3o
74. Fraser, G. (24 January 2025), 'X refused to take down video viewed by Southport killer', *BBC News*, https://www.bbc.co.uk/news/articles/c2egz1089pwo.
75. Fraser, G. (24 January 2025), 'X refused to take down video viewed by Southport killer', *BBC News*, https://www.bbc.co.uk/news/articles/c2egz1089pwo.
76. This video was later removed by YouTube for violating YouTube's terms of service: https://www.youtube.com/watch?v=3gLDoHek68Y.
77. Connecticut's Official State Website CT.Gov, The State Tree, available at https://portal.ct.gov/about/state-symbols/the-state-tree accessed 7th March 2025.
78. Town of Newtown, Connecticut, Community Movies, available at https://www.elocallink.tv/m/v/player.php?pid=w5a3x4B8Q41&fp=ctnew18_qol_rev2_iwd#c|ctnew18_qol_rev2_iwd accessed 7th March 2025
79. Town of Newtown, Connecticut, Welcome to the Town of Newtown! available at https://www.newtown-ct.gov/welcome-town-newtown accessed 7th March 2025
80. Schwartzman, P. (14 December 2012), 'Sandy Hook principal is one of the victims', *Boston Globe*, https://www.bostonglobe.com/2012/12/14/sandy-hook-principal-one-victims/kzc7rF5p9Zw9OngBzCJasN/story.html.
81. *BBC News* (25 October 2017), 'Sandy Hook shootings: Four things revealed by FBI files', https://www.bbc.co.uk/news/world-us-canada-41749336.

82 *BBC News* (25 October 2017), 'Sandy Hook shootings: Four things revealed by FBI files', https://www.bbc.co.uk/news/world-us-canada-41749336.

83 This American Life (15 March 2019), 'Beware the Jabberwock', https://www.thisamericanlife.org/670/beware-the-jabberwock.

84 Freeman, H. (2 May 2017), 'Sandy Hook father Leonard Pozner on death threats: "I never imagined I'd have to fight for my child's legacy" ', *The Guardian*, https://www.theguardian.com/us-news/2017/may/02/sandy-hook-school-hoax-massacre-conspiracists-victim-father.

85 Freeman, H. (2 May 2017), 'Sandy Hook father Leonard Pozner on death threats: "I never imagined I'd have to fight for my child's legacy" ', *The Guardian*, https://www.theguardian.com/us-news/2017/may/02/sandy-hook-school-hoax-massacre-conspiracists-victim-father.

86 This American Life (15 March 2019), 'Beware the Jabberwock', https://www.thisamericanlife.org/670/beware-the-jabberwock.

87 This American Life (15 March 2019), 'Beware the Jabberwock', https://www.thisamericanlife.org/670/beware-the-jabberwock.

88 This American Life (15 March 2019), 'Beware the Jabberwock', https://www.thisamericanlife.org/670/beware-the-jabberwock.

89 Freeman, H. (2 May 2017), 'Sandy Hook father Leonard Pozner on death threats: "I never imagined I'd have to fight for my child's legacy" ', *The Guardian*, https://www.theguardian.com/us-news/2017/may/02/sandy-hook-school-hoax-massacre-conspiracists-victim-father.

90 This American Life (15 March 2019), 'Beware the Jabberwock', https://www.thisamericanlife.org/670/beware-the-jabberwock.

91 Kavanagh, J. & Rich, M. D. (2018), 'Truth Decay: An Initial Exploration of the Diminishing Role of Facts and Analysis in American Public Life', Rand Foundation, available at https://www.rand.org/pubs/research_reports/RR2314.html accessed 17 January 2025.

92 Correspondence with Professor Lewis Griffin.

93 For example, in January 2025 Meta announced that it will no longer use the independent fact-checkers who flag 'misinformation' on

its platforms in the USA. See Kaplan, J. (7 January 2025), 'More Speech and Fewer Mistakes', available at https://about.fb.com/news/2025/01/meta-more-speech-fewer-mistakes/ accessed 14 January 2025.

94 Jenni Stancombe quoted by Wright, G. (August 2024), '17-year-old charged with murder of three girls in Southport attack', *BBC News*, available at https://www.bbc.co.uk/news/articles/cj50ljn44j8o#:~:text=In%20a%20message%20widely%20shared,don't%20need%20this.%22 accessed 17 January 2025.

95 Cybersecurity expert David Benford says that you can download Link Gopher from the Chrome Web Store or Firefox Add-ons.

96 Kelly, H. (15 July 2024), 'How to avoid falling for misinformation and conspiracy theories', *Washington Post*, available at https://www.washingtonpost.com/technology/2024/misinformation-ai-twitter-facebook-guide/.

97 With thanks to David Benford.

98 Christian Fuchs uses a similar activity in his book. For more detail on this topic, look at Fuchs, C. (April 2021), *Social Media: A Critical Introduction*, Los Angeles: Sage Publications.

Chapter 3

1 Ringrose, J., Gill, R., Livingstone, S. & Harvey, L. (May 2012), 'A qualitative study of children, young people and "sexting": A report prepared for the NSPCC: National Society for the Prevention of Cruelty to Children', available at https://eprints.lse.ac.uk/44216/1/__Libfile_repository_Content_Livingstone%2C%20S_A%20qualitative%20study%20of%20children%2C%20young%20people%20and%20%27sexting%27%20%28LSE%20RO%29.pdf

2 Ringrose, J. & Regehr, K. (December 2023), 'Recognizing and addressing how gender shapes young people's experiences of image-based sexual harassment and abuse in educational settings', *Journal of Social Issues*, vol. 79, issue 4: *Sexual Harassment Among Young People*, pp. 1107–55, available at https://spssi.

onlinelibrary.wiley.com/doi/epdf/10.1111/josi.12575 accessed 17 December 2024, and Ringrose, J., Regehr, K. & Whitehead, S. (2022), ' "Wanna trade?": Cisheteronormative homosocial masculinity and the normalization of abuse in youth digital sexual image exchange', *Journal of Gender Studies*, vol. 31, no. 2, pp. 243–61 available at https://www.tandfonline.com/doi/epdf/10.1080/09589236.2021.1947206?needAccess=true accessed 17 December 2024; Ringrose, J., Regehr, K. & Milne, B. (7 December 2021), 'Understanding and Combatting Youth Experiences of Image-Based Sexual Harassment and Abuse', available at https://www.ascl.org.uk/ASCL/media/ASCL/Our%20view/Campaigns/Understanding-and-combatting-youth-experiences-of-image-based-sexual-harassment-and-abuse-full-report.pdf.

3   This event is also outlined in more detail in our book: Ringrose, J., Regehr, K., *Teens, Social Media and Image Based Abuse* (Palgrave, forthcoming). A report on this work can be found at 'Understanding and Combatting Youth Experiences of Image-Based Sexual Harassment and Abuse', 7 December 2021, available at https://www.ascl.org.uk/ASCL/media/ASCL/Our%20view/Campaigns/Understanding-and-combatting-youth-experiences-of-image-based-sexual-harassment-and-abuse-full-report.pdf

4   In September 2021 the *Wall Street Journal* published the Facebook Files, https://www.wsj.com/articles/the-facebook-files-11631713039. The anonymous source was revealed one month later, in October 2021, as former Facebook employee Frances Haugen: Horwitz, J. (3rd October 2021) 'The Facebook Whistleblower, Frances Haugen, Says She Wants to Fix the Company, Not Harm It', *The Wall Street Journal*, available at https://www.wsj.com/articles/facebook-whistleblower-frances-haugen-says-she-wants-to-fix-the-company-not-harm-it-11633304122 accessed 7th March 2025. The Facebook Files included revelations about Instagram's internal research on teenage girls: Wells, G., Horwitz, J. and Seetharaman, D., 'Facebook Knows Instagram Is Toxic for Teen Girls, Company Documents Show', *The Wall Street*

Journal, available at https://www.wsj.com/articles/facebook-knows-instagram-is-toxic-for-teen-girls-company-documents-show-11631620739?mod=hp_lead_pos7&mod=article_inline accessed 29 July 2024.

5. Tech Policy Press, (January 2024) Transcript of the US Senate Judiciary Committee Hearing on Big Tech and the Online Child Sexual Exploitation Crisis, available at https://www.techpolicy.press/transcript-us-senate-judiciary-committee-hearing-on-big-tech-and-the-online-child-sexual-exploitation-crisis/ accessed 29 July 2024.

6. Barnett, K. (January 2024), '5 key takeaways from Meta, TikTok, X, Snap's Congressional hearing on kids' online safety', The Drum, available at https://www.thedrum.com/news/2024/01/31/5-key-takeaways-meta-tiktok-x-snap-s-congressional-hearing-kids-online-safety accessed 21 January 2025.

7. Bruner, R. (16 July 2016), 'A Brief History of Instagram's Fateful First Day', *Time Magazine,* available at https://time.com/4408374/instagram-anniversary/ accessed 29 July 2024.

8. *The Instagram Effect* (7 February 2022), BBC Three, https://www.bbc.co.uk/iplayer/episode/m00149j7/the-instagram-effect accessed 20 August 2024.

9. For more on this subject see the work of Professor Rosalind Gill: Gill, R., 'Changing the perfect picture: Smartphones, social media and appearance pressures', available at https://www.city.ac.uk/__data/assets/pdf_file/0005/597209/Parliament-Report-web.pdf accessed 25 February 2025.

10. Fuchs, C. (April 2021), *Social Media: A Critical Introduction*, Los Angeles: Sage Publications.

11. Chayka, K. (16 January 2024), 'The tyranny of the algorithm: why every coffee shop looks the same', *The Guardian*, available at https://www.theguardian.com/news/2024/jan/16/the-tyranny-of-the-algorithm-why-every-coffee-shop-looks-the-same?CMP=oth_b-aplnews_d-5 accessed 18 October 2024.

12. Mental Health Foundation with YouGov, Body Image Report, Executive Summary 2019, available at https://www.mentalhealth.

org.uk/explore-mental-health/articles/body-image-report-executive-summary#:~:text=New%20body%20image%20statistics,image%20in%20the%20last%20year accessed 29 July 2024.

13 Beat, Online Safety and Eating Disorders, August 2022, available at https://www.beateatingdisorders.org.uk/get-information-and-support/about-eating-disorders/research/online-safety-and-eating-disorders/ accessed 29 July 2024.

14 *The Instagram Effect* (7 February 2022), BBC Three, https://www.bbc.co.uk/iplayer/episode/m00149j7/the-instagram-effect accessed 20 August 2024.

15 *Wall Street Journal* (29 September 2021), 'Facebook Knows Instragram Is Toxic for Teen Girls, Company Documents Show', available at https://www.wsj.com/articles/facebook-knows-instagram-is-toxic-for-teen-girls-company-documents-show-11631620739 accessed 5 December 2024.

16 Pedalino, F. & Camerini, A.-L. (2022), 'Instagram Use and Body Dissatisfaction: The Mediating Role of Upward Social Comparison with Peers and Influencers among Young Females', *Int J Environ Res Public Health*. 29;19(3):1543 doi: 10.3390/ijerph19031543

17 Frances Haugen speaking in the documentary *The Instagram Effect*: BBC Three, *The Instagram Effect* (February 2022), available at https://www.bbc.co.uk/iplayer/episode/m00149j7/the-instagram-effect accessed 29 July 2024.

18 Milmo, D. (11 October 2022), 'Molly Russell: how a teenager's death put social media on trial', *The Guardian*, https://www.theguardian.com/news/audio/2022/oct/11/molly-russell-how-a-teenagers-death-put-social-media-on-trial accessed 20 August 2024.

19 Dermott O'Leary, recalling interviewing Ian Russell (Molly's father), speaking at 'The Smartphone Trap: How Algorithmic Addiction works and what you can do about it', at King Alfred's School, 27 November 2024.

20 Milmo, D. (11 October 2022), 'Molly Russell: how a teenager's death put social media on trial', *The Guardian*, https://www.theguardian.com/news/audio/2022/oct/11/molly-russell-how-a-teenagers-death-put-social-media-on-trial accessed 20 August 2024.

21. Katz, A. & El Asam, A. (2020), 'The CyberSurvey: In their own words: The digital lives of schoolchildren', pp. 1–56, https://www.internetmatters.org/wp-content/uploads/2020/10/Internet-Matters-CyberSurvey19-Digital-Life-Web.pdf accessed 29 July 2024.
22. Katz, A. & El Asam, A. (2020), 'The CyberSurvey: In their own words: The digital lives of schoolchildren', p. 7, available at https://www.internetmatters.org/wp-content/uploads/2020/10/Internet-Matters-CyberSurvey19-Digital-Life-Web.pdf accessed 29 July 2024.
23. Milmo, D. (11 October 2022), 'Molly Russell: how a teenager's death put social media on trial', *The Guardian*, available at https://www.theguardian.com/news/audio/2022/oct/11/molly-russell-how-a-teenagers-death-put-social-media-on-trial accessed 20 August 2024.
24. Ian Russell speaking on *This Morning* in 2022, 'Molly Russell's Father Urges Change To Help Make Social Media Safer For Children', available at https://www.youtube.com/watch?v=LbF7M5ytDcM accessed 5 December 2024.
25. Katz, A. & El Asam, A. (2020), *Refuge and Risk: Life Online for Vulnerable Young People*, s.l.: Internet Matters, p. 24, available at https://www.internetmatters.org/wp-content/uploads/2021/01/Internet-Matters-Refuge-And-Risk-Report.pdf accessed 29 July 2024.
26. Orben, A., Meier, A., Dalgleish, T. et al., 'Mechanisms linking social media use to adolescent mental health vulnerability', *Nature Reviews Psychology* 3, 407–23 (2024).
27. *Good Morning Britain* (2021), 'Molly Russell's Father Wants Social Media Companies To Take Responsibility For Harmful Content', available at https://www.youtube.com/watch?v=1ev11Z6WUNY.
28. Milmo, D. (11 October 2022), 'Molly Russell: how a teenager's death put social media on trial', *The Guardian*, https://www.theguardian.com/news/audio/2022/oct/11/molly-russell-how-a-teenagers-death-put-social-media-on-trial accessed 20 August 2024.
29. Milmo, D. (11 October 2022), 'Molly Russell: how a teenager's death put social media on trial', *The Guardian*, https://www.theguardian.com/news/audio/2022/oct/11/molly-russell-how-

a-teenagers-death-put-social-media-on-trial accessed 20 August 2024.

30   Livingstone and Third (2017), 'Children and Young People's Rights in the Digital Age: An Emerging Agenda', *New Media and Society*, 19 (5) 657–70.

31   *Good Morning Britain* (2021), 'Molly Russell's Father Wants Social Media Companies To Take Responsibility For Harmful Content', available at https://www.youtube.com/watch?v=ievi1Z6WUNY. See also Milmo, D. (30 September 2022), ' "The bleakest of worlds": how Molly Russell fell into a vortex of despair on social media', *The Guardian*, available at https://www.theguardian.com/technology/2022/sep/30/how-molly-russell-fell-into-a-vortex-of-despair-on-social-media#:~:text=But%20the%20darker%20side%20of,%2C%20self%2Dharm%20and%20depression accessed 29 July 2024.

32   Milmo, D. (23 September 2022), 'Molly Russell inquest hears defence of Instagram content policies', *The Guardian*, available at https://www.theguardian.com/uk-news/2022/sep/23/molly-russell-inquest-hears-defence-of-instagram-content-policies#:~:text=The%20court%20also%20heard%20that,death%2C%20suicidal%20feeling%20and%20burial accessed 29 July 2024.

33   *BBC News* (27 September 2022), 'Molly Russell: Posts left psychiatrist unable to sleep – inquest', available at https://www.bbc.co.uk/news/uk-england-london-63049167 accessed 29 July 2024. My previous work has explored how images had impact on professionals who have to see these materials in order to carry out their job and the real harm and trauma these can inflict. See Regehr, C., Regehr, K., Birze, A. & Duff, W. (2023), 'Troubling Records: Managing and Conserving Mediated Artifacts of Violent Crime', *Archivaria* 95 (Spring) 6–40, https://archivaria.ca/index.php/archivaria/article/view/13895; Regehr, C., Regehr, K. & Birze, A. (2022), 'Traumatic Residue, Mediated Remembering and Video Evidence of Sexual Violence: A Case Study', *International Journal of Law and Psychiatry* 81 (2) https://

doi.org/10.1016/j.ijlp.2022.101778; Birze, A., Regehr, C. & Regehr, K. (2022), 'Organizational Support for the Potentially Traumatic Impact of Video Evidence of Violent Crime in the Criminal Justice System: "We're almost making more victims"', *International Review of Victimology*, https://journals.sagepub.com/doi/10.1177/02697580221112436; Birze, A., Regehr, K. & Regehr, C. (2022), 'Workplace Trauma in a Digital Age: The Impact of Video Evidence of Violent Crime on Criminal Justice Professionals', *Journal of Interpersonal Violence* 38 (1–2) https://journals.sagepub.com/doi/10.1177/08862605221090571; Regehr, K., Regehr C. & Birze A. (2021), Regehr, K., Regehr, C., Goel, V., Sato, C., Lyons, K., & Rudzicz, F. (2024). 'Technology-Facilitated Violence Against Public Health Professionals'. Journal of Loss and Trauma, 1–26. https://doi.org/10.1080/15325024.2024.2406509

34 Milmo, D. (11 October 2022), 'Molly Russell: how a teenager's death put social media on trial', *The Guardian*, available at https://www.theguardian.com/news/audio/2022/oct/11/molly-russell-how-a-teenagers-death-put-social-media-on-trial accessed 20 August 2024.

35 Ian Russell speaking after the inquest into his daughter Molly's death. 'I hope the world will be safer', says Molly Russell's father after inquest, *Guardian News*, available at 1min 8 seconds https://www.youtube.com/watch?v=iUC_2h94Dsc accessed 6 December 2024. For more on Langone's testimony see: 'Molly Russell: Instagram posts seen by teen were safe, Meta says', *BBC News*, 26 September 2022, https://www.bbc.co.uk/news/uk-england-london-63034300#:~:text=Ms%20Lagone%20told%20the%20court,they%20were%20experiencing%20suicidal%20thoughts accessed 29 July 2024.

36 Sky News (September 2022), 'Meta defends "safe" Instagram posts seen by Molly Russell', available at https://news.sky.com/story/instagram-posts-seen-by-molly-russell-were-safe-apps-wellbeing-boss-says-12705824 accessed 21 February 2025.

37 Conversations and correspondence with Amir Malik, autumn 2024.

38 Quote read by Ian Russell on *BBC News*: 'Brianna Ghey's mother

and Molly Russell's father join forces to combat online harm', *BBC News*, 15 February 2024, available at https://www.bbc.co.uk/news/uk-68309102 accessed 29 July 2024.

39 Milmo, D. (11 October 2022), 'Molly Russell: how a teenager's death put social media on trial', *The Guardian*, available at https://www.theguardian.com/news/audio/2022/oct/11/molly-russell-how-a-teenagers-death-put-social-media-on-trial accessed 20 August 2024.

40 'Molly Russell inquest: Father makes social media plea', *BBC News* (30 September 2022), https://www.bbc.co.uk/news/uk-england-london-63073489 accessed 29 July 2024.

41 Milmo, D. (11 October 2022), 'Molly Russell: how a teenager's death put social media on trial', *The Guardian*, https://www.theguardian.com/news/audio/2022/oct/11/molly-russell-how-a-teenagers-death-put-social-media-on-trial accessed 20 August 2024.

42 Ian Russell speaking after the inquest into his daughter Molly's death. ' "I hope the world will be safer", says Molly Russell's father after inquest', *Guardian News*, available at https://www.youtube.com/watch?v=iUC_2h94Dsc accessed 6 December 2024.

43 Molly Rose Foundation, available at https://mollyrosefoundation.org/ accessed 6 December 2024.

44 Molly Rose Foundation, available at https://mollyrosefoundation.org/ accessed 6 December 2024.

45 Sellman, M. (7 June 2024), 'Secondary schools join forces to ban smartphones for under-14s', *The Times*, available at https://www.thetimes.com/article/cb7212c8-c49a-42f1-9a81-61e868f261b8 accessed 6 December 2024.

46 The Secretary of State for Digital, Culture, Media and Sport at the time, Michelle Donelan, said in a statement: 'The inquest has shown the horrific failure of social media platforms to put the welfare of children first', adding, 'We owe it to Molly's family to do everything in our power to stop this happening to others. Our Online Safety Bill is the answer and through it we will use the full force of the law to make social media firms protect young people from horrendous

pro-suicide material.' As reported in *BBC News* (30 September 2022), 'Molly Russell inquest: Father makes social media plea', https://www.bbc.co.uk/news/uk-england-london-63073489

47 Online Safety Act Explainer, May 2024, available at https://www.gov.uk/government/publications/online-safety-act-explainer/online-safety-act-explainer accessed 6 December 2024.

48 Ian Russell discusses posts which are 'legal but harmful' on *Good Morning Britain* (2021), 'Molly Russell's Father Wants Social Media Companies To Take Responsibility For Harmful Content', available at https://www.youtube.com/watch?v=ievi1Z6WUNY accessed 5 December 2021.

49 Light, B., Burgess, J. & Duguay, S. (2016), 'The walkthrough method: An approach to the study of apps', *New Media and Society*, vol. 20 no. 2, pp. 881–900, available at https://journals.sagepub.com/doi/10.1177/1461444816675438

50 'Molly Russell's Father Urges Change To Help Make Social Media Safer For Children' (2022), *This Morning*, available at https://www.youtube.com/watch?v=LbF7M5ytDcM accessed 19 December 2024.

51 Bullying in Snapchat was also reported to take place in the comments on videos.

52 Regehr, Shaughnessy and Smales (2025), 'Digital Nutrition: rethinking digital literacy', in press.

53 Regehr, Shaughnessy and Smales (2025), 'Digital Nutrition: rethinking digital literacy', in press.

54 How to change group privacy settings, WhatsApp Help Center, available at https://faq.whatsapp.com/1131457590844955/?cms_platform=web accessed 6 December 2024.

55 'What is cyberbullying: Guide to online bullying for parents', Internetmatters.org, available at https://www.internetmatters.org/issues/cyberbullying/learn-about-it/ accessed 6 December 2024

56 'Child Exploitation and Online Protection Safety Centre', available at https://www.ceop.police.uk/Safety-Centre/ accessed 6 December 2024.

57 Ringrose, J., Regehr, K. & Whitehead, S. (2021), 'Teen girls'

experiences negotiating the ubiquitous dick pic: Sexual double standards and the normalization of abuse in teen digital image exchange', *Sex Roles*, 85: 558–76, available at https://link.springer.com/article/10.1007/s11199-021-01236-3; Ringrose, J., Regehr, K. & Whitehead, S. (2021), ' "Wanna trade?": Cisheteronormative homosocial masculinity and the normalization of abuse in youth digital sexual image exchange', *Journal of Gender Studies* 31(2) 243–61, available at https://www.tandfonline.com/doi/epdf/10.1080/09589236.2021.1947206?needAccess=true; Ringrose, R. & Regehr, K. (2023), 'Recognizing and addressing how gender shapes young people's experiences of image-based sexual harassment and abuse (IBSHA) in educational settings', *Journal of Social Issues* 79(4) 1251–81, available at https://spssi.onlinelibrary.wiley.com/doi/full/10.1111/josi.12575

58 Ringrose, J., Mishna, F., Milne, B., Regehr, K. & Slane, A. (2022), 'Young People's Experiences of Image-Based Sexual Harassment and Abuse in England and Canada: Toward a Feminist Framing of Technologically Facilitated Sexual Violence', *Women's Studies International Forum* 93(5) 102615/

59 Ringrose, J., Regehr, K. & Milne, B. (2021), 'Understanding and Combatting Youth Experiences of Image-Based Sexual Harassment and Abuse', available at https://www.ascl.org.uk/ASCL/media/ASCL/Our%20view/Campaigns/Understanding-and-combatting-youth-experiences-of-image-based-sexual-harassment-and-abuse-full-report.pdf accessed 29 July 2024.

60 X Help Center, Adult Content, available at https://help.x.com/en/rules-and-policies/adult-content accessed 11 December 2024.

61 British Board of Film Classification and Revealing Reality (January 2020), 'Young people, Pornography and Age-verification', p. 6, available at BBFC-Young-people-and-pornography-Final-report-2401.pdf (revealingreality.co.uk) accessed 29 July 2024.

62 Children's Commissioner (January 2023), 'A lot of it is actually just abuse: Young people and pornography', p. 5, available at https://www.childrenscommissioner.gov.uk/report/a-lot-of-it-is-actually-just-abuse-young-people-and-pornography/ accessed 29 July 2024.

63 Children's Commissioner (January 2023), 'A lot of it is actually just abuse: Young people and pornography', p. 8, available at https://www.childrenscommissioner.gov.uk/report/a-lot-of-it-is-actually-just-abuse-young-people-and-pornography/ accessed 29 July 2024.

64 British Board of Film Classification and Revealing Reality (January 2020), 'Young people, Pornography and Age-verification', p. 50, available at BBFC-Young-people-and-pornography-Final-report-2401.pdf (revealingreality.co.uk) accessed 29 July 2024.

65 British Board of Film Classification and Revealing Reality (January 2020), 'Young people, Pornography and Age-verification', p. 46, available at BBFC-Young-people-and-pornography-Final-report-2401.pdf (revealingreality.co.uk) accessed 29 July 2024.

66 British Board of Film Classification and Revealing Reality, 'Young people, Pornography and Age-verification', January 2020BBFC-Young-people-and-pornography-Final-report-2401.pdf (revealingreality.co.uk) p. 32, p. 46, accessed 14 January 2025. There was a big disparity in this statistic between the children identifying as LGB (61% of those who've seen it have learnt from pornography—n=56) and those identifying as heterosexual (41% of n=59324).

67 British Board of Film Classification and Revealing Reality, 'Young people, Pornography and Age-verification, January 2020BBFC-Young-people-and-pornography-Final-report-2401.pdf (revealingreality.co.uk) p. 33, p. 46, accessed 29 July 2024.

68 Children's Commissioner (January 2023), 'A lot of it is actually just abuse: Young people and pornography', available at https://www.childrenscommissioner.gov.uk/report/a-lot-of-it-is-actually-just-abuse-young-people-and-pornography/, p. 4. p. 12, accessed 29 July 2024.

69 Fritz, N. et al. (2020), 'A Descriptive Analysis of the Types, Targets, and Relative Frequency of Aggression in Mainstream Pornography', *Archives of Sexual Behavior*, Springer US, 49(8), pp. 3041 doi: 10.1007/s10508-020-01773-0.

70 Fritz, N. et al. (2020), 'A Descriptive Analysis of the Types, Targets, and Relative Frequency of Aggression in Mainstream Pornography', *Archives of Sexual Behavior*, Springer US, 49(8), pp. 3041–doi: 10.1007/s10508-020-01773-0.

71 Children's Commissioner (January 2023), 'A lot of it is actually just abuse: Young people and pornography', p. 5, available at https://www.childrenscommissioner.gov.uk/report/a-lot-of-it-is-actually-just-abuse-young-people-and-pornography/ accessed 29 July 2024.
72 Children's Commissioner (January 2023), 'A lot of it is actually just abuse: Young people and pornography', p. 8, available at https://www.childrenscommissioner.gov.uk/report/a-lot-of-it-is-actually-just-abuse-young-people-and-pornography/ accessed 29 July 2024.
73 Children's Commissioner (January 2023), 'A lot of it is actually just abuse: Young people and pornography', p. 8, available at https://www.childrenscommissioner.gov.uk/report/a-lot-of-it-is-actually-just-abuse-young-people-and-pornography/ accessed 29 July 2024.
74 Sharpe, M. & Mead, D. (2021), 'Problematic Pornography Use: Legal and Health Policy Considerations', *Current Addiction Reports*, 8, pp. 556–67 doi: 10.1007/s40429-021-00390-8.
75 Government Equalities Office (15 January 2021), 'The relationship between pornography use and harmful sexual behaviours', available at https://www.gov.uk/government/publications/the-relationship-between-pornography-use-and-harmful-sexual-behaviours/the-relationship-between-pornography-use-and-harmful-sexual-behaviours, accessed 30 July 2024.
76 Ringrose, J., Regehr K. & Milne, B. (2021), 'Understanding and Combatting Youth Experiences of Image-Based Sexual Harassment and Abuse, available at https://www.ascl.org.uk/ASCL/media/ASCL/Our%20view/Campaigns/Understanding-and-combatting-youth-experiences-of-image-based-sexual-harassment-and-abuse-full-report.pdf accessed 29 July 2024.
77 Ofcom (15 March 2024), 'Encountering violent online content starts at primary school', available at https://www.ofcom.org.uk/online-safety/protecting-children/encountering-violent-online-content-starts-at-primary-school/#:~:text=Children%20first%20see%20violent%20online,new%20research%20commissioned%20by%20Ofcom accessed 21 November 2024.
78 euConsent available at https://euconsent.eu/ accessed 6 December 2024.

79 Metz, S. (4 May 2023), 'Law requiring porn sites verify user ages takes effect in Utah', *The Independent*, available at https://www.independent.co.uk/news/world/americas/porn-hub-sites-utah-law-age-b2332444.html accessed 6 December 2024.

80 Ofcom (December 2023), 'Implementing the Online Safety Act: Protecting children from online pornography', available at https://www.ofcom.org.uk/online-safety/protecting-children/implementing-the-online-safety-act-protecting-children/ accessed 6 December 2024.

81 Gerken, T. (January 2025), 'All porn sites must "robustly" verify UK user ages by July', available at https://www.bbc.co.uk/news/articles/cwye3qw7gv7o accessed 21 January 2025.

82 Bows, H., 'Introduction', and Keene, S., 'Defining Rough Sex Via Mainstream Pornography', in Jonathan Herring (ed.) (2022), *'Rough Sex' and the Criminal Law: Global Perspectives*, available at https://www.emerald.com/insight/search?q=Jonathan%20Herring accessed 10 January 2025.

83 Keene, S., 'Defining Rough Sex Via Mainstream Pornography', in Jonathan Herring (ed.) (2022), *'Rough Sex' and the Criminal Law: Global Perspectives*, available at https://www.emerald.com/insight/search?q=Jonathan%20Herring accessed 10 January 2025.

84 Children's Commissioner (16 December 2021), 'The things I wish my parents had known: young people's advice on talking to your child about online sexual harassment', available at https://www.childrenscommissioner.gov.uk/news/the-things-i-wish-my-parents-had-known-young-peoples-advice-on-talking-to-your-child-about-online-sexual-harassment/ accessed 20 August 2024.

85 Ramey, Carl R. (1994), 'In the Battle Over TV Violence, The Communications Act Should Be Cheered Not Changed!', *Federal Communications Law Journal*, vol. 47 issue 2, Article 31, available at https://www.repository.law.indiana.edu/cgi/viewcontent.cgi?referer=&httpsredir=1&article=1070&context=fclj accessed 20 August 2024.

86 Ringrose, R. Regehr, K., and Milne, B., 'Understanding and

Combatting Youth Experiences of Image-Based Sexual Harassment and Abuse', available at https://www.ascl.org.uk/ASCL/media/ASCL/Our%20view/Campaigns/Understanding-and-combatting-youth-experiences-of-image-based-sexual-harassment-and-abuse-full-report.pdf and Ringrose, R. & Regehr K. (2023), 'Recognizing and addressing how gender shapes young people's experiences of image-based sexual harassment and abuse (IBSHA) in educational settings', *Journal of Social Issues*. 79(4) 1251–81.

87 Ringrose, J., Regehr, K. & Milne, B., 'Understanding and Combatting Youth Experiences of Image-Based Sexual Harassment and Abuse, available at https://www.ascl.org.uk/ASCL/media/ASCL/Our%20view/Campaigns/Understanding-and-combatting-youth-experiences-of-image-based-sexual-harassment-and-abuse-full-report.pdf accessed 29 July 2024.

88 Ringrose and Regehr (in press), *Teens, Nudes and Image Based Abuse*, Basingstoke and London: Palgrave Macmillan.

89 Ringrose and Regehr (in press), *Teens, Nudes and Image Based Abuse*, Basingstoke and London: Palgrave Macmillan.

90 Ringrose, J., Regehr K. & Milne, B. (2021), 'Understanding and Combatting Youth Experiences of Image-Based Sexual Harassment and Abuse', available at https://www.ascl.org.uk/ASCL/media/ASCL/Our%20view/Campaigns/Understanding-and-combatting-youth-experiences-of-image-based-sexual-harassment-and-abuse-full-report.pdf accessed 29 July 2024.

91 UK Government, 'Cyberflashing to become a criminal offence', 13 March 2022, https://www.gov.uk/government/news/cyberflashing-to-become-a-criminal-offence accessed 30 July 2024.

92 Ringrose and Regehr (in press), *Teens, Nudes and Image Based Abuse*, Basingstoke and London: Palgrave Macmillan.

93 Milmo, D. (30 September 2022), 'Social media firms "monetising" misery', says Molly Russell's father after inquest', *The Guardian*, https://www.theguardian.com/uk-news/2022/sep/30/molly-russell-died-while-suffering-negative-effects-of-online-content-rules-coroner accessed 29 July 2024.

Chapter 4

1. Dr Caitlin Shaughnessy and Dr Katharine Smales.
2. Regehr, Shaughnessy and Smales (2025), 'Digital Nutrition: rethinking digital literacy', in press.
3. Regehr, Shaughnessy and Smales (2025), 'Digital Nutrition: rethinking digital literacy', in press.
4. Regehr, Shaughnessy and Smales (2025), 'Digital Nutrition: rethinking digital literacy', in press.
5. Regehr, Shaughnessy and Smales (2025), 'Digital Nutrition: rethinking digital literacy', in press.
6. Rear, J. (1 May 2020), 'The best kids smart watch for parents to buy', *The Telegraph*, available at https://www.telegraph.co.uk/recommended/kids/best-kids-smart-watch-parents-buy/ – 'Oddly you can turn off the friends chat in school mode but you can't turn off the family chat. I've read enough parental advice columns to know that relatives (often grandparents) are not good at respecting boundaries in this regard and would happily spend all day chatting to your children, much to the chagrin of their teachers. Watch out for that.'
7. 'Using your mobile or smartphone', RNID, https://rnid.org.uk/information-and-support/technology-and-products/using-your-mobile-or-smartphone/
8. Tan, H. L., Aplin, T., McAuliffe, T. & Gullo, H. (2022), 'An exploration of smartphone use by, and support for people with vision impairment: a scoping review', *Disability and Rehabilitation: Assistive Technology*, 19(2), 107–32. https://doi.org/10.1080/17483107.2022.2092223
9. Extracts from a letter to Gillian Keegan from JDRF (now Breakthrough T1D), 4 October 2023: Letter to Gillian Keegan about the use of mobile phones in schools, available at https://breakthrought1d.org.uk/news/letter-to-gillian-keegan-about-the-use-of-mobile-phones-in-schools/
10. 'The Smartphone Generation Needs Computer Help' (2019), *The*

Atlantic, available at https://www.theatlantic.com/sponsored/grow-google-2019/smartphone-generation-computer-help/3127/ accessed 21 November 2024.

11 In 2014 the National Institute for Health and Care Excellence (NICE) suggested that children should have TV-free days or have two-hour limits on the time spent in front of screens. This advice has since been removed from their website, but you can see its announcement reported in news articles, for example: Arthur, C. (23 September 2014), 'Of course children need limits on their screen time – but how to enforce it?', *The Guardian*, available at https://www.theguardian.com/commentisfree/2014/sep/23/children-restrict-screen-time-nice-how-enforce-it accessed 21 November 2024.

12 Karim, J., 'Illinois Commencement 2007, pt 2', available at https://youtu.be/24yglUYbKXE accessed 20 September 2024.

13 Karim, J., 'Illinois Commencement 2007, pt 2', available at https://youtu.be/24yglUYbKXE accessed 20 September 2024.

14 'The History of YouTube, Part 1, One Time on the Internet' (22 September 2021), available at https://podcasts.apple.com/gb/podcast/22-the-history-of-youtube-part-1/id1547910392?i=1000536242614

15 'The History of YouTube, Part 1, One Time on the Internet' (22 September 2021), available at https://podcasts.apple.com/gb/podcast/22-the-history-of-youtube-part-1/id1547910392?i=1000536242614

16 'The History of YouTube, Part 1, One Time on the Internet' (22 September 2021), available at https://podcasts.apple.com/gb/podcast/22-the-history-of-youtube-part-1/id1547910392?i=1000536242614

17 Pew Research Center (July 2020), 'Parenting Children in the Age of Screens', available at https://www.pewresearch.org/internet/2020/07/28/parenting-children-in-the-age-of-screens/ accessed 6 December 2024.

18 In an open letter to *The Guardian* in 2017, an international group of scientists described the concept of screen-time as 'simplistic

and arguably meaningless'. Available at *The Guardian*, 6th Jan, 2017, 'Screen time guidelines need to be built on evidence, not hype', available at https://www.theguardian.com/science/head-quarters/2017/jan/06/screen-time-guidelines-need-to-be-built-on-evidence-not-hype accessed 8 October 2024.

19 'Encourage using screens in ways that build creativity and connection with family and friends', available at https://www.aacap.org/AACAP/Families_and_Youth/Facts_for_Families/FFF-Guide/Children-And-Watching-TV-054.aspx#:~:text=Between%2018%20and%2024%20months,limit%20activities%20that%20include%20screens.

20 The Advertising Standards Agency which regulates advertising, including advertising to children, published the following advice on 23 March 2023, 'Recognising ads: Social media and influencer marketing' (available at https://www.asa.org.uk/advice-online/recognising-ads-social-media.html#children accessed 29 January 2025). This advice states 'The ASA's research on labelling influencer marketing (available at https://www.asa.org.uk/news/clarity-for-consumers-why-ad-is-essential-in-paid-influencer-posts.html accessed 29 July 2025) found that social media users really struggle to tell apart advertising content from non-advertising content in this space, especially (but not only) when influencers use the same editorial style for both types of content. This is not all that surprising when you consider that most users are scrolling through a vast amount of content, at pace, swiftly moving from one piece of content to the next, within their already busy lives. When influencers and brands seek to seamlessly blend editorial and advertising, the onus is not on the consumer to do the work to establish when they are engaging with an ad – that is the responsibility of brands and influencers. It's therefore, especially important for those involved in influencer marketing to take particular care to ensure their advertising is obviously recognizable as such.' If it does count as advertising then the ASA advises that 'there are many different rules that could apply and the product being advertised'. In relation to children specifically it says:

'Although most social media platforms require users to be at least 13 years old to sign-up to access the platform, there are some where this is not the case e.g., YouTube. As such, any influencer marketing content that is directed at under-12s is likely to need to do more than simply include an "ad" label upfront. The ASA is yet to rule on any examples but for further guidance on the principles and examples in other media, see 'Recognising ads: Children (available at https://www.asa.org.uk/advice-online/recognising-ads-children.html accessed 29 January 2025'). This advises that 'When a marketing communication is directed at under-12s (through the selection of media and/or the content), highly immersive or significantly integrated into the surrounding editorial content and unlikely to be identified clearly from the context in which it appears, it will require enhanced disclosure. This means disclosures should be prominent, interruptive, and adequately indicate the commercial intent.'

21 Fang, K. et al. (2019), 'Screen time and childhood overweight/obesity: A systematic review and meta-analysis', *Child care, health and development*, vol. 45 (5), pp. 744–53, available at https://pubmed.ncbi.nlm.nih.gov/31270831/

22 Saunders et al. (20 November 2013), 'Associations of Sedentary Behavior, Sedentary Bouts and Breaks in Sedentary Time with Cardiometabolic Risk in Children with a Family History of Obesity', PLOS One, available at https://doi.org/10.1371/journal.pone.0079143; Thorp, A. et al. (2011), 'Sedentary Behaviors and Subsequent Health Outcomes in Adults: A Systematic Review of Longitudinal Studies, 1996–2011', *American Journal of Preventive Medicine*, vol. 41, issue 2, August 2011, pp. 207–15, doi: 10.1016/j.amepre.2011.05.004.

23 Fang K. et al. (2019), 'Screen time and childhood overweight/obesity: A systematic review and meta-analysis', *Child: Care, Health and Development*, vol. 45 (5), pp. 744–53, available at https://pubmed.ncbi.nlm.nih.gov/31270831/

24 Sweetser, P., Johnson, D., Ozdowska, A. & Wyeth, P. (2012), 'Active versus Passive Screen Time for Young Children', *Australasian*

Journal of Early Childhood, 37(4), pp. 94–8, available at https://journals.sagepub.com/doi/10.1177/183693911203700413

25 A study from 2020 found that 'passive' and 'active' activity on social media had different consequences for well-being. It found that 'passive' engagement with social media created feelings of social comparisons and envy, while 'active' engagement supported social capital and identity and stimulated feelings of social connectedness. Kim et al. (2020), 'Differential associations between passive and active forms of screen time and adolescent mood and anxiety disorders', *Social Psychiatry and Psychiatric Epidemiology*, 55: 1469–78, available at https://link.springer.com/article/10.1007/s00127-020-01833-9

26 Haidt, J. (2024), *The Anxious Generation*, London: Allen Lane.

27 Guidance of Royal College of Paediatrics and Child Health (2019), author's own copy. This screen-time guidance is no longer available online, but you can see it referred to and referenced via other sources including the press release from the Royal College of Paediatrics and Child Health, 4 January 2019, 'Build screen time around family activities, not the other way round, parents told', available at https://www.rcpch.ac.uk/news-events/news/build-screen-time-around-family-activities-not-other-way-round-parents-told accessed 21 November 2024 and The British Association for Counselling and Psychotherapy, 'New guidance for parents about children's screen time', 4 January 2019, https://www.bacp.co.uk/news/news-from-bacp/2019/4-january-new-guidance-for-parents-about-children-s-screen-time/ accessed 21 October 2024.

28 Martinelli, K., 'Neurodivergent Kids and Screen Time', Child Mind Institute, available at https://childmind.org/article/screens-and-neurodivergent-kids/#:~:text=These%20benefits%20can%20significantly%20enhance,soothing%20and%20help%20manage%20anxiety

29 Martinelli, K., 'Neurodivergent Kids and Screen Time', Child Mind Institute, available at https://childmind.org/article/screens-and-neurodivergent-kids/#:~:text=These%20benefits%20can%20

significantly%20enhance,soothing%20and%20help%20manage%20anxiety.
30. BBC, Children's Hour, available at https://www.bbc.co.uk/programmes/p0421yjh
31. 'Encourage using screens in ways that build creativity and connection with family and friends', available at https://www.aacap.org/AACAP/Families_and_Youth/Facts_for_Families/FFF-Guide/Children-And-Watching-TV-054.aspx#:~:text=Between%2018%20and%2024%20months,limit%20activities%20that%20include%20screens

Chapter 5

1. Coldplay – 'A Sky Full of Stars', Live @ Glastonbury 2024, available from 2 mins 35 seconds: https://www.dailymotion.com/video/x91h6je accessed 24 January 2025.
2. The History of the Eatwell Guide, available at https://my-bmi.co.uk/education/the-history-of-the-eatwell-guide/ accessed 17 October 2024.
3. See Van Tulleken, C. (2024), *Ultra-Processed People: Why Do We All Eat Stuff That Isn't Food . . . and Why Can't We Stop?*, London: Penguin.
4. Regehr, K., Shaughnessy, C., Zhao, M. & Shaughnessy, N. (2024), 'Safer Scrolling: How algorithms popularise and gamify online hate and misogyny for young people', https://www.ascl.org.uk/ASCL/media/ASCL/Help%20and%20advice/Inclusion/Safer-scrolling.pdf accessed 29 July 2024.
5. Orben, A. (2022), 'Digital Diet: A 21st century approach to understanding digital technologies and development', *Infant and Child Development*, 31(1); Internet Matters (2022), 'Balance Screen Time: How to Create a balanced digital diet', available at https://www.internetmatters.org/resources/creating-a-balanced-digital-diet-with-screen-time-tips/ accessed 17 October 2024; The Wellbeing Thesis (2023), 'Digital Wellbeing – How to have a

healthy digital diet', available at https://thewellbeingthesis.org.uk/foundations-for-success/digital-wellbeing-how-to-have-a-healthy-digital-diet/ accessed 17 October 2024.

6 Orben, A. (2022), 'Digital Diet: A 21st century approach to understanding digital technologies and development', *Infant and Child Development*, 31(1); Internet Matters (2022), 'Balance Screen Time: How to Create a balanced digital diet', available at https://www.internetmatters.org/resources/creating-a-balanced-digital-diet-with-screen-time-tips/

7 Regehr, Shaughnessy and Smales (2025), 'Digital Nutrition: rethinking digital literacy', in press.

8 US Department of Health, Education, and the US Department of Agriculture (USDA) (1992), Food Guide Pyramid, available at https://www.dietaryguidelines.gov/sites/default/files/2019-05/2000%20Dietary%20Guidelines%20for%20Americans.pdf accessed 17 October 2024.

9 Orben, A. (2022), 'Digital Diet: A 21st century approach to understanding digital technologies and development', *Infant and Child Development*, 31(1).

10 Regehr, Shaughnessy and Smales (2025), 'Digital Nutrition: rethinking digital literacy', in Press.

11 Bonini and Treré argue for the term algorithmic resistance because the industry term 'gaming the algorithm' does not sufficiently account for the subversive and political quality of these movements. See Bonini, T. & Treré, E. (2024), *Algorithms of Resistance: The Everyday Fight Against Platform Power*, Cambridge, MA: The MIT Press, 1st ed.

12 Bonini, T. & Treré, E. (2024), *Algorithms of Resistance: The Everyday Fight Against Platform Power*, Cambridge, MA: The MIT Press, 1st ed., p. 2.

13 Bonini, T. & Treré, E. (2024), *Algorithms of Resistance: The Everyday Fight Against Platform Power*, Cambridge, MA: The MIT Press, 1st ed.

14 According to former TikTok employee and whistleblower Andrew Kaung, 'the algorithms' fuel is engagement, regardless of whether

the engagement is positive or negative.' Reported in Spring, M., '"It stains your brain": How social media algorithms show violence to boys', *BBC News*, 2 September 2024, https://www.bbc.co.uk/news/articles/c4gdqzxypdzo accessed 11 February 2025.
15 Regehr, Shaughnessy and Smales (2025), 'Digital Nutrition: rethinking digital literacy', in press.
16 Regehr, Shaughnessy and Smales (2025), 'Digital Nutrition: rethinking digital literacy', in press.
17 Regehr, Shaughnessy and Smales (2025), 'Digital Nutrition: rethinking digital literacy', in press.

Chapter 6

1 'Our Mission', Redemption Roasters, available at https://www.redemptionroasters.com/our-mission accessed 15 November 2024.
2 Millennials (born 1981 – 1996 according to the Pew Research Centre: https://www.pewresearch.org/short-reads/2019/01/17/where-millennials-end-and-generation-z-begins/) are old now, by the way.
3 Impress, 20 July 2023, Spotlight On | Daisy Greenwell, Positive News editor, available at https://www.impressorg.com/spotlight-on-daisy-greenwell-positive-news-editor/ accessed 11 February 2025, see also Daisy Greenwell on Instagram @daisygreenwell
4 See Greenwell, D. (29 February 2024), 'I was terrified of giving my child a phone - so I made a pact with 10,000 other parents not to', iNews, available at https://inews.co.uk/inews-lifestyle/terrified-child-phone-pact-parents-2930468 accessed 11 February 2025, and Moshakis, A., 30 June 2024, '"We wanted to change the norm on smartphone use": grassroots campaigners on a phone-free childhood', *The Guardian*, available at https://www.theguardian.com/lifeandstyle/article/2024/jun/30/we-wanted-to-change-the-norm-on-smartphone-use-grassroots-campaigners-on-a-phone-free-childhood accessed 11 February 2025.
5 Banfield-Nwachi, M. (February 2024), ' "It went nuts": Thousands

join UK parents calling for smartphone-free childhood', *The Guardian*, available at https://www.theguardian.com/technology/2024/feb/17/thousands-join-uk-parents-calling-for-smartphone-free-childhood accessed 15 November 2024.
6. Personal communication with Daisy Greenwell.
7. Year nine in the UK includes children aged thirteen to fourteen years old.
8. Impress, 20 July 2023, Spotlight On | Daisy Greenwell, Positive News editor, available at https://www.impressorg.com/spotlight-on-daisy-greenwell-positive-news-editor/ accessed 11 February 2025.
9. Transcript: US Senate Judiciary Committee Hearing on 'Big Tech and the Online Child Sexual Exploitation Crisis', Tech Policy Press, available at https://www.techpolicy.press/transcript-us-senate-judiciary-committee-hearing-on-big-tech-and-the-online-child-sexual-exploitation-crisis/ accessed 19 December 2024.
10. Department for Science Innovation and Technology and The Rt. Hon Peter Kyle MP, First UK–US online safety agreement pledges closer cooperation to keep children safe online, available at https://www.gov.uk/government/news/first-uk-us-online-safety-agreement-pledges-closer-co-operation-to-keep-children-safe-online, reported Vallance, S. & Singleton, T. (10 October 2024), '"Argument won" on smartphones in schools', minister says, *BBC News*, available at https://www.bbc.co.uk/news/articles/c8915q82qz5o#:~:text=Limited%20evidence&text=The%20UK%20government%20acknowledged%20that,the%20agreement%20to%20address%20this accessed 15 November 2024.
11. Sibbald, B. (1998), 'Why Are Randomised Controlled Trials Important', *BMJ*, 316:201
12. Cancer Research UK, 'How Does Smoking Cause Cancer', available at https://www.cancerresearchuk.org/about-cancer/causes-of-cancer/smoking-and-cancer/how-does-smoking-cause-cancer accessed 26 February 2025.

13 Johnathan Haidt has compiled much of the evidence here. See Haidt, Twenge and Rausch (ongoing) 'Social Media and Mental Health: A Collaborative Review', available at https://docs.google.com/document/d/1w-HOfseF2wF9YIpXwUUtP65-olnkPyWcgF5BiAtBEy0/edit?tab=t.0 accessed 25 February 2025.

14 Amy Orben uses the concept of digital stress to describe the process through which adolescents ruminate on online experiences. Orban et al. cite a cross-sectional study (Reinecke et al. (2017) which found that younger users' (age 14–34 years and 35–49 years) perception of social pressure to be constantly available was related to communication load (measured by questions about the amount of use, as well as the urge to check email and social media) and Internet multitasking, whereas this was not the case for older users aged 50–85 years. Orben, A., Meier, A., Dalgleish, T. et al., 'Mechanisms linking social media use to adolescent mental health vulnerability', *Nature Reviews Psychology* 3, 407–23 (2024), https://doi.org/10.1038/s44159-024-00307-y Reinecke, L., Aufenanger, S., Beutel, M.E., Dreier, M., Quiring, O., Stark, B., Wölfling, K., & Müller, K.W. (2016): 'Digital Stress over the Life Span: The Effects of Communication Load and Internet Multitasking on Perceived Stress and Psychological Health Impairments in a German Probability Sample', *Media Psychology*, DOI: 10.1080/15213269.2015.1121832

15 @elonmusk (October 26 2022) 'Entering Twitter HQ – let that sink in!' available at https://x.com/elonmusk/status/1585341984679469056?lang=en accessed 24 January 2025.

16 @elonmusk, 30 October 2022, 'My title is Chief Twit right there in the bio. No idea where the CEO is', available at https://x.com/elonmusk/status/1586685737591709696 accessed 24 January 2025.

17 @elonmusk, 28 October 2022, 'the bird is freed', available at https://x.com/elonmusk/status/1585841080431321088 accessed 24 January 2025.

18 Lotan, G. et al. (2011), 'The Arab Spring| the revolutions were tweeted: Information flows during the 2011 Tunisian and Egyptian

revolutions', *International Journal of Communication*, vol. 5, available at https://ijoc.org/index.php/ijoc/article/view/1246.

19 'Hope to Nope: Graphics and Politics 2008 to 2018' exhibition at the Design Museum, 28 March to 12 August 2018, as described at https://astrofella.wordpress.com/2018/07/05/hope-to-nope-graphics-and-politics-design-museum/ and see Lowery, W. (17 January 2017), 'Black Lives Matter: the birth of a movement', *The Guardian*, available at https://www.theguardian.com/us-news/2017/jan/17/black-lives-matter-birth-of-a-movement.

20 Whitehead, T. (2015), 'Paris Charlie Hebdo attack: Je Suis Charlie hashtag one of most popular in Twitter history', available at https://www.telegraph.co.uk/news/worldnews/europe/france/11336879/Paris-Charlie-Hebdo-attack-Je-Suis-Charlie-hashtag-one-of-most-popular-in-Twitter-history.html accessed 15 November 2024.

21 Gerbaudo, P. (2012), *Tweets and the Streets: Social Media and Contemporary Activism*, London: Pluto Press.

22 Gerbaudo, P. (2012), *Tweets and the Streets: Social Media and Contemporary Activism*, London: Pluto Press.

23 Slacktivism is defined as 'activity that uses the internet to support political or social causes in a way that does not need much effort, for example creating or signing online petitions' by the *Cambridge Dictionary*, at https://dictionary.cambridge.org/dictionary/english/slacktivism accessed 10 December 2024.

24 Gladwell, M. (2010), 'Small Change', *The New Yorker*, available at https://www.newyorker.com/magazine/2010/10/04/small-change-malcolm-gladwell?currentPage=all

25 Dean, J. (2005), 'Communicative Capitalism: Circulation and the Foreclosure of Politics', *Cultural Politics*, vol. 1, issue 1, pp. 51–74, at p. 70, available at https://commonconf.wordpress.com/wp-content/uploads/2010/09/proofs-of-tech-fetish.pdf accessed 15 November 2024.

26 BBC (2020), 'Trump in Tweets', available at https://www.bbc.co.uk/iplayer/episode/p08hsxd5/trump-in-tweets accessed 15 November 2024.

27 BBC (2020), 'Trump in Tweets', available at https://www.bbc.

co.uk/iplayer/episode/p08hsxd5/trump-in-tweets accessed 15 November 2024.

28. *BBC News*, (May 2020), 'Twitter hides Trump tweet for "glorifying violence"', available at https://www.bbc.co.uk/news/technology-52846679 accessed 21 February 2025.

29. *BBC News* (January 2021), 'Twitter "permanently suspends" Trump's account', available at https://www.bbc.co.uk/news/world-us-canada-55597840 accessed 15 November 2024.

30. Allyn, B. (25 April 2022), 'Elon Musk bought Twitter. Here's what he says he'll do next', available at https://www.npr.org/2022/04/25/1094671225/elon-musk-bought-twitter-plans accessed 15 November 2022.

31. @elonmusk, 15 November 2023, 'You have said the actual truth', available at https://x.com/elonmusk/status/1724908287471272299?ref_src=twsrc%5Etfw%7Ctwcamp%5Etweetembed%7Ctwterm%5E1724908287471272299%7Ctwgr%5E170a909cd2afffd9522e72920ec78d5651b07acc%7Ctwcon%5Es1_&ref_url=https%3A%2F%2F accessed 15 November 2024.

32. Dealbook Summit, 2023. Lincoln Center on November 29, 2023 in New York City. Available at 11 mins 19 seconds: https://www.youtube.com/watch?v=2BfMuHDfGJI accessed 3 December 2024. Also reported in *Le Monde* with AFP (November 2023), 'Musk regrets controversial post but won't bow to advertiser '"blackmail"', available at https://www.lemonde.fr/en/pixels/article/2023/11/30/musk-regrets-controversial-post-but-won-t-bow-to-advertiser-blackmail_6301678_13.html# accessed 15 November 2024.

33. Dealbook Summit, 2023. Lincoln Center on November 29, 2023 in New York City. Available at 13 mins 22 seconds: https://www.youtube.com/watch?v=2BfMuHDfGJI accessed 3 December 2024. Also reported in *France 24*, (30th November 2023) 'Musk apologizes for comment seen as anti-Semitic but accuses fleeing advertisers of "blackmail"' available at https://www.france24.com/en/technology/20231130-musk-says-he-regrets-controversial-post-but-

lashes-out-over-fleeing-advertisers-blackmail accessed 7th March 2025

34   Heater, B. (6 August 2024), 'X files antitrust suit against advertising groups over "systematic illegal boycott"', *TechCrunch* available at https://techcrunch.com/2024/08/06/x-files-suit-against-advertising-groups-over-systematic-illegal-boycott/ accessed 11 December 2024.

35   Statement on the Global Alliance for Responsible Media (GARM), available at https://wfanet.org/leadership/garm/about-garm accessed 15 November 2024.

36   Statement on the Global Alliance for Responsible Media (GARM), available at https://wfanet.org/leadership/garm/about-garm accessed 24 January 2025

37   Maruf, R. and Duffy, C., CNN, (9 August 2024), 'Elon Musk's X just sued a nonprofit advertising group out of existence', available at https://edition.cnn.com/2024/08/09/tech/elon-musk-garm-advertisers-lawsuit/index.html accessed 24 January 2024.

38   Scarcella, M., Reuters (11 October 2024), 'Elon Musk's X drops Unilever from advertiser boycott lawsuit', available at https://www.reuters.com/legal/elon-musks-x-drops-unilever-advertiser-boycott-lawsuit-2024-10-11/ accessed 24 January 2024.

39   Statement on the Global Alliance for Responsible Media (GARM), available at https://www.wfanet.org/knowledge/item/2024/08/09/wfa-discontinues-garm accessed 24 November 2024.

40   X News (11 October 2024), 'X is pleased to have reached an agreement with Unilever', available at https://x.com/XNews/status/1844737849456771425?lang=en-GB accessed 26 February 2025.

41   Stempel, J., Reuters (25 March, 2024), 'Musk's X Corp loses lawsuit against hate speech watchdog', available at https://www.reuters.com/technology/musks-x-corp-loses-lawsuit-against-hate-speech-watchdog-2024-03-25/ accessed 24 January 2025.

42   The Associated Press, NPR (21 November 2023), 'Musk's X sues Media Matters over its report on ads next to hate groups' posts', available at https://www.npr.org/2023/11/21/1214338766/

musks-x-sues-media-matters-over-its-report-on-ads-next-to-hate-groups-posts accessed 24 January 2025.

43 Advertising companies are concerned not just with understanding how many people are on a social media platform but also what their engagement levels are. These engagement levels are used by social media companies to provide advertisers with metrics to demonstrate their platforms' suitability for advertisers' brands.

44 Personal correspondence with Prof. Lewis Griffin, November 2024.

45 Wakabayashi, D. & Maheshwari, S. (20 Feb 2019), New York Times, 'Advertisers Boycott YouTube After Pedophiles Swarm Comments on Videos of Children', available at https://www.nytimes.com/2019/02/20/technology/youtube-pedophiles.html accessed 24 January 2025

46 Alexander, J., The Verge (21 Feb 2019), 'YouTube terminates more than 400 channels following child exploitation controversy / And it's deleted tens of millions of comments', available at https://www.theverge.com/2019/2/21/18234494/youtube-child-exploitation-channel-termination-comments-philip-defranco-creators accessed 24 January 2025.

47 Kumar, S. (2019), 'The algorithmic dance: YouTube's Adpocalypse and the gatekeeping of cultural content on digital platforms', *Internet Policy Review*, 8(2). https://doi.org/10.14763/2019.2.1417

48 Conklin, A., Fox Business (22 July 2020), 'Brands that pulled Facebook ads with #StopHateForProfit campaign', available at https://www.foxbusiness.com/technology/brands-facebook-ads-stop-hate-profit accessed 24 January 2025. See also Aziz, A. (June 2020) 'Facebook Ad Boycott Campaign "Stop Hate For Profit" Gathers Momentum And Scale: Inside The Movement For Change', Forbes.com, available at https://www.forbes.com/sites/afdhelaziz/2020/06/24/facebook-ad-boycott-campaign-stop-hate-for-profit-gathers-momentum-and-scale-inside-the-movement-for-change/ accessed 21 January 2025.

49 GARM: Brand Safety Floor + Suitability Framework, available at https://wfanet.org/l/library/download/urn:uuid:7d484745-41cd-4cce-a1b9-a1b4e30928ea/

garm+brand+safety+floor+suitability+frame work+23+sept.pdf accessed 15 November 2024.

50 Stetson, S. (30 March 2023), 'Meta launches brand suitability controls and third party verification for feed powered by AI', available at https://www.facebook.com/business/news/brand-safety-suitability-feed-control-verification/ accessed 15 November 2024.

51 Meta Business Help Centre, About Inventory Filter, available at https://en-gb.facebook.com/business/help/3001448133206080?id=1769156093197771 accessed 24 January 2025.

52 Correspondence and conversation with Tom Connaughton, former MD of Spotify.

53 About B Corp Certification, available at https://www.bcorporation.net/en-us/certification/ accessed 24 January 2025.

54 See The Byproducts of Buying Products, this chapter and the work of Dr Photini Vrikki cited therein.

55 Hank, M. (November 2024), 'Netflix documentary Buy Now! uncovers stealthy marketing tactics', *National Post*, available at https://nationalpost.com/entertainment/television/netflix-documentary-buy-now-uncovers-stealthy-marketing-tactics accessed 25 February 2025.

56 'Emissions from ChatGPT are much higher than from conventional search', available at https://limited.systems/articles/google-search-vs-chatgpt-emissions/#:~:text=If%20all%20search%20queries%20are,Emissions%20would%20increase%20by%2060x accessed 24 January 2024.

57 Heikkila, M., MIT Technology Review (December 2023), 'Making an image with generative AI uses as much energy as charging your phone', available at https://www.technologyreview.com/2023/12/01/1084189/making-an-image-with-generative-ai-uses-as-much-energy-as-charging-your-phone accessed 24 January 2025.

58 'Ecosia, Like Google but Greener', available at https://www.ecosia.org/

59 Rangappa, A. (12 December 2022), 'The Not-So-Invisible Hand in

Twitter's Marketplace of Ideas', available at https://asharangappa.substack.com/p/the-not-so-invisible-hand-in-twitters accessed 15 November 2024.

60 Hern, A. (6 April 2022), 'Pinterest announces ban on all climate misinformation', available at https://www.theguardian.com/technology/2022/apr/06/pinterest-announces-ban-on-all-climate-misinformation accessed 15 November 2024. It is also worth noting that Pinterest was one of the sites which Molly Russell had an account with and viewed harmful content on. At the time of the inquest Pinterest's head of community operations, Judson Hoffman, apologized after admitting the platform was 'not safe' when the fourteen-year-old used it. Mr Hoffman said he 'deeply regrets' posts viewed by Molly on Pinterest before her death, saying it was material he would 'not show to my children'. Available at Giordano, C. (23 September 2022), 'Molly Russell: Coroner issues warning as Instagram videos of "distressing nature" shown', *The Independent*, available at https://www.independent.co.uk/news/uk/home-news/molly-russell-inquest-instagram-videos-warning-b2174079.html accessed 6 December 2024.

61 'Brand safety on Pinterest', available at https://business.pinterest.com/en-gb/brand-safety/ accessed 21 November 2024.

62 Alfred, R. (29 September 2010), '1920: Radio Goes Commercial', available at https://www.wired.com/2010/09/0929ready-made-radio-receivers/ accessed 26 November 2024.

63 Federal Communications Commission, 'History of Commercial Radio', available at https://www.fcc.gov/media/radio/history-of-commercial-radio accessed 15 November 2024.

64 This mission statement was created by Lord Reith for the BBC as a corporation, in the 1930s. BBC, 'Mission, values and public purposes', available at https://www.bbc.com/aboutthebbc/governance/mission accessed 21 November 2024.

65 'The history of the BBC pips,', Royal Museums Greenwich, available at https://www.rmg.co.uk/stories/topics/bbc-pips-history-royal-observatory-greenwich-time-service, accessed 21 November 2024

66 WNET (PBS) pledge breaks (12 December 1993), available at

https://www.youtube.com/watch?v=YcgYzybciMU accessed 15 November 2024.

67 *The Moderators*, available at www.bbc.co.uk/programmes/m0024vtx accessed 26 November 2024. There is currently academic work being done at the University of Bristol on the experiences of moderators – see Haime, Z. et al. (2024), 'Experiences of moderation, moderators, and moderating by online users who engage with self-harm and suicide content', *medRxiv* doi: https://doi.org/10.1101/2024.02.15.24302878 accessed 21 November 2024.

68 David Willner, a member of Facebook's original team of moderators, quoted on the Radio 4 series *The Moderators*, available at www.bbc.co.uk/programmes/m0024vtx accessed 26 November 2024.

69 Regehr, C., Regehr, K., Birze, A. & Duff, W. (2023), 'Troubling Records: Managing and Conserving Mediated Artifacts of Violent Crime', *Archivaria* 95 (Spring) 6–40, available at https://archivaria.ca/index.php/archivaria/article/view/13895; Regehr, C., Regehr, K. & Birze, A. (2022), 'Traumatic Residue, Mediated Remembering and Video Evidence of Sexual Violence: A Case Study', *International Journal of Law and Psychiatry* 81 (2) https://doi.org/10.1016/j.ijlp.2022.101778; Birze, A., Regehr, C. & Regehr, K. (2022) 'Organizational Support for the Potentially Traumatic Impact of Video Evidence of Violent Crime in the Criminal Justice System: "We're almost making more victims"', *International Review of Victimology*, https://journals.sagepub.com/doi/10.1177/02697580221112436; Birze, A., Regehr, K. & Regehr, C. (2022), 'Workplace Trauma in a Digital Age: The Impact of Video Evidence of Violent Crime on Criminal Justice Professionals', *Journal of Interpersonal Violence* 38 (1–2) https://journals.sagepub.com/doi/10.1177/08862605221090571; Regehr, K., Birze, A. and Regehr, C. (2021), 'Technology facilitated re-victimization: How video evidence of sexual violence contributes to mediated cycles of abuse, *Crime, Media, Culture* 10.1177/17416590211050333.

70 Regehr, Shaughnessy and Smales (2025), 'Digital Nutrition: rethinking digital literacy, in press.

71 Dr Sarah T. Roberts, paraphrased from the full quote: 'The fundamental role of content moderation of social media is actually a brand management function for the firms. The firms dreamt up content moderation not because they were necessarily concerned about users, but because they had to manage their own relationships with advertisers. And it turns out that a lot of mainstream advertisers don't want their ad for cookies or coffee or automobiles or whatever to be displayed next to some Nazi propaganda, right? And so that's why content moderation really came into being.' From the BBC radio series *The Moderators*, available at www.bbc.co.uk/programmes/m0024vtx accessed 26 November 2024.

72 BBC Editorial Guidelines, available at https://www.bbc.co.uk/editorialguidelines/ accessed 26 November 2024.

73 Kleinman, Z. (11 November 2024), 'I was moderating hundreds of horrific and traumatising videos', available at https://www.bbc.com/news/articles/crr9q2jz7y0o accessed 15 November 2024.

74 See *Good Morning Britain* (2021), 'Molly Russell's Father Wants Social Media Companies To Take Responsibility For Harmful Content', available at https://www.youtube.com/watch?v=ievi1Z6WUNY accessed 5 December 2024.

75 Kuenssberg, L. (11 January 2025), 'Molly Russell's dad warns UK "going backwards" on online safety and urges PM to act', *BBC News*, available at https://www.bbc.co.uk/news/articles/cp3j5kp8501o accessed 15 January 2025.

76 Green, D. A. (11 January 2025), 'The coming battle between social media and the state', *Financial Times*, available at https://www.ft.com/content/917c9535-1cdb-4f6a-9a15-1a0c83663bfd accessed 15 January 2025.

77 ITU website: https://www.itu.int/en/Pages/default.aspx

78 Watson, C. (11 April 2018), 'The key moments from Mark Zuckerberg's testimony to Congress', *The Guardian*, available at https://www.theguardian.com/technology/2018/apr/11/mark-zuckerbergs-testimony-to-congress-the-key-moments.

79 Griffin, A. (11 April 2018), 'Zuckerberg Congress hearing: The most

excruciating moments from the Facebook boss' questioning', *The Independent*, available at https://www.independent.co.uk/tech/facebook-mark-zuckerberg-hearing-congress-moments-whatsapp-twitter-a8299511.html accessed 3 December 2024.

80 'Senator Asks How Facebook Remains Free, Mark Zuckerberg Smirks: "We Run Ads"', *NBC News*, available at 32 seconds https://www.youtube.com/watch?v=n2H8wx1aBiQ accessed 3 December 2024.

81 *Wall Street Journal* Podcasts (August 2023), 'How Instagram's Algorithm Connects and Promotes Paedophile Network', available at https://www.wsj.com/podcasts/tech-news-briefing/how-instagrams-algorithm-connects-and-promotes-pedophile-network/a683c0b4-2e6f-4661-9973-10bd455db895 accessed 15 November 2024.

82 Forbes Breaking News (January 2024), 'Mark Zuckerberg Faces Grilling By Judiciary Committee Senators' | Hearing Of The Week, available at https://www.youtube.com/watch?v=SsiJFOXOQx4 accessed 15 November 2024.

83 'Transcript: US Senate Judiciary Committee Hearing on "Big Tech and the Online Child Sexual Exploitation Crisis"' (31 January 20024), available at https://www.techpolicy.press/transcript-us-senate-judiciary-committee-hearing-on-big-tech-and-the-online-child-sexual-exploitation-crisis/

84 Green, D. A. (11 January 2025), 'The coming battle between social media and the state', *Financial Times*, available at https://www.ft.com/content/917c9535-1cdb-4f6a-9a15-1a0c83663bfd accessed 14 January 2025.

85 The Digital Services Act, available at https://commission.europa.eu/strategy-and-policy/priorities-2019-2024/europe-fit-digital-age/digital-services-act_en accessed 15 November 2024.

86 Green, D. A. (11 January 2025), 'The coming battle between social media and the state', *Financial Times*, available at https://www.ft.com/content/917c9535-1cdb-4f6a-9a15-1a0c83663bfd accessed 14 January 2025.

87 Meta Platforms Inc., 'Annual Report Pursuant to Section 13 or 15(d)

of the Securities Exchange Act of 1934, For the fiscal year ended December 31, 2023', available at https://www.sec.gov/Archives/edgar/data/1326801/000132680124000012/meta-20231231.htm accessed 21 January 2025.

88 Riemer, K. & Peter, S. (2021), 'Algorithmic audiencing: Why we need to rethink free speech on social media', *Journal of Information Technology*, 36(4), 409–26 https://doi.org/10.1177/02683962211013358

89 Riemer, K. & Peter, S. (2021), 'Algorithmic audiencing: Why we need to rethink free speech on social media', *Journal of Information Technology*, 36(4), 409–26 https://doi.org/10.1177/02683962211013358

90 Waldron, J. (2012), *The Harm in Hate Speech*, Cambridge, MA: Harvard University Press.

91 Brown, R. (2016), 'Defusing hate: a strategic communication guide to counteract dangerous speech', US Holocaust Memorial Museum Washington, DC, https://www.ushmm.org/confront-genocide/how-to-prevent-genocide/hate-speech-and-incitement-to-genocide/defusing-hate-a-guide-to-counteract-dangerous-speech

92 Howard, J. W. (May 2019), 'Free Speech and Hate Speech', *Annual Review of Political Science*, vol. 22, pp. 93–109, although as previously noted Elon Musk has stated that the word 'cisgender' is hate speech.

93 Arun, A., Chhatani, S., An, J. & Kumaraguru, P. (2024), 'X-posing Free Speech: Examining the Impact of Moderation Relaxation on Online Social Networks', *Proceedings of the 8th Workshop on Online Abuse and Harms* (WOAH 2024), pp. 201–11, Mexico City, Mexico: Association for Computational Linguistics.

94 Regehr, Shaughnessy and Smales (2025), 'Digital Nutrition: rethinking digital literacy, in press.

95 Cohen, J. E. (2017), 'Law for the Platform Economy Symposium – Future-Proofing Law: From RDNA to Robots', *U.C.D.L. Rev.* 51, pp. 133–204.

96 Reports and Publications of the Surgeon General, US Department of Health and Human Services, available at https://www.hhs.gov/

surgeongeneral/reports-and-publications/index.html accessed 15 November 2024.

97 'Parents Under Pressure: The U.S. Surgeon General Advisory on the Mental Health and Well-Being of Parents', available at https://www.hhs.gov/surgeongeneral/priorities/parents/index.html accessed 15 November 2024.

98 In reporting on the new Surgeon General advisory on parenting, the *New York Times* contextualized contemporary parenting within a generational history situating the term 'parenting' as relatively new. That is, in the 1970s, 'parent' was only a noun rather than a verb, and generally parents did adult things while kids did kid things independently. Kids played outside, as the saying goes 'until the streetlamps came on'. In the 1980s, expert commentary on how to parent emerged with a focus on physical safety. But in the 1990s, there were developments in neuroscience, and culturally, we started to think about the impact of our actions on our kids. Women rested speakers on their bellies following recommendations to play classical music to babies in utero and suggestions emerged that your every interaction with your child could influence your child's development, behaviour and outcomes of success. The Surgeon General's report references 'intensive parenting', a term coined in the 1990s to describe a much more labour-intensive and time-consuming form of parenting. In fact, a study (Hays, S. (1996), *The cultural contradictions of motherhood*, New Haven, Connecticut: Yale University Press) suggested that working mothers spent as much time with their children as stay-at-home mothers did in the 1970s, because they dedicated so much out-of-work time to this 'job' – exercise, socializing, personal grooming all can now be done with the kids for their benefit. From: https://podcasts.apple.com/gb/podcast/the-parents-arent-all-right/id1200361736?i=1000672343331.

99 'Parents Under Pressure: The U.S. Surgeon General Advisory on the Mental Health and Well-Being of Parents' (2024), available at https://www.hhs.gov/surgeongeneral/priorities/parents/index.html accessed 15 November 2024 p. 14

100 *The Daily* (October 2024), 'The Parents Aren't All Right', available at https://podcasts.apple.com/gb/podcast/the-parents-arent-all-right/id1200361736?i=1000672343331 Accessed 15 November 2024.

101 *The Daily* (October 2024), 'The Parents Aren't All Right', available at https://podcasts.apple.com/gb/podcast/the-parents-arent-all-right/id1200361736?i=1000672343331

102 Chayka, K. (2024), 'The tyranny of the algorithm: why every coffee shop looks the same', *The Guardian*, available at https://www.theguardian.com/news/2024/jan/16/the-tyranny-of-the-algorithm-why-every-coffee-shop-looks-the-same?CMP=oth_b-aplnews_d-5 accessed 18 October 2024.

Conclusion

1 For more on this see Bond, E. & Phippen, A. (2022), *Safeguarding Adults Online: Perspectives on Rights to Participation*, London: Polity Press.

2 I have worked with Mentors in Violence Prevention (MVP) programme, 1 January 2017, updated 25 April 2024, available at https://education.gov.scot/resources/mentors-for-violence-prevention-mvp-an-overview/ accessed 30 August 2024.

3 Conversations and correspondence with Amir Malik, autumn 2024.

4 Fry, Hannah (2018), *Hello World: How to Be Human in the Age of the Machine*, London, Doubleday.

5 See Kaplan, J. (7 January 2025), 'More Speech and Fewer Mistakes', available at https://about.fb.com/news/2025/01/meta-more-speech-fewer-mistakes/ accessed 14 January 2025.

6 *BBC News* (5 November 2024), 'Fall of Berlin Wall: How 1989 reshaped the modern world', available at https://www.bbc.co.uk/news/world-europe-50013048 accessed 21 November 2021; and 'Opening and fall of the Berlin Wall', The Official Website of Berlin, available at https://www.berlin.de/en/history/8482274-8619314-opening-and-fall-of-the-berlin-wall.en.html

7 *The Ellen DeGeneres Show*, 'President Obama and Ellen Discuss the

Road to Equality' (12 February 2016), available at https://www.youtube.com/watch?v=RecREW7iZz8 accessed 21 November 2024.
8 In 2020 BuzzFeed reported bullying allegations against Ellen DeGeneres which eventually led to her show being cancelled. See Yandoli, K. L. (17 July 2020), 'Former Employees Say Ellen's "Be Kind" Talk Show Mantra Masks a Toxic Work Culture', available at https://www.buzzfeednews.com/article/krystieyandoli/ellen-employees-allege-toxic-workplace-culture accessed 26 November 2024.

Glossary of Terms

1 Simon, H. (1971), 'Designing Organizations for an Information-Rich World', in Greenberger, M. (ed), *Computers, Communications and the Public Interest*, Baltimore, MD: The Johns Hopkins Press.
2 Williams, J. (2018), *Stand Out in Our Light: Freedom and Resistance in the Attention Economy*, Cambridge, New York, Melbourne, New Delhi: Cambridge University Press.
3 Bhargava, V. & Velasquez, M. (2021), 'Ethics of the Attention Economy: The Problem of Social Media Addiction', *Business Ethics Quarterly* 31:3 (July 2021), pp. 321–59 at p. 345 doi: 10.1017/beq.2020.32
4 About B Corp Certification, available at https://www.bcorporation.net/en-us/certification/ accessed 24 January 2025.
5 Dimock, M. (17 January 2019), 'Defining generations: Where Millennials end and Generation Z begins', available at https://www.pewresearch.org/short-reads/2019/01/17/where-millennials-end-and-generation-z-begins/ accessed 12 November 2024.
6 Baby Boomers, Britannica online, available at https://www.britannica.com/topic/baby-boomers
7 Silent Generation, Britannica online, available at https://www.britannica.com/topic/Silent-Generation
8 NHS Mental Health Conditions: Body Dysmorphia, available at https://www.nhs.uk/mental-health/conditions/body-dysmorphia/

9. Bot definition from the Merriam Webster dictionary, available at https://www.merriam-webster.com/dictionary/bot
10. 'What is a bot?', available at Amazon at https://aws.amazon.com/what-is/bot/
11. Information Commissioners Office: Cookies definition, available at https://ico.org.uk/for-the-public/online/cookies/
12. Cambridge Dictionary definition of digital native, available at https://dictionary.cambridge.org/dictionary/english/digital-native
13. This term has been disputed in academic circles but it is now widely used in the media and so I use it here. For more information about how it is has been discredited see Sorrentino, P. (2018), 'The Mystery of the digital natives' existence: Questioning the validity of the Prenskian metaphor', First Monday, available at https://firstmonday.org/ojs/index.php/fm/article/download/9434/7598 accessed 27 November 2024.
14. Government Response: Fact Sheet on the CDU (Government's Counter-Disinformation Unit and Rapid Response Unit) and the RRU (Rapid Response Unit), published 9 June 2023, available at https://www.gov.uk/government/news/fact-sheet-on-the-cdu-and-rru#:~:text=What%20is%20mis%2Fdisinformation%3F,political%2C%20personal%20or%20financial%20gain accessed 12 November 2024.
15. Cinelli, M., De Francisci Morales, G., Galeazzi, A., Quattrociocchi, W. & Starnini, M. (2 March 2021), 'The echo chamber effect on social media', *Proc Natl Acad Sci U S A* 118(9):e2023301118 doi: 10.1073/pnas.2023301118.
16. Pariser, E. (2012), *The Filter Bubble: What the Internet Is Hiding from You*, London: Penguin.
17. Valentine, A. & Wukowitz, L. (2013), 'Using the filter bubble to create a teachable moment', Pennsylvania Libraries: Research and Practice, p. 28, doi:10.5195/palrap.2013.18.
18. Generation X definition, Britannica online, available at https://www.britannica.com/topic/Generation-X
19. Pew Research Centre (2019), 'Where Millennials End and Generation Z Begins', available at https://www.pewresearch.org/

short-reads/2019/01/17/where-millennials-end-and-generation-z-begins/
20 Gerlitz, C. & Helmond, A. (2013), 'The like economy: Social buttons and the data-intensive web', *New Media and Society*, vol. 15, issue 8, https://doi-org.libproxy.ucl.ac.uk/10.1177/14614448124723
21 MIT Sloan School, https://mitsloan.mit.edu/ideas-made-to-matter/machine-learning-explained
22 IBM, Machine Learning definition, available at https://www.ibm.com/topics/machine-learning
23 IBM, Machine Learning definition, available at https://www.ibm.com/topics/machine-learning
24 Dimock, M. (17 January 2019), 'Defining generations: Where Millennials end and Generation Z begins', available at https://www.pewresearch.org/short-reads/2019/01/17/where-millennials-end-and-generation-z-begins/ accessed 12 November 2024.
25 Government Response: Fact Sheet on the CDU (Government's Counter-Disinformation Unit and Rapid Response Unit) and the RRU (Rapid Response Unit), published 9 June 2023, available at https://www.gov.uk/government/news/fact-sheet-on-the-cdu-and-rru#:~:text=What%20is%20mis%2Fdisinformation%3F,political%2C%20personal%20or%20financial%20gain accessed 12 November 2024.
26 University of Edinburgh, Business School, 'How to Harness Social (Media) Natives in Turbulent Times', available at https://www.business-school.ed.ac.uk/about/news/how-to-harness-social-media-natives-in-turbulent-times
27 Kavanagh, J. & Rich, M. D., 'Truth Decay: An Initial Exploration of the Diminishing Role of Facts and Analysis in American Public Life', available at https://www.rand.org/pubs/research_reports/RR2314.html accessed 4 September 2024.
28 Pariser, E. (2012), *The Filter Bubble: What the Internet Is Hiding from You*, London, Penguin.
29 Valentine, A. & Wukowitz, L. (2013), 'Using the filter bubble to create a teachable moment', Pennsylvania Libraries: Research and Practice, p. 28, doi:10.5195/palrap.2013.1.